CSHSE National Standards Covered in this Text

The Council for Standards in Human Service Education (CSHSE) devel
departments and help students understand the knowledge, values, and
guidelines reflect the interdisciplinary nature of human services.

STANDARD

Professional History

Understanding and Mastery...

Historical roots of human services
Creation of human services profession
Historical and current legislation affecting services delivery
How public and private attitudes influence legislation and the interpretation of policies related to human services
Differences between systems of governance and economics
Exposure to a spectrum of political ideologies
Skills to analyze and interpret historical data application in advocacy and social changes

Human Systems

Understanding and Mastery...

Theories of human development
How small groups are utilized, theories of group dynamics, and group facilitation skills
Changing family structures and roles
Organizational structures of communities
An understanding of capacities, limitations, and resiliency of human systems
Emphasis on context and the role of diversity in determining and meeting human needs
Processes to effect social change through advocacy (e.g., community development, community and grassroots organizing, local and global activism)
Processes to analyze, interpret, and effect policies and laws at local, state, and national levels

Human Services Delivery Systems

Understanding and Mastery...

Range and characteristics of human services delivery systems and organizations
Range of populations served and needs addressed by human services
Major models used to conceptualize and integrate prevention, maintenance, intervention, rehabilitation, and healthy functioning
Economic and social class systems, including systemic causes of poverty
Political and ideological aspects of human services
International and global influences on services delivery
Skills to effect and influence social policy

Adapted from the October 2010 Revised CSHSE National Standards

STANDARD	CHAPTER
Information Management	
Understanding and Mastery...	
Obtain information through interviewing, active listening, consultation with others, library or other research, and the observation of clients and systems	2, 3, 5, 7, 8, 9, 10, 11
Recording, organizing, and assessing the relevance, adequacy, accuracy, and validity of information provided by others	2, 3, 5, 7, 11
Compiling, synthesizing, and categorizing information	2, 3, 5, 7, 9, 10, 11
Disseminating routine and critical information to clients, colleagues, or other members of the related services system that is provided in written or oral form and in a timely manner	2, 3, 4, 5, 6, 7, 11
Maintaining client confidentiality and appropriate use of client data	
Using technology for word processing, sending email, and locating and evaluating information	2, 4, 5, 6, 7, 9, 10, 11
Performing elementary community-needs assessment	3, 10
Conducting basic program evaluation	3, 10, 11
Utilizing research findings and other information for community education and public relations and using technology to create and manage spreadsheets and databases	2, 4, 5, 7, 11
Planning and Evaluating	
Understanding and Mastery...	
Analysis and assessment of the needs of clients or client groups	3, 10
Skills to develop goals, and design and implement a plan of action	2, 3, 7, 10
Skills to evaluate the outcomes of the plan and the impact on the client or client group	2, 3, 10, 11
Program design, implementation, and evaluation	2, 3, 6, 7, 10, 11
Interventions and Direct Services	
Understanding and Mastery ...	
Theory and knowledge bases of prevention, intervention, and maintenance strategies to achieve maximum autonomy and functioning	
Skills to facilitate appropriate direct services and interventions related to specific client or client group goals	3, 10
Knowledge and skill development in case management, intake interviewing, individual counseling, group facilitation and counseling, location and use of appropriate resources and referrals, and use of consultation	
Interpersonal Communication	
Understanding and Mastery...	
Clarifying expectations	2
Dealing effectively with conflict	7
Establishing rapport with clients	7
Developing and sustaining behaviors that are congruent with the values and ethics of the profession	1, 7

CSHSE National Standards Covered in This Text

STANDARD	CHAPTER
Administration	
Understanding and Mastery...	
Managing organizations through leadership and strategic planning	2, 3
Supervision and human resource management	2
Planning and evaluating programs, services, and operational functions	2, 3, 7, 10, 11
Developing budgets and monitoring expenditures	2, 3, 6, 10, 11
Grant and contract negotiation	8, 9, 10, 11
Legal/regulatory issues and risk management	1, 9
Managing professional development of staff	2, 11
Recruiting and managing volunteers	2, 11
Constituency building and other advocacy techniques such as lobbying, grassroots movements, and community development and organizing	2, 4, 5, 7
Client-Related Values and Attitudes	
Understanding and Mastery...	
The least intrusive intervention in the least restrictive environment	
Client self-determination	
Confidentiality of information	5
Worth and uniqueness of individuals (e.g., ethnicity, culture, gender, sexual orientation, age, and other expressions of diversity)	2
Belief that individuals, services systems, and society change	
Interdisciplinary team approaches to problem solving	2
Appropriate professional boundaries	
Integration of the ethical standards outlined by the National Organization for Human Services and Council for Standards in Human Service Education	
Self-Development	
Understanding and Mastery...	
Conscious use of self	
Clarification of personal and professional values	
Awareness of diversity	2
Strategies for self-care	
Reflection on professional self (e.g., journaling, development of a portfolio, project demonstrating competency)	

Grant Writing and Fundraising Tool Kit for Human Services

. . . .

Jill C. Dustin

Old Dominion University

PEARSON

Boston Columbus Indianapolis New York San Francisco Upper Saddle River
Amsterdam Cape Town Dubai London Madrid Milan Munich Paris Montréal Toronto
Delhi Mexico City São Paulo Sydney Hong Kong Seoul Singapore Taipei Tokyo

Editorial Director: Craig Campanella
Editor in Chief: Ashley Dodge
Editorial Product Manager: Carly Czech
Editorial Assistant: Nicole Suddeth
Vice President/Director of Marketing: Brandy Dawson
Executive Marketing Manager: Wendy Albert
Marketing Assistant: Frank Alarcon
Manufacturing Buyer: Romaine Denis

Creative Director: Jayne Conte
Full-Service Project Management: Aishwarya Dakshinamoorthy
Composition: PreMediaGlobal
Printer/Binder: RR Donnelley
Production Project Manager: Romaine Denis
Interior Design: Joyce Weston Design
Cover Designer: Bruce Kenselaar

Library of Congress Cataloging-in-Publication Data
Dustin, Jill C.
    Grant writing and fundraising tool kit for human services / Jill C. Dustin.
        p. cm.
    Includes bibliographical references and index.
    ISBN-13: 978-0-205-08869-0
    ISBN-10: 0-205-08869-4
    1. Proposal writing for grants—United States.   2. Fund raising—United States.   3. Nonprofit organizations—United States.   I. Title.
    HG177.5.U6D87 2013
    658.15'224—dc23
                                                                                        2012016916

5   16

ISBN-10: 0-205-08869-4
ISBN-13: 978-0-205-08869-0

Contents

. . . .

4. Developing and Implementing a Marketing Strategy: Tools and Techniques   54

. . . .

5. Identifying and Managing Funding Sources   77

Preface

· ·

All successful fundraising campaigns typically begin with the awareness that the agency is in need of money. The amount of money needed varies, but this amount sets the stage for the agency's fundraising goals. Whether the fundraising effort is a one-shot endeavor to subsidize a particular, non-reoccurring project, or an ongoing annual campaign, it starts and finishes with the goal. The success or failure of the fundraising campaign is measured incrementally by how far above or how far below the goal the campaign finishes.

Grant writing, as the name implies, is the process of writing a grant to obtain funds for an agency or project. For almost all nonprofit organizations, these grants are essential in order for organizations to survive. However, remarkably few administrators have any formal training in grant writing. Grant writing skills can be developed. With the right tools, even the most novice grant writers can compose winning grants.

Grant Writing and Fundraising Tool Kit for Human Services provides the nuts and bolts for developing successful grant writing skills and fundraising plans. Because human service agencies rely heavily on outside sources to fund their organizations and programs, it behooves human service practitioners to develop and sharpen their grant writing and fundraising skills.

For many human service practitioners, grant writing and fundraising are topics about which they may not be zealous. However, many positions are created as a result of outside funding, and most agencies rely on external funding to keep their organizations active and programs running. Therefore, practitioners who possess grant writing and fundraising skills are highly sought after by agencies.

Audience

This book was designed as a primary textbook for undergraduate and graduate students in human services, social work, counseling, psychology, public administration, and other related disciplines. Other targeted groups who could benefit from this book are human service practitioners, administrators, and other individuals charged with grant writing and fundraising responsibilities for an organization or program.

Grant Writing and Fundraising Tool Kit for Human Services provides easy-to-follow guidelines and instructions to grant writing and fundraising. Fundraising and grant writing skills are often secondary to other skills utilized by human service practitioners. Therefore, this book is user friendly and written in such a way that will motivate even the most apprehensive professional in developing and implementing a funding plan.

Unique Features

One of the unique features of this book is its focus on grant writing *and* fundraising, two topics that go hand in hand with agency funding yet are rarely combined into one book. Therefore, this book provides a more focused emphasis on two areas of agency funding: grant writing and fundraising.

In the fundraising section of the book, a number of unique topics are covered, including

- pulling a team together (e.g., board members, volunteers)
- marketing (e.g., branding, websites, emails, printed materials)
- developing and maintaining a prospect and donor list
- building relationships with prospects and donors
- processing donations
- understanding the ethics of fundraising (e.g., maintaining confidentiality)

The grant writing section contains a number of unique features and topics as well. Among these are

- exploring grant possibilities (e.g., foundations)
- searching funding databases
- implementing and managing grants

This book provides comprehensive information on these topics, as opposed to including this information as subtopics incorporated within other chapters.

Organization

Part 1 of this book is devoted to all things fundraising. It is divided into seven chapters, each focusing on a vital aspect of a successful fundraising campaign. Chapter 1 provides essential information needed to prepare nonprofits for fundraising, including definitions of pertinent terms related to nonprofits and fundraising, information on registering nonprofits for fundraising, explanations of unrestricted and restricted funds, ethical considerations regarding fundraising, and common fundraising pitfalls. Chapter 2 provides valuable tips on pulling a fundraising team together, including ideas on motivating members of the fundraising team. Chapter 3 presents practical guidelines for creating a fundraising plan, from writing the case statement to evaluating the plan. Chapter 4 provides an overview of marketing strategies and marketing plans and presents a deluge of marketing techniques ranging from agency branding to website marketing. It concludes with tips on improving the success of the marketing endeavor. Chapter 5 offers tools and techniques inherent in identifying and locating target markets, tapping into various funding sources, and effectively managing donor information. Chapter 6 presents a variety of fundraising ideas, from the familiar capital campaign to some unique fundraising options such as a golf ball drop. Part 1 wraps up with Chapter 7 that offers a number of valuable tips for fundraising success. Ways to cultivate relationships with donors and potential donors, process donations, express appreciation to donors, and manage fundraising documents are suggested. Part 1, in its entirety, provides indispensable fundraising guidance, tips, protocol, tools, and trends.

Part 2 of this book is dedicated to grant writing. It provides an abundance of tips and resources to benefit, not only the first-time grant writer but also the veteran professional.

Each of its four chapters highlights key features of the grant writing process. Chapter 8 explores grant writing considerations for agencies to contemplate during the early planning stage of their campaign, including the role that collaboration plays, the importance of time management, and the pros and cons of contracting with a professional grant writer. Chapter 9 provides an overview of the various types of grants and offers information on a range of funding databases and resources. Chapter 10 presents the steps involved in the grant writing process, details information on each element of a grant proposal, and offers insight into the review process. Part 2 concludes with Chapter 11. This final chapter provides a guide to successfully executing, managing, and closing a funded project. The grant writing section of the book offers a collection of invaluable resources and suggestions to lead nonprofit agencies in developing and implementing successful grant writing initiatives.

Obtaining and/or sharpening grant writing and fundraising skills can be extremely gratifying. Not only will it benefit the agencies and their programs; for the individual writing the grants and developing fundraising plans, these skills can be intellectually stimulating and energizing.

Get Connected with MySearchLab with eText

Provided with this text, MySearchLab with eText provides engaging experiences that personalize, stimulate, and measure student learning. Pearson's MyLabs deliver proven results from a trusted partner in helping students succeed. Features available with this text include

- a *complete eText*—just like the printed text, you can highlight and add notes to the eText online or download it to your iPad.
- *assessment*—chapter quizzes, topic-specific assessment, and flashcards offer and report directly to your grade book.
- *writing and research assistance*—a wide range of writing, grammar, and research tools and access to a variety of academic journals, census data, Associated Press newsfeeds, and discipline-specific readings help you hone your writing and research skills.

MySearchLab with eText can be packaged with this text at no additional cost—just order the ISBN on the back cover. Instructors can also request access to preview MySearchLab by contacting your local Pearson sales representative or visiting www.mysearchlab.com.

Acknowledgments

The success of *Grant Writing and Fundraising Tool Kit for Human Services* would not be possible without the support and contributions of numerous people. First and foremost my deepest appreciation goes to my family and friends for their encouragement, support, patience, and tolerance while I worked diligently on this book over the past 2 years.

I am grateful for my esteemed colleagues who encouraged me to write this book and provided insight and guidance throughout this journey. Thanks also to the countless number of students who inspired my work.

I would also like to express my gratitude to the team at Pearson including, but certainly not limited to, Carly Czech, editorial product manager, and Crystal Parenteau, development manager. My appreciation also goes out to the following reviewers who offered valuable suggestions and recommendations as I developed this manuscript: Gregg Allinson, Beaufort County Community College; Yvonne Barry, John Tyler Community College; Jeff Cohen, St. Edwards University; Maureen Donahue-Smith, Elmira College; Stephany Hewitt, Trident Technical College; Melanie Horn, California State University at Fullerton; Wade Luquet, Gwynedd-Mercy College; Carmen V. Negron, New York City College of Technology; Lauren Polvere, Clinton Community College; Mary Ray, Great Basin College; and Lia Willis, Columbia College.

Dedication

This book is dedicated to Tony. For all you do, for who you are, I will be forever grateful that you came into my life. In the words of Brian Wilson, "God only knows what I'd be without you."

CHAPTER 1

Gearing Up for Fundraising

What You Need to Know

Before delving into the ins and outs of fundraising, it is essential to understand some relevant terms regarding nonprofit organizations. Because the type of nonprofit can play a role in fundraising efforts, knowing the differences between nonprofit and charitable nonprofit organizations is essential.

Nonprofit versus Charitable Nonprofit Organizations

According to Hoffman (1992), all charities are nonprofits, but all nonprofits are not charities. The Internal Revenue Service (2009) states that nonprofit status is a state law concept. Nonprofit organizations may be eligible for certain benefits, such as state property, sales, and income tax exemptions; however, organizing as a nonprofit at the state level does not necessarily grant the organization exemption from federal income tax. To qualify as exempt from federal income taxes, the organization must meet specific requirements that are set forth by the Internal Revenue Service (IRS). Examples of nonprofit organizations that may qualify for exemption from federal income tax include state chartered credit unions, business leagues, fraternal societies, social welfare organizations, and veterans organizations.

Nonprofit charitable organizations are organizations that are organized and operated exclusively for exempt purposes as set forth by the IRS under section 501(c)(3). Charitable organizations are eligible to receive tax-deductible contributions (Internal Revenue Service, 2009). The primary purpose of nonprofit charitable organizations is to improve some part of society without a profit motive. In other words, they cannot be organized or operated to benefit private interests such as the creator, the creator's family, or shareholders of the organization. The programs and services offered through nonprofit charitable organizations

Learning Objectives
- Describe the differences between nonprofit and charitable nonprofit organizations.
- Explain the Federal Trade Commission's role in fundraising efforts.
- Describe the differences between unrestricted and restricted funds.
- Recognize the significance of ethics in fundraising.
- Identify fundraising pitfalls.

All charities are nonprofits, but all nonprofits are not charities.

are funded through private donations, service fees, corporate and private foundation grants, commercial activity, and government grants (Usry, 2008b).

As is evident, the term *nonprofit* can refer to a nonprofit charitable organization that qualifies for exemption from federal taxes. It can also refer to a nonprofit organization that is not a charitable organization and, as such, may qualify for some state benefits but does not qualify for federal income tax exemptions.

Regardless of the type of nonprofit, any nonprofit that depends on donations to obtain the necessary financial support to operate must register with the regulators in states where it intends to solicit funds. Registration is designed not only to aid states in keeping detailed records of nonprofits and third-party fundraisers, but also to help protect donors from being defrauded by phony nonprofits.

Nonprofit versus Not-for-Profit Organizations

The terms *nonprofit* and *not-for-profit* are often used interchangeably. In most cases, mingling the terms does not cause any problems because most people believe they refer to the same type of organization. Differences in these terms, however, do become important when the government or a tax entity recognizes a difference. In the United States, the IRS (2009) defines a not-for-profit as an organization devoted to some sort of activity, such as a hobby, which does not operate as a legal entity in and of itself (i.e., it does not have a governing board that officially represents the group). A nonprofit, on the other hand, refers to an organization or agency founded for purposes other than profit making.

Administration

Understanding and Mastery of . . . legal/regulatory issues and risk management

Critical Thinking Question: The Federal Trade Commission is the federal government's chief consumer protection agency. How is the fundraising work of nonprofit organizations influenced by the work of the Federal Trade Commission?

Nonprofit Fundraising Registration

Billions of dollars are donated to nonprofit charitable organizations each year. Unfortunately, 1% of all charitable donations is misused or collected fraudulently (Usry, 2008a). State governments have assumed the role of overseeing nonprofit charitable organizations through registration and reporting; however, the Federal Trade Commission is the federal government's foremost consumer protection agency. For those states where such laws have been ratified, the attorney general's office generally takes on the responsibility for the registration of, the reports about, and enforcement of laws pertaining to charitable giving (Usry, 2008a).

The laws regarding the information charitable organizations are obliged to submit along with their annual reports and registration applications vary in each state. Examples of documents and information that may be required, depending on the state, include IRS 501(c)(3) determination letters, audit paperwork, bylaws, fundraising contracts, IRS 990 forms, notarized signatures, and fees. In addition, each state maintains its own fee structures for both the initial and recurring registration and reporting costs (Usry, 2008a). In most states that require registration, organizations must renew annually, and deadlines for renewal vary from state to state. Not properly registering, prior to fundraising, risks penalties and could result in felony charges. In some cases, nonprofits have had to return donations received due to registering too late or not registering at all (Fritz, 2010f).

Unified Registration Statement

In 1997, the Unified Registration Statement (URS) was developed, and in 1998, it was released. The URS represents an attempt to merge the information and data requirements of those states that require registration of nonprofit organizations, which solicit for funds within their jurisdictions. The effort is managed by the National Association of State Charities Officials and the National Association of Attorneys General. It is a part of the Standardized Reporting Project, whose goal is to simplify, economize, and standardize compliance under the states' solicitation laws. As of August 2010, 37 states required registration of nonprofits conducting charitable solicitations and accepted the URS, whereas 3 states required registration of nonprofits conducting charitable solicitations and did not accept the URS (Multi-State Filer Project, 2010).

The URS endeavor consists of three stages: (a) assembling an inventory of registration information requirements from all states; (b) constructing a form which includes all (or most) of these requirements; and (c) persuading states to agree to this "standardized" format as a replacement for their own forms. States typically require both registration (at least an initial registration) and annual financial reporting (The Unified Registration Statement, 2010).

The subject of multi-state registration and reporting has become even more critical for nonprofit organizations due to the use of the Internet in fundraising. Prior to the Internet, agencies with sizeable budgets could afford to launch fundraising campaigns, which extended beyond their jurisdictions or across their state borders. As a result, smaller nonprofits rarely had to file multi-state registrations to fundraise. Today, however, both Internet and email fundraising have become popular and economical means to soliciting contributions. This has lead to many smaller organizations having to complete numerous state applications in order to solicit and collect donations. The more applications, the more the administrative processing costs to the organization and to the states (Usry, 2008a). The URS, therefore, is an alternative to filing all the individual registration forms created by each of the cooperating states (Multi-State Filer Project, 2010).

> The subject of multi-state registration and reporting has become even more critical for nonprofit organizations due to the use of the Internet in fundraising.

Even if an agency does not solicit donations in a particular state, an agency may have to register in that state to accept donations from individuals who reside there. For example, New York and Florida require registration from any nonprofit that accepts donations from their respective state residents. According to Fritz (2010f), local and regional organizations may want to consider using donation software that allows the organization to block donations received from residents of other states.

Understanding the differences between nonprofit organizations and nonprofit charitable organizations as well as state registration requirements is essential, especially in regard to their impact

Administration

Understanding and Mastery of . . . legal/regulatory issues and risk management

Critical Thinking Question: Agencies wishing to fundraise must register with the state or states from which the agency plans to fundraise. Why may an agency need to register in a state in which the agency does not plan to solicit donations?

on different types of fundraising, which will be discussed shortly. First, however, it is necessary to be familiar with two additional terms in regard to nonprofit fundraising, *unrestricted funds* and *restricted funds*. The differences in these funds, and how these distinctions impact fundraising activities, will now be discussed.

Unrestricted versus Restricted Funds

An agency's funds are often categorized as either unrestricted or restricted funds. Unrestricted funds are available for the agency to use toward any purpose. Unrestricted funds are often used to pay for the operating expenses of the organization. In contrast, restricted funds are funds whose assets are limited to a designated purpose as per the donor's request or are raised for a specific purpose or project such as a capital campaign used to fund a building expansion. Unrestricted funds can be either temporarily restricted or permanently restricted. Temporarily restricted funds have donor-imposed restrictions that can be satisfied in one of two ways: the passage of a defined period (i.e., a time restriction) or by performing defined activities (i.e., a purpose restriction). An example of temporarily restricted funds would be a gift from a donor with the aim of supporting a particular program. Permanently restricted funds are restricted by the donor for a particular purpose or time constraint that never expires. The intent of a permanently restricted fund is that the principal balance of the gift will remain as an investment forever. With permanently restricted funds, the agency utilizes the interest and investment returns. Because of the flexibility of unrestricted funds, many organizations consider them more desirable; however, they tend to be more difficult to raise. A general rule of thumb is to use restricted funds for a particular expense whenever possible and to put unrestricted funds aside for expenses for which raising money to support the expenses is more difficult (Nonprofits Assistance Fund, n.d.; WWF, 2006).

> **Because of the flexibility of unrestricted funds, many organizations consider them more desirable; however, they tend to be more difficult to raise.**

Both unrestricted and restricted funding can be raised from any funding source. In practice, however, some types of fundraising are more likely to garner restricted funds than others, and vice versa. For example, some fundraising events, such as silent auctions, are more likely to raise unrestricted funds because they are less likely to be subject to restrictions from outside funding sources. On the other hand, legacy fundraising may be built around the donors' interests, and as a result, be set up to fund a specific program.

The aforementioned sections provide an overview of information central to nonprofit fundraising including nonprofit status, registration requirements, and funding categories. The subject of ethics is intertwined throughout all aspects of fundraising, from start to finish. A number of recent controversies at major nonprofits regarding the ethics of fundraising have generated public outcry. As a result, professional organizations have responded by establishing or revising ethical standards for their members.

Understanding the Ethics of Fundraising

In the current economic climate, agencies may be tempted to seek funding wherever they can find it. This can lead to serious mistakes in decision-making and, at times, unethical behavior. During the most difficult times, it becomes even more imperative that leaders of nonprofit agencies closely examine their fundraising plan and remain disciplined about the way they raise money.

The leaders of the organization—the board, the executive director—set the stage for the ethical behavior of the agency. As stated by Schmidt (2004), a truly ethical agency can exist only when its leaders embrace ethical decision-making and recognize the importance of values other than the organization's bottom line. One guiding principle of the nonprofit world is that no one individual is to profit from the organization. Many presume that individuals working in the nonprofit sector always operate with the highest of standards; unfortunately, this is not always the case. A few chapters of United Way and the American Red Cross have found themselves depicted in a negative light due to unethical behavior. Specifically, United Way of America was accused of excessive expenditures of top management (e.g., first-class plane tickets, chauffeur-driven limousines) and setting up of satellite organizations with questionable activities (e.g., hiring an executive's son without conducting a search for other qualified candidates). The American Red Cross has been involved in several scandals, including accusations of padding bank accounts, embezzlement of funds to support a crack cocaine habit, forgery of signatures on purchase orders, and theft of over $1 million in Red Cross funds by a chief executive and his bookkeeper. Perhaps the most egregious scandal took place after the 9/11 tragedy when the Red Cross was accused of using millions of dollars donated to them specifically for survivors of 9/11 and families of those killed for other Red Cross operations. Unethical behavior and gross negligence in nonprofit organizations can result in sharp declines in charitable contributions.

The Association of Fundraising Professionals (AFP) (2009) is the governing body which fosters the development and growth of fundraising professionals and the profession. Its mission is to advance philanthropy by facilitating ethical and effective fundraising. The AFP Code of Ethical Principles and Standards (2008) provides standards in regard to member obligations, solicitation and use of philanthropic funds, presentation of information, and compensation and contracts.

Organizations must ensure that their philanthropic activities are steeped in integrity. From choosing the fundraising team to processing donations, ethical fundraising practices are paramount to the integrity and future of the organization.

Interpersonal Communication

Understanding and Mastery of . . . developing and sustaining behaviors that are congruent with the values and ethics of the profession

Critical Thinking Question: In what ways can a human service professional make certain that his or her fundraising activities are congruent with the ethics of the profession?

Unethical behavior and gross negligence in nonprofit organizations can result in sharp declines in charitable contributions.

Interpersonal Communication

Understanding and Mastery of . . . developing and sustaining behaviors that are congruent with the values and ethics of the profession

Critical Thinking Question: How can an agency help ensure an ethical fundraising campaign if it has no prior fundraising experience?

Fundraising Pitfalls

Fundraising blunders can be costly. Nonprofits confronted with increased needs, yet facing reduced budgets, cannot afford to make costly mistakes. Following are 15 common fundraising pitfalls agencies should avoid. Information on ways to avoid each pitfall can be found in the chapters noted after each item.

1. *Failing to have a solid team in place.* A successful fundraising initiative is only as strong as the team of individuals who oversee the fundraising effort. All members of the team must be involved in the fundraising effort in some way. Overworked staff and volunteers are a recipe for failure. The entire fundraising team must have defined roles and responsibilities, including an accurate estimate of the time commitment each position requires. See Chapter 2.

2. *Failing to motivate the fundraising team.* Motivated team members are successful fundraisers. Motivated team members never wait to be asked, are often the first to identify needs, and are usually the first to take action. Team members must be motivated to motivate potential donors. When motivation is absent, so are contributions. See Chapter 2.

3. *Failing to have a mission statement.* The mission statement is the heart of the agency. It guides the work of the organization including its fundraising efforts. It makes it possible for potential donors to determine if the agency's cause matches the donor's values. See Chapters 2, 3, 5, 6, and 7.

4. *Failing to have clear and measurable goals and objectives.* Clear and measurable goals and objectives are the only means by which the success of a fundraising initiative can be measured. Goals and objectives must be realistic and put in writing for all parties to see. See Chapter 3.

5. *Failing to plan adequately.* Successful fundraising entails careful and recurring planning. Every task, from the initial startup to the final evaluation, must be identified and delegated. See Chapters 3, 4, and 5.

6. *Failing to effectively time the fundraising initiatives.* Timing is everything. Fundraisers that are scheduled at a time when they will be competing with other major activities such as scheduling a casino night fundraiser during the same week as the annual art auction can spell disaster. See Chapter 3.

7. *Failing to develop an evaluation plan and evaluation tools.* A comprehensive evaluation plan and the tools needed to carry it out are essential to ensuring that the fundraising campaign stays on track. Creating a fundraising plan without taking the time to evaluate how things are going makes it close to impossible to stay on track and reach the funding goals. See Chapter 3.

8. *Failing to ask for donations.* It may seem obvious, but to raise money, agencies must ask for donations. Some agencies hold back when asking for contributions. Agencies that are uncomfortable asking for gifts are likely receiving far less than what is possible. See Chapters 3, 5, and 7.

9. *Failing to seek consultation.* Nonprofits without fundraising experience must seek professional assistance and fundraising training prior to delving into a fundraising initiative. Not doing so can be disastrous. See Chapters 3 and 4.

10. *Failing to effectively market the agency and its fundraising initiatives.* Effective marketing is an essential element of successful fundraising. If people are not aware that their support is needed, they will not know to offer their support. See Chapter 4.

11. *Failing to diversify funding sources.* The best fundraising campaigns are those that tap into a variety of funding sources. Organizations that put all their eggs in one basket, so to speak, are more likely to run into problems should their funding source dry up. See Chapter 5.

12. *Failing to stand behind the charity.*   Board members and other fundraising team members must contribute to the best of their abilities. Potential donors are more likely to give when they are aware that members of the nonprofit team lead by example. See Chapter 5.

13. *Failing to have good record-keeping practices.*   Nonprofits must keep accurate records. Accurate records are vital to furnishing expense and income records, pledge information, prospect lists, donor information, and in-kind gifts. Good record-keeping practices provide information on what worked and what did not work. This information is a valuable resource for future fundraising campaigns. See Chapters 5 and 7.

14. *Failing to choose the best types of fundraisers.*   Offering a variety of fundraisers keeps donors and potential donors interested in the fundraising initiative. Ongoing campaigns can be supplemented with easy fundraisers or fundraising events. In the same vein, repeating the same old fundraiser over and over again can lead to boredom. Boredom can result in flat to declining revenue. See Chapter 6.

15. *Failing to acknowledge contributions.*   Contributions are the bread and butter of a nonprofit's sustainability. Donors must be acknowledged, thanked, and cultivated for the long-term success of the nonprofit. Not doing so can result in donor attrition. See Chapter 7.

Donations keep nonprofits going. When fundraising campaigns are unsuccessful, it is usually due to one or more of these pitfalls. To ensure that organizations make the most of their fundraising opportunities, knowing what *not* to do is just as critical as knowing what to do.

Summary

Tough economic times have made it more and more difficult for nonprofit organizations and charitable nonprofit organizations to meet their financial needs. The term *nonprofit* can refer to nonprofit charitable organizations that qualify for federal tax exemptions, or it can refer to nonprofit organizations that are not charitable organizations and do not qualify for federal tax exemptions. All nonprofit organizations must register in their state and in any state in which they solicit donations. In 1998, the URS was released. It represents an attempt to merge the information and data requirements of states that require registration of nonprofits that solicit for funds within their jurisdictions. An organization's funds are classified as either unrestricted or restricted. Unrestricted funds are available for the agency to use toward any purpose, whereas restricted funds are raised for a particular purpose or project. The leaders of the organization set the stage for ethical behavior of the nonprofit. The Association of Fundraising Professionals (AFP) (2009) is the governing body that promotes ethical behavior of fundraising professionals and the profession. Successful fundraising initiatives require that nonprofits are in tune with the terms, requirements, and ethical standards that govern fundraising. In addition, they must avoid common fundraising pitfalls. Nonprofits faced with reduced budgets and increased needs cannot afford to make costly mistakes.

The following questions will test your application and analysis of the content found within this chapter. For additional assessment, applying, analyzing, synthesizing, and evaluating chapter content with practice, visit **MySearchLab.com**

1. Which of the following types of organizations are organized and operated exclusively for exempt purposes as set forth by the IRS under section 501(c)(3)?
   a. Nonprofit organizations
   b. Exempt organizations
   c. Nonprofit charitable organizations
   d. Not-for-profit organizations

2. Even if an agency does not solicit donations in a particular state, an agency may have to register in that state to
   a. accept donations from individuals who live in that state.
   b. conduct future fundraising activities in that state.
   c. prevent a lawsuit.
   d. accept unrestricted funds.

3. Restricted funds are funds whose assets are designated or raised for a specific purpose. Unrestricted funds are funds that are available for the agency to use toward any purpose. Which of the following fundraising methods would an agency needing to raise unrestricted funds choose to lessen the likelihood that the funds will be restricted?
   a. Legacy fundraising
   b. Corporate fundraising
   c. Giving circle
   d. Silent auction

4. Flower Power, a new nonprofit, community beautification project, is putting together a fundraising campaign. No one at the organization has any fundraising experience, but this doesn't stop them from moving forward. They need to raise $500 and decide to hold a yard sale at a neighborhood church. Each Flower Power volunteer commits to bring a minimum of 10 items for the sale. All the volunteers show up for the yard sale with their items in hand. They realize that there are no tables set up, no money box, and no structure. None of the items are priced and no one seems to be able to agree on prices or the best way to display the items. To top it off, only seven people stop by and the organization raises only $22. The most likely reason the fundraiser was not successful was the organization's failure to
   a. ask for donations.
   b. seek consultation.
   c. have a mission statement.
   d. motivate the fundraising team.

5. Although nonprofit organizations and not-for-profit organizations are similar in many ways, they are also different. In what ways do nonprofit organizations differ from not-for-profit organizations?

6. The Unified Registration Statement (URS) represents an attempt to merge the information and data requirements of those states that solicit for funds and require registration of nonprofit organizations. The URS endeavor consists of what three stages?

7. Restricted funds are those funds whose assets are limited to a designated purpose, per the donor's wish, or are raised for a specific project. What are three types of funding sources that typically garner restricted funds?

8. An ethical agency is steeped in the ethical behavior of its leaders. Unfortunately, some leaders of nonprofit agencies do not operate with high ethical standards. Describe three ways in which an agency can ensure that it is operating with integrity and high ethical standards.

CHAPTER 2

Pulling the Team Together

· ·

The success of the fundraising campaign begins with the ability of the organization to recruit and retain a team of individuals committed to the viability and financial well-being of the agency. The journey through successful fundraising begins and ends with the fundraising team; and the survival of the agency rests on the team's ability to raise funds. The task of fundraising is immeasurably strengthened when a genuine partnership exists among all team members. The focus of this chapter is on the nuts and bolts associated with the fundraising team, including pulling the team together, choosing leaders, the fundraising responsibilities of the members, and motivating the team. Team members hold many significant roles within an organization, and each role is vital to the overall success of "The Team!"

Pulling the Fundraising Team Together

Team members provide key contacts and referrals, knowledge and skills, and, in many cases, their personal financial support to the agency. It is pertinent to note that although this chapter addresses a variety of committees and fundraising team members, each agency develops its own fundraising team based on a number of factors. For example, large agencies serving sizeable numbers of consumers, and offering numerous programs and services, are more likely to develop comprehensive fundraising teams that include many of the committees and individual members discussed in this chapter. On the other hand, smaller agencies may set up modest fundraising committees comprised of a board, a few staff members, and several volunteers. Whether the team consists of a number of fundraising committees or just one, all-inclusive committee, the goal of the team is the same: to secure the continued success of the nonprofit through the raising of funds sufficient to support its mission.

The forthcoming sections will describe the fundraising responsibilities of each team member, beginning with the executive director and

Learning Objectives

- Describe the fundraising responsibilities of the various team members.
- Recognize characteristics of effective fundraising team members.
- Apply recommended guidelines to running effective meetings.
- Apply recommendations for recruiting fundraising team members.
- Employ suggestions for motivating fundraising team members.

· ·

The journey through successful fundraising begins and ends with the fundraising team; and the survival of the agency rests on the team's ability to raise funds.

ending with the volunteers. In addition, team member characteristics will be high-lighted, and when applicable, recruiting tips will be provided.

Executive Director

Leadership from the executive director is essential. First and foremost, the executive director must have a clear vision of the fundraising needs of the agency and share this vision with others in order to instill unity among all team members. The executive director needs to support the concept that fundraising is a shared responsibility among all members of the agency including the staff, board, committees, and volunteers. If the executive director considers fundraising to be the sole responsibility of the fundraising committee, it is likely that other agency affiliates will feel the same way. The executive director must create a culture of fundraising that is ingrained in the philosophy of the organization. Jenne and Henderson (2000) state that the working relationship between the executive director and the board, staff, volunteers, funding organizations, clients, and other service agencies can substantially influence the agency's success and reputation in the community.

The executive director is accountable for the day-to-day operations of the agency in order to achieve the organization's goals and objectives. He or she recommends the annual budget to the board for approval and carefully manages the agency's resources within the constraints of the budget guidelines according to existing laws, bylaws, and regulations. This can be a difficult task to accomplish year after year. One of the major responsibilities of the executive director is to ensure that the agency meets its mission. Doing so requires raising the necessary funds to support programs and services that can make a difference in the lives of its consumers. As such, a chief task of the executive director is fundraising.

Fundraising Responsibilities of the Executive Director

The executive director plays a fundamental role in the fundraising campaign. His or her responsibilities and tasks pertaining to fundraising can range from recruiting team members to writing and submitting grant proposals. Specifically, executive directors

- recruit members to the board of directors who are well suited to carrying out the organization's fundraising needs.
- serve as the liaison to the board and collaborate with them in developing and implementing the fundraising plan.
- set up the fundraising committees comprised of board members, staff, and volunteers.
- provide board, fundraising committee, and staff with fundraising education, training, and assistance.
- ensure that all fundraising activities are carried out with high ethical standards.
- provide board members with useful information about the organization that the board can convey to potential donors.
- identify resource requirements and research funding sources.
- establish strategies to approach funders.

- assure that contributions are accepted and used in a responsible manner.
- ensure that donors are acknowledged and are regularly informed about the nonprofit.
- submit proposals and administer fundraising records and documentation.

The executive director is critical in terms of management, leadership, and guidance and holds many roles that are essential in maintaining the sustainability of the nonprofit. Although the fundraising responsibilities of the executive director will vary depending on the size, purpose, and composition of the agency, effective leaders are both personally and professionally motivated to fundraise.

Chairs

The fundraising team is comprised of the agency's board and a number of committees and campaign divisions. Each of these collective groups is headed by a leader, known as the chair. A promising fundraising campaign begins with its chairs. Without dynamic, hard-working, motivated, and experienced chairs, it is unlikely that the fundraising endeavor will be successful.

Fundraising Responsibilities of Chairs

The fundraising responsibilities of the chairs will differ depending on whether the chair is the leader of the board or leader of one of the agency's various committees. However, there are some typical responsibilities that chairs share in regard to a nonprofit's fundraising campaign. The following list represents typical tasks:

- Recruit board and committee members including co-chairs, if needed and applicable.
- Set policies, priorities, and goals for fundraising programs.
- Manage all fundraising efforts within the board or committee's domain.
- Execute the fundraising plan.
- Identify, evaluate, and rate major potential funders.
- Communicate the mission of the agency to key constituents and make the case for support.
- Schedule appointments with major potential donors and solicit their donations.
- Serve as the public spokesperson for the agency and its fundraising campaign and make statements to the media.
- Recruit core groups of individuals to serve as solicitation team captains, when needed and appropriate.
- Work with the team captains in recruiting solicitors, when needed and applicable.
- Create meeting agendas, run scheduled board or committee meetings, engage members in meaningful and productive discussions, and arrange additional meetings as needed.
- Review the ongoing performance of the board or committee's fundraising responsibilities and tasks.
- Review the board or committee's achievements as they relate to the board or committee's goals and objectives.

- Keep other chairs informed of the board or committee's progress by routinely reporting back to them.
- Attend annual board planning meetings and educational events.
- Ensure proper donor and volunteer recognition by reviewing the gift acknowledgment process.
- Establish benefits and incentives for volunteers to maintain and enhance donor-volunteer relations.

Chairs play an instrumental role in the fundraising team; therefore, knowing the characteristics of effective chairs can assist agencies in choosing the best leaders.

Characteristics of Effective Chairs

If 1,000 individuals are polled and asked to list characteristics that describe the perfect chair, chances are there would be a 1,000 different lists; however, a number of the characteristics would probably be included on the majority of the lists. Following are some of the most essential characteristics one should look for when choosing chairs.

- *Ethical.* One of the most salient characteristics of effective chairs is that they are ethical. They live above the line. They are moral, honorable, and trustworthy. They strive to achieve an ideal character: They are the same on the outside as they are on the inside. Such leaders are honest, admirable, humble, and can be trusted because they remain true to their inner values. They take responsibility for their actions and give credit where credit is due. They acknowledge their team members. They are respectful and do not speak negatively about others. Ethical leaders "walk the talk!"
- *Enthusiastic.* Effective chairs are enthusiastic. People respond more optimistically to leaders who are excited about their work and about their leadership roles. Effective leaders are a source of inspiration. They approach tasks with confidence and are zealous about their work. Leaders who are genuinely enthusiastic and excited are contagious and irresistible. People want to be around them and want to be a part of their teams.
- *Assertive.* Quality leaders are assertive. They are able to clearly state their expectations in order to avoid misunderstandings. They are confident communicators, in both speaking and listening. They express their feelings and beliefs honestly but in a way that demonstrates respect and dignity for the team members. Assertive chairs inspire team members to put forth their best effort.
- *Dedicated.* Effective chairs are dedicated. They inspire their teams by leading by example and always working toward the goals and objectives at hand. They are willing to take on responsibilities, make sacrifices, and put the needs of the agency and the team first. They go the extra mile and are sincere and dedicated to their work. Good leaders are committed to meeting deadlines no matter how early in the morning or how late into the evening they need to work.
- *Open-minded.* Excellent leaders are open-minded. They avoid favoritism and appreciate the unique qualities of each team member. They suspend judgment and avoid jumping to conclusions while listening to all sides of an issue. They actively seek input from the team and welcome new ways of doing things based on this input.

- *Organized.* Quality chairs are organized. They operate in efficient, purposeful, and methodical ways. They are proactive and focus on the goals at hand. They base decisions on the impact the decisions will have on moving toward the overall vision. Organized leaders are responsive. They address matters in a reasonable timeframe. Team members look to leaders in times of unfamiliarity and uncertainty and find comfort in leaders who are prepared, orderly, responsive, and organized.
- *Creative.* Talented leaders are creative; they think outside the box. They have fresh ideas and have the ability to visualize things that others may not see. They are able to see the possibilities and move the team in new directions.
- *Transparent.* The best leaders believe in the free flow of information between them and the team members. Processes, decisions, responsibilities, and developments are transparent and readily available and directly accessible to the entire team. The information is provided in such a way that is easily understandable.
- *Humorous.* Effective leaders are able to use humor to invigorate and motivate the team. A sense of humor is essential to relieving stress and reducing boredom. They are able to rein in negative emotions by getting people to laugh. No matter how serious the situation may become, exceptional leaders maintain a sense of humor and are able to raise the morale of the team.

In addition to the aforementioned characteristics, it is beneficial that chairs possess the experience, knowledge, and skills specific to their committee's focus. It is also useful to consider characteristics especially crucial to fundraising, such as former fundraising experience and strong marketing and managerial skills. In addition, the chair should have clout in the community. The leader's influence and leverage in the community should be proportionate to the amount of funds needed to be raised. Because chairs guide their committee's responsibilities in regard to the entire fundraising plan, it is essential that they gain the respect, trust, and confidence of the executive director, other committees, staff, and volunteers. A healthy, positive partnership among all fundraising team members is necessary for the overall success of the fundraising effort. The finest chairs are able to look ahead and see the job in its entirety. They have a far-reaching vision. They are able to see the overall fundraising strategy and do not focus on one fundraising activity or project.

Recruiting Chairs

Chairs have the primary responsibility of establishing, overseeing, and achieving the nonprofit's vision. With that said, the average volunteer chairperson typically spends less than 10 hours per month doing work associated with the position. Therefore, one of the most pivotal roles of chairs is to work in tandem with their committees to turn the board or committee's energy and attention toward projects that matter the most—advancing the agency in the community and taking it to the next level.

The recruitment process for securing qualified chairs is an essential activity. Agencies can start by matching the organization's strategic plan with qualities and skills needed in its leaders to carry out the strategic plan. Reviewing the strategic plan is especially valuable if a new plan has been created. According to Martinelli and Biro (2010), the new plan may have implications regarding agency leadership. For example, the strategic plan may have determined that the leadership needs to be more diverse. When recruiting chairs, following these steps can increase the likelihood of securing competent leaders:

1. *Review bylaws.* The recruiting process begins with reviewing the agency's bylaws to determine the specific requirements of chairs. This will assist agencies in determining who is eligible to serve. The bylaws may also mandate a process for selecting the chairs, for example, some bylaws may require that a committee oversee the chair recruitment and nomination process. Agencies must be in compliance with the bylaws as bylaws are legal documents.

2. *Create profiles.* Create profiles of potential chairs, including sought-after expertise, skills, knowledge, and experience. Once the profiles are created, job descriptions can be written. The job descriptions clarify the responsibilities of the chairs. Job descriptions should be clear and should state, in behavioral terms, precisely the expectations the agency has of its chairs.

3. *Develop a list of possible chairs.* Next, a preliminary list of possible chairs is developed. The list should match the recruiting priorities of the agency. Martinelli and Biro (2010) recommend considering a number of potential recruits by "throwing the net wide."

4. *Rank the prospects.* After identifying the initial list of potential chairs, the prospects should be examined more carefully and ranked based on how well the candidates' qualifications match the agency's and committee's needs.

5. *Invite candidates to visit the organization.* Once the leading candidates are identified they should be offered an opportunity to visit the organization, if they are unfamiliar with it (Martinelli & Biro, 2010). During this visit, candidates should be provided time to observe programs and services in action, speak with the executive director and staff, and attend a board meeting to get an idea of how the board conducts business and makes decisions.

6. *Invite prospects to an orientation.* The next step in the recruitment process is to invite prospective chairs to attend an orientation session. Orientation sessions provide candidates with an opportunity to learn more about roles and responsibilities of the board and committees, as well as the individual responsibilities of the chairs. The executive director should be present to convey the importance of the position the candidates are being asked to consider. During the orientation, prospective chairs should be provided with an opportunity to ask questions and to confirm their willingness to serve as chair.

7. *Review and begin election process.* Following the orientation sessions, candidates who participated in all aspects of the recruiting process are reviewed and the election process ensues. The election process follows the organization's bylaws. For example, bylaws may require that a slate of names be brought to the board of directors for action. In determining the best fit for the chair positions, boards can further screen candidates by answering the following questions. First, does the candidate appear committed to the mission and enthusiastic about the vision of the agency? Second, can the candidate provide the necessary time and energy to

the organization? Third, does the candidate possess the skills, knowledge, experience, and other talents that match the agency's recruiting priorities? Fourth, when making decisions, does it look as if the candidate can place the agency's interests and objectives above his or her own personal and professional interests?

8. *Select chair.* Chairs are selected based on the outcome of the aforementioned process. Some agencies may be tempted to rely on "whoever is available at the time." The overall performance of the board and its committees depends on selecting a recruitment process that gives consideration, energy, and time toward choosing the best leaders. Often, problems in board and committee performance can be traced to an agency's casual or haphazard recruiting process.

Once chairs have been recruited, selected, and orientated, and they have confirmed their commitment to their new roles and to the agency, it is time for them to begin planning and preparing for committee meetings. Chairs play such a vital role in the fundraising process. Therefore, it is essential for them to have loyal committee members who hold the same passion and enthusiasm as do their leaders. One of the major downfalls of any committee is the committee meeting. The chair is ultimately responsible for ensuring group cohesiveness and ensuring that the fundraising plan is on track.

Running Effective Meetings

For the most part, people approach committee meetings with trepidation. They may view meetings as boring, lengthy, and monotonous. As a new chair, these perceptions can be intimidating. New leaders are rarely trained on how to conduct meetings that capture the attention and enthusiasm of the committee members. However, committee and board meetings are a fundamental necessity for any successful fundraising campaign; they provide face-to-face contact between members and focus energy on the fundraising plan. As Forhan (2008) states, when done properly, meetings can build community and provide members with a means to share ideas, debate issues, and make decisions.

Quality meetings do not occur on their own; they are planned. By following some basic guidelines, even the most novice chair can hold and run meetings that are stimulating, effective, and successful. Forhan (2008) suggests that chairs of Parent-Teacher Organizations (PTO) be mindful of a number of factors in order to run successful meetings. These factors include preparation, marketing, punctuality, collaboration, arranging space, agendas, introductions, enthusiasm, minute taking, bylaws, keeping on task, and neutrality. Many of these factors are relevant to running nonprofit committee and board meetings. Following are some suggested ways that chairs of nonprofits can incorporate these factors into planning and running successful committee meetings.

> Quality meetings do not occur on their own; they are planned. By following some basic guidelines, even the most novice chair can hold and run meetings that are stimulating, effective, and successful.

- *Prepare.* Preparation is the key to any successful meeting. Chairs should prepare, in advance, to lead the meeting. For those inexperienced with presiding over meetings, reading *Robert's Rules of Order* can be helpful. *Robert's Rules of Order* is a set of rules and conduct for meetings that allows everyone to be heard and decisions to be made without confusion. It can be adapted to suit the needs of any organization. Chairs can also prepare by asking former chairs for guidance and by reading books and articles about meeting management.

- *Promote.* Chairs should promote meetings in as many ways as possible, such as through agency websites, newsletters, emails, and word of mouth. Members should be made aware of the reasons why attendance is important and what will be accomplished during the meeting. This will help dispel any beliefs that meetings will be a waste of time.

- *Be punctual.* Chairs should start and end meetings on time. Punctuality breeds punctuality. Standards should be set by modeling the behavior expected of the committee. Chairs should arrive early enough to take care of final preparations, such as arranging the meeting space, making copies of the agenda and other handouts, and preparing refreshments. Meetings should begin and end on time. People have busy schedules and appreciate chairs who respect the time individuals reserve for meetings by starting and ending meetings on time.

- *Collaborate.* Chairs should collaborate and work directly with agency staff by providing advance notice of meeting schedules as well as any needs such as room arrangements and refreshments. Rooms should be left clean and organized as they were prior to the meeting, with chairs properly setup, trash thrown away, and lights turned off.

- *Arrange meeting space.* Meeting space should be based on the type of meeting that will take place and on the number of attendees. For example, arranging the chairs in a circle, or having everyone sit around the same table, can create an atmosphere of cooperation and collaboration. Such a seating arrangement does not send a message that there is a hierarchy among the members.

- *Review meeting agendas.* Chairs should review meeting agendas with the executive director in advance of each meeting. Topics should be targeted for the executive director's report to the committee, and the amount of time needed for the report should be identified. If possible, agendas should be sent to committee members prior to the date of each meeting. This allows members to better prepare for meetings. Agendas should include specific topics such as "new business," "unfinished business," and "committee reports," along with the date, time, and place of the next meeting. Prior to the start of each meeting, hard copies of the agenda should be distributed to the participants. This enables attendees to keep track of the progress of meetings and take notes if they wish. Time at the end of each meeting should be reserved for open discussions.

- *Introduce.* Each meeting should begin with introductions. Chairs should not assume that all attendees know one another. It is a good idea to provide nametags, begin each meeting with a warm welcome, and have everyone introduce themselves.

- *Be enthusiastic.* Set a positive tone at each meeting. Enthusiasm is contagious! Because new members may feel overwhelmed and intimidated, they should be looked after. By maintaining an enthusiastic tone and by nurturing new members, all members will feel more comfortable. Treat each member as a future leader of the agency.

- *Take minutes.* Minutes should be taken at all meetings. Taking minutes is a vital, legal function at committee meetings and must be taken whenever people vote and even when people do not vote. The minutes should list the date, time, and place of the meeting, the meeting notes, all motions, the names of people who make motions and second motions, and the outcomes of votes. Minutes should be kept for the agency's records.
- *Know the bylaws, policies, standing rules, and standards.* It is essential to be familiar with the organization's bylaws, policies, standing rules, and standards. This will lessen the possibility of being caught off guard with unexpected issues. When caught off guard by an outspoken committee member regarding a controversial topic, chairs should consider postponing the issue until the next meeting to allow time to investigate the issue.
- *Encourage appropriate discussions.* Chairs should encourage attendees to speak to the issues at hand but discourage repetitive or argumentative discussions. Discussions can be managed by alternating, as much as possible, between pro and con points of view to ensure that both sides are heard. Side conversations, crosstalk, and detailed committee reports should be discouraged.
- *Remain neutral.* Chairs must remain publicly neutral according to *Robert's Rules of Order*. The chair's role is to preside over meetings and not influence attendees' decisions. Chairs vote only when needed to break a tie, and they must stay out of debates as sharing personal feelings can sway other committee members.

Meetings provide a means for fundraising teams to gather to discuss ideas, make recommendations, and formulate action plans. They are also social events where members can get together to network, interact, and build relationships. When meetings are "done right," chances are they will be more productive and lead to fewer and shorter meetings.

Now that the important role of chairs has been covered, the focus will now shift to the members of the board of directors. The board of directors manage, implement, and maintain the organization's mission, goals, and objectives. Boards ensure successful planning and see that all of the agency's resources are managed effectively. The role of the board is vital to the overall success of the nonprofit.

Interpersonal Communication

Understanding and Mastery of ... Clarifying expectations

Critical Thinking Question: How might executive directors and chairs of fundraising committees clearly clarify their expectations of committee members and staff?

Board of Directors

The most valuable volunteers of an agency are its board of directors or board of trustees. According to the Center for Community Change (2010), the primary responsibility of the board is to govern the organization and ensure its ultimate success. The mission statement declares why an organization exists and is the foundation upon which a long-range strategic plan can be developed. The long-range strategic plan, with its clearly stated programmatic initiatives and their respective costs, guides the development of the fundraising strategy. From this fundraising plan, fundraising campaigns are created and initiated (Poderis, 2009e). Money and resources are necessary for an organization to fund its programs and services and satisfy its mission. As one can clearly see, the mission statement is the focus of all fundraising efforts. The involvement of the board in fundraising is no longer a benefit; it is a necessity. Therefore, fundraising is the most fundamental duty of a nonprofit's board, and few nonprofits are successful in raising funds without the board's involvement.

Why is the involvement of the board so critical to the organization's fundraising initiatives? Following are some answers to this frequently posed question:

- Donors are likely to view the board members' involvement in fundraising as evidence of the agency's community support and credibility (Center for Community Change, 2010). Board members are volunteers, and their participation in fundraising shows their commitment to the organization. Even when staff members are involved in fundraising activities, funders may view the staff members' involvement as somewhat motivated by the need to raise money to subsidize their salaries.
- Board members' personal financial contributions to the organization's fundraising initiative are essential philanthropic advertising (Zimmerman & Lehman, 2004). Prospective key funders often inquire into whether the board members have contributed. Answering, "Yes, 100% of the board has contributed to the fundraising campaign!" demonstrates, to potential donors, the board's level of commitment and confidence in the agency (Center for Community Change, 2010).
- Many nonprofit organizations have limited staff. The staff is likely to have their hands full, running programs and managing the organization. The board's assistance with fundraising is essential. It helps free up some of the staff's time, so staff can focus more energy on administering programs and services.
- Board members' involvement in fundraising is critical because their personal contacts are indispensable in the nonprofit's fundraising plans. Organizations need to bring all of their contacts together to access potential funders. Board involvement significantly increases the list of personal contacts.
- Board members are well suited to do the asking. Although prospective funders must be interested in the agency, it is the individuals who ask for donations that make people want to donate. One of the main reasons a person or business contributes to a nonprofit organization is that the right person asks.
- Board members are in a position to recruit new members, with clout and connections, to the board of trustees or board of directors (Zimmerman & Lehman, 2004). These new recruits can help ensure the success of the fundraising endeavor.
- Because the board of directors are charged with ensuring the success of the agency, board members are in a prime position to oversee the agency's fundraising efforts. The agency's executive director will likely look to the board for guidance in developing and implementing the fundraising plan.

Board members are the lifeline of the fundraising plan and must include individuals who are able to select, implement, run, manage, and evaluate fundraising campaigns. Without their guidance and support, it is unlikely that the fundraising endeavor will be successful.

Fundraising Responsibilities of the Board of Directors

In addition to approving the nonprofits' budget, board members set the pace of the fundraising effort by committing to give, soliciting major donors, and recruiting volunteers (Poderis, 2009e). Following are some examples of common tasks and responsibilities of board members in regard to the agency's fundraising plan:

- Attend board meetings on a regular basis and actively participate in fundraising activities.
- Provide input into the fundraising plan.
- Serve as an advocate for the agency.
- Serve on one or two committees or task forces.
- Volunteer for and accept fundraising assignments and thoroughly complete them and complete them on time.
- Recruit volunteers to serve on the fundraising team.
- Appeal to peers for donations.
- Identify and cultivate new donors/prospects.
- Accompany staff on key visits to funders and make introductions for staff to follow up.
- Assist with recognizing and thanking funders.
- Oversee the fiscal integrity of the agency's funds.
- Actively participate in the board's fundraising evaluation and fundraising planning efforts.

It is clear that the board plays a key role in the fundraising efforts of an agency. Just as critical is the role of the development committee. The development committee adds crucial expertise and connections to enhance and improve the fundraising initiatives and results.

Characteristics of Effective Board of Directors

There are a number of characteristics that make up effective boards. This section highlights some of the most fundamental characteristics that help prevent board members from becoming disengaged. Specifically, effective boards are diverse, passionate, enthusiastic, alert, and active.

- *Diverse.* The board should be diverse and should resemble the population of the community and surrounding area as much as possible. Not only is ethnic and racial diversity essential, diversity in gender, sexual orientation, age, socioeconomic status, ability/disability, religion, expertise, fundraising experience and skills, subject matter, and ways of thinking, are just as vital. The goal is to achieve the agency's mission by utilizing the diversity of the board through teamwork.
- *Passionate.* A quality board is passionate about the organization and its cause. Board members must believe in the agency's cause. They must also believe that the agency is making a positive difference in the lives of the consumers it serves and in the community in general. They must identify with and articulate the agency's mission and defend it with fervor.

**Planning
and Evaluating**

Understanding and Mastery of ... Program
design, implementation, and evaluation

Critical Thinking Question: What individual skills
are vital to developing successful fundraising
campaigns and evaluating the results of campaigns?

· ·

- *Enthusiastic.* A successful board is enthusiastic and optimistic about the organization. Board members are confident that problems can be overcome and are creative in their ability to look at problems and find ways to rise above them.
- *Alert.* Boards must be alert. Effective boards are alert to indicators of trouble before a crisis erupts. Whether the problem is financial, managerial, or one regarding a conflict of interest, sound boards take necessary steps to resolve such issues.
- *Active.* Effective boards are active. Board members do not simply show up for scheduled meetings; they participate in discussions and help shape the vision and future direction of the agency. They actively assist with projects, committee work, fundraising, and events.

Recruiting Board Members

When recruiting board members it is essential to keep this in mind: The organization is essentially "hiring" individuals for one of the most important jobs in the entire agency, that of governance and leadership (Gottlieb, 2008). Although board positions are filled by volunteers, the position is an appointment just as significant as the leader of a for-profit company. With that said, agencies must recruit the right people with the skills needed to assist the agency in achieving its fundraising goals.

In regard to fundraising objectives, one of the first questions an organization should consider as it begins to recruit for board members is, What are our fundraising goals and objectives and what expertise and skills might we need on our board to attain those goals and objectives? Another consideration may be to seek individuals with knowledge and expertise in the agency's service areas. For example, an agency that serves victims of intimate partner violence may want board expertise in that specialty area. As the organization changes, grows, or expands its vision, the expertise sought in its board members may change as well. As stated in the preceding section, another critical component is to ensure diversity among board members.

Recruiting board members is not unlike the recruiting process when hiring a paid employee. Specifically, recruiting board members can be broken down into the following steps:

1. *Know what the agency is looking for.* What qualities are needed? What skills or talents are necessary?
2. *Recruit candidates for each position.* Candidates should be recruited for each open position as opposed to recruiting candidates from the same pool for all open positions. By using a competitive process, agencies are more likely to discover the best candidates.
3. *Know how to recruit board members.* As opposed to relying on board members to suggest candidates, because the agency feels desperate to fill board seats, have prospects compete for a seat on the board. Agencies should get the word out about their recruiting efforts through announcements at functions and to networking groups, and through advertising in newsletters, on websites, and on social networking sites.

4. *Get to know the applicants.* Agencies should get to know their applicants just as the applicants get to know the agency. This helps determine if there is a good fit between the applicant and the agency and vice versa. Agencies can get to know the applicants by creating and using an application form, providing candidates with an orientation to the agency and the board, and interviewing prospects using the agency's list of desired qualifications.

5. *Make the transition a smooth one.* Agencies should make the board members' transition to the agency and to the position as smooth as possible.

6. *Have contracts signed.* Once board members have been chosen and voted in, new members should sign a contract and formally take on the governing duties of the organization.

7. *Request disclosures.* New members should disclose any conflicts of interest regarding any outside relationships they have which may be perceived as influencing their actions or decisions.

8. *Provide comprehensive orientation.* New board members should be given a comprehensive orientation to become more familiar with the agency and its role in the community.

9. *Put them to work.* Finally, new members should be put to work by providing them with a variety of activities and committees from which to choose.

If executed properly, recruiting board members is neither a quick nor easy process. Such a meticulous process is necessary to ensure effective administration and oversight of the nonprofit's fundraising plan. The amount of energy and time spent on recruiting and securing qualified board members can yield significant rewards in the form of a successful and profitable fundraising campaign.

Development Committee

Most organizations can benefit from setting up a development committee. A development committee is especially useful when the majority of the board of directors lack experience and skills in fundraising. A development committee is also beneficial when an agency is in need of initiating or managing an endowment or capital campaign. Doing so, especially without the assistance of a development committee, would drain too much of an agency's resources and efforts. The committee can also be helpful when there is a program or project that necessitates raising funds rapidly; when assistance is needed to put on a large, special event each year; or when the objective of the agency is to raise funds from a specific source such as a local organization or business.

It is significant to note that some agencies hire their development committee Director and sometimes employ all or some of the members of their development committee. However, there are quite a few development committees entirely comprised of volunteers. Those made up of volunteers can provide the volunteer point of view that can inspire and motivate the board's fundraising campaign. Development committees oversee and advise on the agency's fundraising campaign. Specifically, development committees are useful when the board of directors is doing everything it can to raise funds, but it is not sufficient.

Nonprofits with solid development operations are likely to have secondary committees for ongoing fundraising endeavors. Examples of these ongoing fundraising committees include capital campaigns, annual funds, underwriting campaigns, and sponsorships. The majority of the members of these ongoing fundraising committees are usually trustees, but these committees are also comprised of fundraising leaders who are not trustees. The chairs of these secondary fundraising campaign committees are likely to sit on the development committee (Poderis, 2009f).

Fundraising Responsibilities of the Development Committee

A development committee can identify, recruit, and research funding prospects and decide on the number of types of fundraising events, which will take place during the year. The committee can also write proposals. Each agency can choose the role of its development committee based on the needs of the organization. Following are examples of typical responsibilities often assigned to the development committee:

- Set policies, priorities, goals, and objectives for fundraising programs for the current fiscal year.
- Collaborate with the executive director and the board of directors to determine the short-term and long-term financial needs of the organization.
- Preserve the quality of the board of directors' future by determining what skills are needed and recruiting board members who possess the necessary skills.
- Identify and recruit community leaders to serve on the development committee and cultivate relationships with community leaders.
- Recruit key volunteer leadership and solicitors for the agency's fundraising campaign.
- Orient new board members to the organization and to the quality of the governance board the agency is working to achieve.
- Obtain training for the board of directors, including training on marketing, corporate solicitation, and proposal writing.
- Communicate with the board of directors to ensure that they are making a valuable contribution.
- Work with the board of directors in organizing fundraising activities that take into account each board member's distinct skills, knowledge, and talents.
- Communicate with board members to make sure they are satisfied with their experience on the board.
- Evaluate and assess the organization's progress toward fundraising goals.
- Encourage and motivate the board of directors in their fundraising efforts.
- Identify and rate all prime donor prospects for support (Poderis, 2009f).
- Review the ongoing performance of each campaign.

Characteristics of Effective Development Committees

Recruiting effective development committee members relies on an understanding of the characteristics that make up a successful committee. This section underscores some of the essential characteristics of development committee members.

- *Determined, attentive, adaptable.* One of the main characteristics of effective development committees, according to Poderis (2009b), is temperament. Development committees must have a temperament suitable to serving the agency's needs. They must be determined, attentive, and adaptable.
- *Thick skinned.* They must understand that in regard to fundraising, credit goes to the people who obtain the funds, not to the facilitators. As such, the development committee makes the volunteers shine, even if it is at the expense of the development committee's glory.
- *Humble.* Members need to function in a more supportive role. They must be able to derive pleasure from working in the background and out of the spotlight. In other words, development committees tend to operate in the background.
- *Inspiring.* Development committees inspire agency solicitors and provide them with the tools they need to be successful.
- *Organized.* They must be able to bring a sense of organization and leadership to the fundraising campaign.
- *Donor-driven.* They are donor-driven as opposed to institution driven. They are mindful and protective of the reputation and mission of the agency. They are in the best position to say "no" to appeals that demand too much from the organization or undermine the agency's purpose.

Effective development committee members possess a variety of characteristics; therefore, attention must be given to recruiting qualified and talented members.

Recruiting Development Committee Members

When recruiting members of the development committee, a number of guidelines can be helpful. The following segment provides suggested steps for recruiting development committee members:

1. *Seek diversity.* As with all nonprofit recruiting endeavors, it is imperative that an agency ensures diversity among its development committee. The most effective development committees are those that bring a diverse group of individuals together with a range of opinions and perspectives.
2. *Recruit a board member as chair.* Because the development committee is usually a standing committee of the board, it is useful to recruit a board member to serve as the chair of the development committee. The development committee chair must be an organized and outstanding leader who can inspire and encourage committee members.
3. *Secure both board and non-board members.* The development committee members should include both board members and non-board members. The development committee can be an excellent training ground for prospective board members (Capital Venture, 2010).
4. *Ensure that the recruit has the time.* It is essential that members who are recruited to the development committee have the time to serve and have demonstrated enthusiasm and passion for the agency.

5. *Confirm that the position duties can be met.* If the organization has a fundraising requirement, potential development committee members must be able to meet the requirement.
6. *Verify the recruit's ability to oversee judicial and fiduciary duties.* In addition, members of the development committee must be able to fulfill the board's judicial oversight and fiduciary duties.
7. *Provide a position description.* Prospective development committee members should be provided with a position description of the expectations and requirements of serving on the committee.
8. *Provide orientation.* They should also be given an orientation to the agency, so they can decide whether the agency is a suitable match for them.

The executive director, staff, board of directors, and the development committee are central faces of the agency in the community. With this in mind, their role in selecting members of the fundraising committee is all the more important. The fundraising campaign becomes another central face of the agency, and the selection of its members is essential in developing a high-quality fundraising plan.

Fundraising Committee

Fundraising committees are fundamental to the viability and economic welfare of agencies. Committees may be ad hoc committees, standing teams recruited to help raise funds and awareness, or comprised of board members. They serve to share information, build relationships, and raise money to meet the continuing needs of the organization. Active, dedicated, and productive committees ensure winning fundraising campaigns. Some agencies may choose to have the fundraising committee responsible for obtaining a certain percentage of the total contributions. In such cases, agencies may choose to hold a public campaign to enlist the support of others for the remaining percentage.

According to Poderis (2009f) the fundraising committee is typically broken into five divisions: major corporate and business gifts, smaller corporate and business gifts, foundations, major individual gifts, and smaller individual gifts. Corporate and individual donors are separated by the size of the gift, whereas foundations, because they are often few and far between, are treated like a single group. In regard to corporations, it is essential to categorize the corporation by the size of the desired gift and not by the size of the corporation. Each of these divisions may be further divided according to the agency's needs.

Fundraising Responsibilities of the Fundraising Committee

Following are examples of some of the typical fundraising committee members' responsibilities and tasks in the overall development and implementation of the fundraising plan:

- Define the agency's short-range, intermediate-range, and long-range funding needs in collaboration with the executive director and the board of trustees or the board of directors.

- Identify, encourage, and procure community leaders to serve on the fundraising committee or a campaign division committee.
- Establish priorities and policies for the fundraising campaign.
- Identify tasks and activities that need to be completed.
- Estimate and evaluate the probable success of fundraising campaigns and activities.
- Produce solicitation materials and train volunteer solicitors for fundraising campaigns.
- Involve the board in fundraising campaigns, and organize fundraising activities, which take into consideration the unique talents of the board members.
- Take the lead in certain types of outreach efforts, such as hosting fundraising parties.
- Make personal donations and encourage board members to contribute.
- Identify and rate all major potential funders for support (Poderis, 2009f).
- Schedule appointments with major prospects and solicit donations.
- Recruit and train key solicitors and volunteer leaders for the agency's fundraising plan (Poderis, 2009c).
- Monitor the fundraising efforts to ensure that ethical practices are in place, that donors are acknowledged, and that fundraising efforts are cost-effective.
- Review and evaluate the ongoing performance of each fundraising campaign and motivate the board in its fundraising efforts.

The duties of the fundraising committee should be divided among the committee members based on the individual member's strengths. Newer members should be given more basic and short-term tasks at first. When they express enthusiasm to take on more duties, they should be given additional responsibilities. All board and committee members should present a united front (Darling, 2010).

Agencies with strong fundraising committees may also have campaign division committees to assist with ongoing fundraising endeavors such as the endowment, annual fund, capital fund, and sponsorship and underwriting campaigns. The chairs of these campaign division committees also sit on the development committee.

Information Management

Understanding and Mastery of ... Using technology for word processing, sending email, and locating and evaluating information

Critical Thinking Question: In what ways can fundraising team members use technology to assist with an agency's fundraising efforts?

Characteristics of Effective Fundraising Committees

Members of effective fundraising committees share common characteristics; specifically, members are

- *Passionate.* Successful fundraising committees are made up of members who are passionate and committed to the mission of the agency.
- *Experts.* Many effective members have come up through the ranks as volunteers within the nonprofit, whereas others are members based on their professional expertise in fundraising.
- *Leaders.* Effective committee members have proven leadership in fundraising. According to NFP Consulting Resources, Inc. (2010), characteristics to consider are members who are known and respected leaders in the community, are able to open

doors to major donors, can recruit additional leaders, have the ability to motivate others, and are able to make major gifts to the agency.

- *Dedicated.* Effective members deem the organization as one of their top philanthropic priorities during their tenure on the fundraising committee.

Recruiting fundraising committee members who possess these characteristics is essential to the success of the fundraising campaign.

Recruiting Fundraising Committee Members

The fundraising committee will ultimately determine the overall success of the agency's fundraising campaign. Therefore, members of the fundraising committee must be carefully chosen for their influence in the community, their generosity, and their eagerness and willingness to work. Along with the chair, previously discussed, it is sometimes a good idea to recruit co-chairs and even couples. The following steps are helpful in recruiting fundraising committee members:

1. *Develop a job description.* The board, along with staff input, should develop a job description that includes participation and attendance expectations, philanthropy, and committee involvement.
2. *Determine the length of service.* The length of service as well as the expectations of time commitment should be established.
3. *Recruit community members.* Although it is common for some board members to serve on fundraising committees, members of the community should be recruited as well. The board can be enlisted to recruit new fundraising committee members. Community members who have an ardent interest in the agency should be invited to serve on the committee. For example, agencies can recruit members from the list of individuals who have attended previous fundraising events or have previously volunteered and helped out at organization-sponsored events. Their interest in the agency is a key element to successful fundraising committees and campaigns.
4. *Recruit community leaders.* Agencies should also consider individuals who are exemplary leaders in the community, such as philanthropists who have been successful with other organizations. Key leadership prospects should be approached to obtain their willingness to have their names included on the nomination list.
5. *Notify prospects.* Prospects should be told that the organization will be interviewing a number of people being considered for the fundraising committee. This will demonstrate to the prospects that the organization is seeking quality members.
6. *Inquire about prospects' knowledge of the organization.* The size of the fundraising committee is not as important as the effectiveness of its leaders and the dedication of its members. Prospects should be asked what they know about the vision and work of the agency, and agencies should answer any questions that prospects have.
7. *Request bios from prospects.* It is useful to request bios from the candidates as well as a list of nonprofit leadership experience and professional accomplishments.

8. *Assign roles.* Recruited volunteer committee members can be assigned to the overall fundraising committee or to a campaign division committee that makes best use of the volunteers' experience, interests, and skills.

In addition to the executive director, chairs, and committee members, agency staff play a vital role in the organization's fundraising initiatives.

Staff

A successful fundraising campaign relies on the help and support of the organization's staff members, those individuals who are responsible for providing the services and programs to its constituents. Staff have first-hand knowledge of the need for funding. The key, however, is to ensure that agencies avoid simply piling on additional job responsibilities on an already overworked and, at times, underpaid staff. As such, it is beneficial for agencies to incorporate fundraising responsibilities into the job descriptions and performance evaluations of its staff; doing so can create a culture of philanthropy.

> A successful fundraising campaign relies on the help and support of the organization's staff members, those individuals who are responsible for providing the services and programs to its constituents.

Nonprofit staff face different challenges than many employees in the public sector. In many instances, the salaries are lower and even though nonprofit staff, for the most part, are aware that they could command higher earnings in the public sector, they are intrinsically motivated to contribute to a charity or cause. However, some organizations face challenges in gaining commitment from staff members.

At times, agencies have difficulty instilling in their staff a strong affiliation with the organization and its work. Without a strong connection between the staff and the organization, staff are generally less motivated to perform with excellence and contribute to the fundraising effort (Axiom Consulting Partners, 2010). Gaining commitment from the organization's staff is based on a number of factors. It is not a one-way street but involves the organization's commitment to the staff as well as the staff's commitment to the organization. According to Boggon (2009), staff in the nonprofit sector typically spend only 18 months working for a cause before moving on to another position. This is especially true of younger and newer recruits. Boggon attributes this to the "curve of involvement." The "curve of involvement" illustrates that the more personal responsibility a staff member takes for the fundraising effort, the more involved the staff member will be in the fundraising endeavor. The levels of involvement range from low, which includes an awareness and interest in the organization and its causes, to high, which includes commitment, ownership, and taking personal responsibility for the organization and its causes. In other words, the more passionate staff are about the cause, the easier it is for them to motivate potential donors.

Based on this assumption, it may also be assumed that the way the organization treats its staff inevitably affects how the staff feel about their jobs. Answers to the following two questions may shed light on the level of staff commitment to the organization's cause and fundraising efforts. First, how does the organization demonstrate its commitment to its staff's fundraising efforts? Second, what can the organization do to enhance its commitment to its staff and thereby increase the staff's commitment to fundraising? The amount of time and effort spent considering these two questions can influence the staff's overall commitment to the fundraising effort. Higher levels of commitment and engagement can increase retention and subsequently reduce undesired staff turnover rates. Leaders of agencies must provide staff with the necessary resources and support to demonstrate the agency's commitment to its staff (Center for Community Change, 2010; Lansdowne, 2006). For example, providing staff with ongoing fundraising training and support can not only bring financial rewards to the organization, but can help staff become more aware of the significant role that fundraising plays in the sustainability of the organization.

When an agency mobilizes its staff to play a role in the fundraising effort, the organization's fundraising capacity is dramatically enhanced. There are a number of fundraising tasks that can be allocated to staff. These tasks will now be discussed.

Fundraising Responsibilities of Staff

Staff must be engaged in the fundraising process. They are in a prime position to provide first-hand knowledge of the organization needs, wants, and what it can do. Staff involvement in the agency's fundraising effort builds ownership and ownership can make all the difference in the success of the campaign. Following are some examples of staff responsibilities and tasks in the overall development and implementation of the fundraising plan. It is important to note that staff responsibilities vary based on the type of organization, its size, and its needs.

- Assist the executive director in developing plans to generate income from various sources and assist with the preparation of the preliminary budget. Assure that expenses are within budget during the year.
- Follow up with the board and committee decisions to assure implementation of such decisions.
- Provide input on the fundraising plan, suggest innovative fundraising ideas, and formulate annual fundraising objectives.
- Organize fundraising campaign and take care of logistics related to fundraising activities such as recruiting, training, supervising, and assessing volunteers.
- Prepare materials for the fundraising campaign, including supporting documents, exhibits, and proposals for the board and committees. Ensure timely submission and dissemination of these materials.
- Improve and develop communication material for the agency, including websites, brochures, posters, and annual reports. Assist with press releases and media stories.
- Conduct research and establish contacts with new and potential funders. Monitor donor websites and identify donor opportunities.
- Foster relationships with existing donors, respond to their requests, and keep them updated about the work of the organization.
- Assist the board in any means possible, including accompanying board and committee members on key visits to funders, asking for money when appropriate, and providing assistance with fundraising events.
- Develop and maintain a fundraising database of donor organizations, agencies, and private corporations offering funding.

- Assist with expressions of gratitude when appropriate.
- Process donations, maintain program records, and prepare annual reports, program reports, and reports on achievement of goals and objectives.

Where staff contribute their insight, knowledge, and work experience to the fundraising campaign, volunteers provide hundreds and hundreds of hours of service to agencies and organizations. Their generous contributions of time, knowledge, and skills are the glue that holds the entire fundraising campaign together.

Although all previously mentioned members of the fundraising team, with the exception of the executive director and paid staff, are likely volunteers, there is also a need for volunteers beyond those serving on the board, in leadership roles, or on one of the committees. Additional volunteers are needed to support the efforts of the board, its committees, and the staff. These volunteers are the foundation of a solid fundraising endeavor, appear in all areas of the fundraising campaign, and provide a unique perspective to the fundraising plan.

Volunteers

Volunteers bring a new dimension to the fundraising campaign by offering an outside perspective and serving as special advocates for the agency. Volunteers are individuals who may not be interested in serving on a board or committee; rather, they may be interested in lending their time to a charity they value.

Fundraising Responsibilities of Volunteers

Volunteers should be invited to give of their time and talent and, when recruited, should be given meaningful work, not just busy work. To be effective, volunteers need support. They need to have their expectations clearly communicated, and they need the tools to succeed. Many organizations underuse volunteers or use them in the wrong way. Well-trained volunteers who are furnished with quality material about the agency and its work can help with a variety of events and can make solicitation calls. It is helpful to appoint a permanent liaison to the volunteer group. The liaison should be someone who is familiar with the organization and its fundraising goals and is available to the volunteers when needed (Hoffman, 1992). Here are some ways volunteers can assist agencies with fundraising efforts:

- Lend a hand with fundraising events as they occur.
- Make suggestions on alternative ways to raise money.
- Open doors for solicitation calls by scheduling meetings and introducing the board and staff to potential funders.
- Provide administrative support when needed.
- Ensure that all inquiries from potential donors are brought to the attention of the fundraising committee.
- Promote the agency and its fundraising activities within the community.
- Assist with direct mailings to appeal for donations from new and prospective donors.

- Assist with grant proposals, capital campaigns, major gift appeals, endowment campaigns, and planned giving efforts.
- Help out with telephone fundraising.
- Assist with hosting special events such as small group luncheons.
- Lend other skills and resources as needed.

Not all people want to volunteer, but for those who do, there are a number of characteristics that effective volunteers share.

Characteristics of Effective Volunteers

Effective volunteers share a number of characteristics, including the following:

- *Dependable.* Effective volunteers are dependable and reliable. They come in when they say they will be in and follow through on projects and assignments.
- *Accountable.* They assume essential responsibilities.
- *Leaders.* They possess exceptional leadership skills.
- *Interpersonal.* They demonstrate concern for relationships between and among people and are excellent communicators.
- *Ethical.* They are ethical and demonstrate high moral values.
- *Devoted.* They take their volunteer work seriously, just as seriously as if they were being paid.
- *Efficient.* The best volunteers work efficiently.
- *Givers.* They appreciate the opportunity to contribute their knowledge and skills for the betterment of the agency and community.
- *Committed.* Effective volunteers demonstrate a sincere interest in the nonprofit and are committed to the organization for which they are willing to serve.

Part of the challenge of recruiting volunteers who possess the aforementioned characteristics is an agency's volunteer recruiting program. Recruiting volunteers requires a commitment by the board to fund a line to recruit and train volunteers to assist with the fundraising campaign.

Recruiting Volunteers

The following steps will ensure a successful recruiting process:

1. Understand what motivates people to volunteer. Gaining commitment from volunteers to give up their personal time, and assist with an agency's fundraising efforts, may not be as difficult a task as it may seem. Volunteers are motivated by a number of factors. By tapping into these motivators, securing volunteers to assist with fundraising activities becomes an easy task.
2. Determine the activities, skills, and knowledge that would add value to the fundraising campaign. Answering a series of questions can serve as a guide to ensuring that the volunteer's roles fit with the agency's needs. For example, what fundraising needs does the organization have that are currently not being met? What else would the agency do in regard to the fundraising campaign if it had the resources and time? What more would the agency do if it had the necessary skills? In what ways

can the core functions of the fundraising team be improved? What other fundraising competencies does the agency need? Which fundraising skills could the agency benefit from learning the most?

3. Proactively tackle attrition before it becomes a concern. Volunteer attrition is a serious problem and tends to be tied to the lack of acknowledgment and recognition, as well as the lack of tools necessary to help the volunteers succeed. Attrition can, therefore, be reduced when agencies clearly communicate their expectations, provide the necessary tools that will allow the volunteers to succeed, and acknowledge the importance of the volunteers' roles to the overall success of the fundraising campaign (Lysakowski, 2005). They must be assured that they will be given meaningful work, not just busy work. Because volunteers are most effective when they receive staff support, assuring them that they will have the support they need is another fundamental pledge.

Volunteer recruitment requires an understanding of the motivations and an understanding of some of the evolving trends in volunteerism. Knowing these trends can open the doors to more creative ways of recruiting:

- Many volunteers also have full-time or part-time jobs, family responsibilities, academic obligations, and other commitments. Therefore, volunteers may look for finite volunteer positions, as opposed to traditional volunteer positions. In other words, many volunteers are interested in assisting on projects that have a beginning and an end as opposed to assisting with the ongoing, daily work of an organization.

- Another trend is the corporate volunteer. Corporate volunteers are encouraged by their employers to participate in community service. Some businesses provide a day or more of leave each year for employees to participate in community service. Agencies can benefit from corporate volunteers by designing team projects, which can be completed in a day.

- Virtual volunteering is a terrific option for agencies looking for innovative ways to recruit volunteers. Virtual volunteering allows volunteers to work from their desks. It is an excellent option for individuals with limited time to travel or restricted mobility, or for those who would like to volunteer for an organization that is not locally based.

- One of the most modern methods to recruiting volunteers is through a site called "the extraordinaries" (2010). The extraordinaries provide a network of experts, ready to volunteer. The concept is called MICRO-volunteering. It is a volunteer collaboration that takes place entirely online. It is designed for millennial-generation employees and the super busy and is perfect for team building. It requires less time from volunteers and less supervision from the nonprofit agency. It is an entirely free service where nonprofits can get help with marketing, fundraising, idea generation, and more. In addition, it provides organizations with an opportunity to network with people interested in the organization's cause. The MICRO-volunteers are people from all over the world who collaborate virtually to help nonprofits solve problems and answer questions. MICRO-volunteering is also promoted to corporations as a turn-key employee volunteering program and, as a result, nonprofits have access to

Administration

Understanding and Mastery of ... Recruiting
and managing volunteers

Critical Thinking Question: Why might it be
essential for agencies to find innovative ways to
recruit volunteers?

· ·

a high-quality labor pool with experts in marketing, public relations (PR), finance, product design, operations, and more. For companies, it offers a way for employees to use their spare time and engage with communities. Employees can use their professional skills and expertise to volunteer for a few minutes while waiting for a meeting to begin, while on a bus to work, or during a lunch break. MICRO-volunteering is touted as a "skills-based employee engagement."

Thinking outside the box can open up a number of volunteer opportunities that would otherwise remain untapped. An agency can overcome barriers that may discourage individuals from volunteering by offering innovative and flexible options to its recruits.

Teamwork: Getting Everyone Onboard

Both paid staff and volunteers have a vital role in the design and implementation of the fundraising campaign. Whether paid or unpaid, organizations need and benefit from competent, caring individuals who assist the agency in its fundraising efforts. It is through the fundraising work of these individuals that nonprofits are able to provide much-needed programs and services. Effective teamwork begins by gaining commitment from both paid staff and volunteers. This requires an understanding of roles, specifically, Who in the agency holds the power in practice and on paper? What tasks are performed by paid staff and what tasks are performed by volunteers? What has the management team discussed in regard to the most effective combination of paid staff and volunteers? Teamwork can ensue only in an environment in which both the paid staff and volunteers feel motivated and have clearly defined and meaningful roles.

Gaining Paid Staff Support for Working with Volunteers

At times, paid staff may be reluctant to work with volunteers. According to Volunteering Ireland (2010) some of paid staff's apprehension may revolve around concerns regarding job security and budget cuts. Some staff may hold feelings that volunteers will be more of a burden than a help due to the additional workload required to train them. Others may be apprehensive about having to manage volunteers without having management experience or concerned about not being able to control the volunteers. Still others may be uneasy about diminished quality of service or about the volunteers being unreliable.

To avoid paid staff from taking their concerns and frustrations out on the volunteers, a number of strategies can be employed to help gain staff support in working with volunteers, including the following:

- Agencies can develop a volunteer policy that clearly defines the purpose of volunteer involvement in the fundraising campaign.
- Nonprofits can include, as a component of staff evaluations, the ability to effectively work with volunteers.
- Volunteer information can be included in employee orientation and ongoing training.

- When hiring new employees, agencies can assess candidates' capabilities in terms of personal volunteer experience and views regarding volunteers.
- Staff can be involved in the creation of meaningful volunteer roles and in the selection and orientation of the volunteers.
- Agencies can recognize those employees who work well with volunteers.

Gaining the support of staff for working with volunteers is one necessary component of teamwork. Another element is gaining the support of volunteers for working with paid staff.

Gaining Volunteer Support for Working with Paid Staff

Some volunteers may be just as apprehensive about working with paid staff as paid staff may be about working with volunteers. The reasons for these concerns vary. Certain volunteers may consider themselves more qualified to perform the job duties than the paid staff. Volunteers may believe they are unappreciated or underappreciated by the paid staff. Some volunteers may feel irritated that staff are getting paid whereas they are doing similar work without pay. Volunteers may also become annoyed when paid staff are credited for the volunteers' brilliant ideas. Volunteers may think that they are doing work that no one else wants to do. They may feel that no one listens to their suggestions and that staff are reluctant to make changes. Some volunteers may believe that staff do not work hard enough. Finally, volunteers may think that they are always told what to do but not asked to participate.

With these concerns and issues in mind, nonprofits can implement a number of strategies to help in gaining the support of fundraising volunteers. For example,

- Agencies can create policies that clearly express the reasons why various types of paid staff are employed and how these link to the work of the volunteers.
- Nonprofits can develop selective target marketing of volunteer recruitment, which carefully matches volunteers to specific tasks.
- Organizations can make effective work relationships with staff a part of the volunteers' position descriptions.
- Staff information can be included in volunteer orientation and ongoing volunteer training.
- Agencies can obtain feedback from volunteers regarding staff members who work well with them.
- Nonprofits can allow volunteers to play appropriate, participatory roles within the agency.

Effective teamwork among staff and volunteers requires clear boundaries and a transparent line of communication and accountability. Doing so increases the likelihood that both paid staff and volunteers will be more satisfied in their roles. Agencies should involve staff and volunteers in defining roles and refining roles over time. Volunteers should be asked what roles they want and do not want to play, in the overall fundraising campaign. Paid staff should be asked what roles they would like to delegate to volunteers. The needs of the paid staff and volunteers should be matched in the best way possible to create a motivated fundraising team.

According to Volunteering Ireland (2010), agencies should avoid situations where people wear different hats. It is better if paid staff do not volunteer for the organization that they work for. If they do, however, they should undertake work that is entirely different from work in which they are paid. This will help avoid future power struggles and unclear disciplinary situations. Board and development committees should avoid roles where they manage a staff member in one situation and are managed by the same staff member in another situation. This can create another potential source of conflict. If a paid position becomes available within an organization, volunteers should be permitted to apply. However, agencies should adhere to the U.S. Equal Employment Opportunity Commission's (EEOC) (2010) recruitment guidelines and advertise extensively, rather than placing someone into a position without giving it much thought.

Whether paid or unpaid, teambuilding involves all levels of the organization, from the executive director to the volunteers. When all levels of the organization are involved, ownership of the fundraising effort is shared by everyone. See Appendix A for an example of an organizational chart of a nonprofit's fundraising team.

Motivating Members of the Fundraising Team

Motivating the team to take an active role stems from the team members' fervent belief that they can truly make a difference. Members must believe that the work they will be involved in is meaningful in the lives of others, in the community, and in the world.

People are moved into taking action based on sentiments and emotions regarding what might be possible when working together to achieve a goal. Fundraising team members must feel that they are stakeholders in the mission, governance, and life of the organization. Team members, who are invested in the overall success of an organization, are more prone to become engaged in the fundraising planning process and take ownership of the fundraising campaign. The following suggestions can aid in motivating fundraising team members to commit to the fundraising effort:

> Motivating the team to take an active role stems from the team members' fervent belief that they can truly make a difference.

- Agencies must ensure that fundraising team members clearly understand, up front, that fundraising is a collaborative effort. Their active participation in fundraising is necessary. By seeking input from the team, members are more likely to take active roles in the overall fundraising campaign.
- By dispelling early on any concerns the team members may have about fundraising, apprehension regarding expectations can be dramatically reduced.
- Agencies should match each team member's fundraising efforts, based on the individual's skills and interests. There are a number of roles and activities that team members can actively participate in, from cultivating prospective donors to writing thank-you notes.
- Agencies should provide the fundraising team with ample information about the organization and sufficient fundraising training, so they can effectively contribute their talents to the overall success of the campaign. Fundraising, for the most part, is a learned skill. The best way to gain knowledge and skills is through preparation, involvement, and participation.

- Agencies should inform the fundraising team members about why the organization needs the money. Agencies should inform team members about where the current funding is coming from and what the current fundraising efforts entail. An organization must take the time to explain to its team what phenomenal programs and services will be funded with the money that will be raised. The fundraising team should have a clear idea of what the world might look like should the fundraising goals be met, and how it might look if the goals are not met.
- Agencies should provide fundraising team members with sufficient training and support in fundraising. The team should be provided with supporting materials and permitted to practice the fundraising skills with seasoned fundraisers and staff. One of the best ways to motivate team members is to have them work with former or current members who have participated in fundraising-related activities. These mentors can share personal experiences regarding previous fundraising campaigns, particularly the successes. Ciconte (2005) says it best, by taking the mystery out of the fundraising experience, even the more reluctant fundraising team members will be more comfortable with fundraising.
- Agencies should follow up with the fundraising team members, through encouragement and support, on their fundraising efforts. Members should be apprised of the overall fundraising effort and publicly thanked. The majority of individuals appreciate being recognized and thanked for what they do. This is certainly true of fundraising team members.

By following these practical tips, agencies will be on the right path to motivating and inspiring their fundraising teams. Motivated teams are successful teams!

Summary

A weak fundraising team can undermine an organization's ability to raise the revenue needed to support its programs and services. Establishing a strong fundraising team requires much time and energy, but it is worth the effort. Fundraising teams are comprised of the executive director, staff, as well as numerous volunteers including chairs and committee members. The chairs serve as the leaders of the board and of the various committees, including development committees, the fundraising committees, campaign division committees, and secondary committees. The board of directors and the various fundraising committees rely on a group of qualified volunteers to serve as board and committee members. A successful fundraising team is complete when additional volunteers, who are not interested in serving on a committee, are secured to lend their hands to a charity they respect. Successful fundraising relies on the dedication, creativity, passion, and preparedness of its team members. Every member of the team serves an integral role in the design and implementation of a profitable fundraising campaign. Through thoughtful and deliberate planning, organizations can recruit, train, support, and motivate a fundraising team that will meet or exceed each organization's expectations.

The following questions will test your application and analysis of the content found within this chapter. For additional assessment, applying, analyzing, synthesizing, and evaluating chapter content with practice, visit **MySearchLab.com**

1. Among some of the responsibilities of this role is to recruit members to the board of directors, serve as the liaison to the board, and ensure that all fundraising activities are carried out with high ethical standards.

   a. Chair of the fundraising committee.
   b. Executive director.
   c. Chair of the board of directors.
   d. Chair of the development committee.

2. When recruiting chairs, a number of steps should be taken to increase the likelihood of securing competent leaders. One of the steps is to review the candidates who participated in all aspects of the recruiting process and begin an election process. The election process must

   a. include a secret ballot.
   b. follow *Robert's Rules of Order*.
   c. follow the organization's bylaws.
   d. take place within 2 weeks of the candidates' interviews.

3. You are a staff member at a local nonprofit agency. The agency is putting together an art auction and your executive director asks you to recruit volunteers to assist with marketing the fundraiser. She suggests that you check out a site called "the extraordinaries." You are not familiar with the site but after some research you learn that "the extraordinaries" specializes in

   a. virtual volunteering.
   b. corporate volunteering.
   c. commercial volunteering.
   d. MICRO-volunteering.

4. You are the volunteer coordinator at a nonprofit organization that assists displaced homemakers in securing employment. You overhear three of your volunteers discussing an upcoming fundraiser. Specifically, the volunteers were saying they felt underappreciated by the paid staff and felt that staff were getting paid for the same type of work that they, the volunteers, are doing. With these concerns in mind, the best course of action for you to take would be to

   a. implement strategies to gain support of the volunteers.
   b. recruit new volunteers.
   c. speak with the staff and let them know how the volunteers are feeling.
   d. let the volunteers know that you overheard them and explain to them why staff get paid for what they do.

5. The fundraising team is comprised of the organization's board and various committees and campaign divisions. Each of these groups is led by a chair. What are three characteristics of effective chairs?

6. The involvement of the board is crucial to an agency's fundraising initiative. Explain two reasons why board involvement is so critical.

7. At times, paid staff may be hesitant to work with volunteers. Describe a strategy that agencies can adopt to help gain staff support for working with volunteers.

8. Fundraising team members must believe that the work they will be doing will make a difference in the lives of others, in the community, and in the world. What steps can agencies take to motivate their fundraising team members?

CHAPTER 3

Creating a Fundraising Plan

In Chapter 2, you were introduced to the fundamentals of pulling the fundraising team together. Once the fundraising team is established, the next step is to create a quality fundraising plan that guides the effort. The first component of a fundraising plan is to identify the fundraising goals. Fundraising goals emphasize the agency's needs and sets the organization's financial goals.

Identifying Fundraising Goals

Agencies must identify their fundraising goals before launching into a fundraising campaign. When developing fundraising goals, it is crucial to involve the board of directors in the process. When the board is actively involved, they are more likely to engage in the fundraising campaign itself.

Fundraising goals help the organization to determine what funds are needed in order to achieve the agency's priorities and ensure its future. Goals also highlight what the money will be used for. In other words, identifying fundraising goals provides information on the amount of money needed to accomplish the agency's goals, the amount of money needed for fundraising initiatives, and an overview of how the money will be spent. Goals must be meaningful, easy to understand, and consistent with the agency's mission and objectives.

Fundraising goals may be fixed or open. Fixed goals are established to meet an end result, such as the cost of renovating a homeless shelter. On the other hand, open goals have no set target amount because the money raised is usually dispersed over a number of programs and services (Alise, 2010). Most organizations will likely have a number of fundraising goals based on the unique needs of the organizations. For example, an agency may need to build a new facility, reduce a deficit, fund a new program, or perhaps develop an emergency fund. Each organization has its own needs. However, the majority of nonprofits have four main

Learning Objectives
- Clarify the differences between fundraising goals and objectives.
- Describe and create a gift chart.
- Identify the five sections of a needs/problem statement.
- Identify resources and estimate the cost of a fundraising plan.
- Identify the different types and components of a case statement.

Fundraising goals help the organization to determine what funds are needed in order to achieve the agency's priorities and ensure its future.

funding needs: program, general operating costs, capital campaigns, and building endowments.

Program funds provide funding needed to support the organization's programs. Examples of program costs include the salaries and benefits for staff members working exclusively on the program; personal equipment costs attributable to these staff members; supplies and materials for each program; and rent, in cases where the program exclusively uses a particular facility (Garcia Abadia, 2009).

General operating costs are the funds needed for nonprofits to sustain their day-to-day operations. Examples of general operating costs include rent, utilities, staff salaries, and office supplies.

Capital campaigns raise money that will be spent to acquire or improve a physical asset. Capital campaigns are commonly referred to as "bricks and mortar" because they are typically used to purchase, construct, or renovate a building (Poderis, 2009d).

Endowments can insure an organization against the future. It is a restricted fund where only interest from the fund can be spent. The principal serves as the anchor of the endowment. Typically only a portion of the earnings or interest from the endowment is spent annually. Usually this amounts to 5% (Fritz, 2010e). This ensures that the original funds grow over time. Endowment funds are typically overseen by professional money managers who invest the money in stocks and bonds (Fritz, 2010e).

Interventions and Direct Services

Understanding and Mastery of . . . Skills to facilitate appropriate direct services and interventions related to specific client or client group goals

Critical Thinking Question: How do fundraising goals and organizational goals affect one another?

Undeniably, fundraising goals and organizational goals affect one another. Oftentimes agencies set program goals that require funds far too grand for the agency to generate. The fundraising goals are dependent on what the organization intends to do in the future. Therefore, agency goals and fundraising goals should be set at the same time. By setting program goals and fundraising goals simultaneously, agencies are more prone to identify more realistic program and fundraising goals (National Consumer Supporter Technical Assistance Center, n.d.). For example, when organizations determine what programs and services they aim to provide in the future, they will be in a better place to identify fundraising goals to ensure they have the resources to support the identified programs and services.

When identifying fundraising goals, it is useful for organizations to answer the following questions:

- How much money is needed to support the daily operations of the organization, as well as fund programs and services?
- Which of the current income sources produces the greatest share of income?
- Is that source expected to decrease, increase, or remain unchanged?
- Which revenue source is the most consistent?
- What income can be counted on by the agency?
- Which income sources are the least consistent?
- What might be here today, but gone tomorrow?
- Which revenue sources, despite size, have the greatest growth potential for the organization?

Once fundraising goals have been established, fundraising objectives can be identified. Fundraising objectives ensure that the agency sufficiently considers what will be achieved and at what cost.

Identifying Fundraising Objectives

Fundraising objectives are an essential component of the plan, as they are the only means by which the success of the fundraising campaign can be measured. If the stated objectives are met, it can then be assumed that the fundraising campaign was a success. Without fundraising objectives, organizations can only speculate as to the fundraising plan's original intent and the effectiveness of the activities undertaken (Sargeant & Jay, 2004).

According to Sargeant and Jay (2004), fundraising objectives should speak of the amount of funds that will be raised; the categories of donors that will provide the funds (i.e., corporate, foundation, individual); and an accurate estimate of the costs of raising funds.

Objectives can also address more specific topics such as donor retention and attrition rates, average gift size, response rates, and return on initial investment. Since the types of fundraising will likely differ, it is quite common to split the objectives into different categories such as restricted/unrestricted funds, capital campaign/annual funds, and uncommitted/committed givers (Sargeant & Jay, 2004).

As stated in Chapter 1, restricted funds are funds received to support a particular cause such as a specific program or service. Unrestricted funds are funds that are donated to support the daily work of the agency and can be spent where needed. Since both of these types of funds serve different agency needs, it is customary for agencies to write separate objectives for each type of fund because the level of flexibility for each fund is quite different.

Capital funds are funds that are contributed to raise "capital" for a significant project such as a new building. Annual funds are contributions made to fund the ongoing costs associated with running the organization. Separate objectives should be established for each fund.

The term *uncommitted givers* refers to individuals who may make a donation based on an agency appeal or may send occasional gifts to support an organization. On the other hand, committed givers refer to individuals who pledge to make regular donations monthly, quarterly, or annually. Sometimes these donations are made through a direct draw from a bank account or through an automatic charge to the donor's credit card. Because separate appeals are typically made to each category of giver, they are often distinguished separately when identifying the fundraising objectives.

The manner in which the objectives are written is just as crucial as the objectives themselves. According to Duggan and Jurgens (2007), the acronym MAPS can be used to describe the characteristics of high-quality objectives. Specifically, they must be Measurable, Action-oriented, Practical, and Specific.

- *Measurable.* Using terms such as *increase* or *boost* is not helpful when trying to determine the effectiveness of a fundraising campaign. Objectives should be measurable, that is, they should be quantifiable in order to determine specifically what needs to be accomplished and when.

- *Action-oriented.* Objectives must be action-oriented. They must be written in a way that specifically states the various activities that will produce the desired outcome.
- *Practical.* Objectives must be practical. Practical objectives are those objectives that are realistic, given the resources available to the organization. If the objective is unattainable, those affiliated with the objective may feel discouraged, and in some cases, resources may be wasted.

The objectives should be related to one aspect of a fundraising activity or to one category of donor. Objectives should be specific, not vague. Additionally, they should be broken down into manageable sequential steps that lead to achieving the objective.

Creating Gift Charts

A gift chart is a valuable planning tool that illustrates the number of gifts and donors needed to raise a certain amount of money. It provides information regarding whether or not there is a sufficient number of donors at each level to meet the agency's fundraising goals. According to Seale (2010) drafting a gift chart is the first step in assessing whether a fundraising campaign goal is achievable, or not ambitious enough.

Gift charts are constructed much like a pyramid, with the top gift on top followed by a number of major gifts, and ending with many smaller gifts. According to Seale (2010) the top gifts are 15 to 25% or more of the total fundraising goal. Approximately 80% of the organization's fundraising goal should come from 20% of the agency's donors.

Gift charts are built downward by dividing the gift size in half and then doubling or tripling the number of donors at each level. Donation levels are rounded up or down to avoid irregular numbers. Because not everyone will say "yes" to the amount the agency is requesting, it is essential to have three or four qualified prospects for each gift being sought. A qualified prospect is a prospect the agency believes would consider a gift at that level. When going down the list, fewer and fewer prospects are needed because individuals who said "no" to higher levels are more prone to give at lower levels.

Gift charts may change over the course of the fundraising campaign or from campaign to campaign. Agencies with well-established donors may want to build gift charts that are top heavy, that is, the charts may include more top tiers than bottom tiers. Conversely, agencies that are just beginning to establish their donor base may choose to build bottom-heavy gift charts (Seale, 2010). Blackbaud, Inc. (2010), provides a useful and free gift range calculator on its website. The tool calculates the number of gifts an organization will need to achieve its fundraising goal. It utilizes agency standards that fundraising professionals have been using for decades. Although the calculator is more suitable for capital campaigns, it can also be adapted for annual requests. See Appendix B for a sample of a generic gift chart. Once the gift chart is completed, names of prospects should be added at each level.

After the gift chart has been constructed, it is time to put it to good use. Two versions should be made of the chart. On the first version, prospect names should be added to each level. This will be the fundraising committee's working document. On the second version, the names of the prospects should be left off. Copies of version 2 can be presented to potential donors when meeting with them. According to Walker (2009) the gift chart can illustrate to the donors the amount of donations needed, the amount raised, and the number of gifts received at each level. It provides a graphic illustration for donors to see exactly where the campaign stands and where they may fit. The gift chart should be updated as the campaign evolves.

The next component of the fundraising plan is the needs/problem statement. The needs/problem statement is used to assure funders that the proposed program, project, or service will meet a vital community need.

Writing the Needs/Problem Statement

A needs/problem statement answers the question, "What need will the agency address?" The needs/problem statement must be clearly connected to the agency's mission and purpose. It should not focus on the organization's needs, but rather on the people the agency serves. It should be supported with evidence such as expert opinions, trends, statistics, and data. It should be directly connected to the agency's ability to respond to the need. The needs/problem statement should be palatable—written without jargon, so it is easily understandable (Carlson & O'Neal-McElrath, 2008). Finally, it should avoid circular reasoning. According to the Foundation Center (2011b), circular reasoning is when the absence of a solution is presented as the actual problem. For example, the circular reason for building a community center for seniors might be, "The problem is that there is no community center for seniors. Building a community center will solve the problem." A better way to demonstrate the need would be to cite what a community center for seniors has meant to a neighboring city by offering specialized programs such as exercise and nutrition programs, scam-prevention education, and senior socials.

A needs/problem statement answers the question, "What need will the agency address?"

Walsh (n.d.) suggests a five-section outline for writing the needs/problem statement. The five sections recommended include the problem, cause, cost, strategy, and barriers. Specifically,

- the problem section introduces the problem or need that the agency is facing. It clarifies why the need must be addressed, and why it is necessary to address the need sooner than later.
- the cause section sheds light on the root causes of the problem and introduces a solution to the problem.
- the cost section describes the impact the problem has on the agency and its services, the cost on those affected by the problem and the consequences, should the problem not be addressed.
- the strategies section explains what the agency is currently doing to solve the problem, where gaps exist, and what the most promising approach is to solving the problem.
- the barriers section discusses the potential barriers to the suggested solution. For example, whether the solution addresses the entire problem or whether the solution meets client expectations.

Information Management

Understanding and Mastery of ... Performing elementary community-needs assessment

Critical Thinking Question: How can an agency ensure that their needs/problem statement accurately reflects the needs of the people served?

A strong needs/problem statement gives the reader a clear picture of the need. It provides the rationale for the funding request and presents statistics, data, and other objective evidence that support the need for a solution to the problem. A needs/problem statement is the source for conceptualizing the agency's program, service, or intervention.

Before organizations estimate the potential cost of the fundraising plan, they must first identify existing resources. Identifying resources that are already available will save time, energy, and funds.

Identifying Existing Resources

Identifying existing resources is a critical step in the fundraising planning process. When agencies have implemented previous fundraising endeavors, they may have some of the necessary information and items needed for future campaigns. For example, organizations may have a donors list and records of their past contributions. Prior fundraising strategies and the amount of money raised for each strategy may be available. Agencies may have information regarding the results of previous market studies that measured public perception and awareness of the organization. There may be copies of marking materials previously used, such as annual reports, brochures, and press releases. Organizations may have a list of volunteers who assisted with previous fundraising efforts and a list of board members who have experience in fundraising. Finally, organizations may possess a detailed description of campaigns that directly addressed the agency's needs statement.

Organizations can save valuable time by identifying existing resources, before estimating the cost of the fundraising plan. It can also help agencies to better plan their future fundraising endeavors. As Mutz and Murray (2010) assert, organizations that look carefully at a campaign postmortem are less likely to experience a disaster with a future campaign.

Once existing resources have been identified, agencies can begin to estimate the actual cost of the fundraising plan. A thorough analysis and estimation of both the direct and indirect costs of the fundraising plan can help organizations to effectively budget money to make money!

Estimating the Cost of the Fundraising Plan

It costs money to raise money. Although some believe that raising money does not come with a price, the opposite is true. To generate funds, an agency must spend. According to Lesley Barker (2010), on average, it costs 20 cents to raise $1. This depends, of course, on the fundraiser and the programmatic elements such as recognition banquets. The key is to raise funds in the most cost-effective way possible. Agencies often engage in a balancing act between revenue raised and the cost to raise revenue. Although direct costs to fundraise (i.e., catering, entertainment, invitations, etc.) are generally clear and acknowledged, many indirect costs are often missing from the equation. An accurate estimated cost of a fundraising plan contains both direct and indirect costs.

Direct costs are those costs that can be identified specially to the fundraising campaign. They are costs that are easily and clearly attributable to a program or service, such as

- printing of flyers, invitations, raffle tickets, programs associated with fundraising events, and other activities related to the fundraising plan.
- food, drinks, and other refreshments.
- postage, shipping, and other mailing expenses related to sending letters and other materials to ask for contributions.
- travel expenses including gas and airline tickets. Travel is often required in order to make connections with potential donors, especially in cases involving major gifts. Major gifts provide significant funding for programs, major projects, and capital campaigns; travel is often necessary.
- material, equipment, and supplies purchased specifically for the fundraising plan.
- communication costs, such as long-distance phone calls specifically associated with the fundraising campaign.
- costs of subscriptions essential in developing and managing the fundraising campaign (e.g., *Chronicle of Philanthropy*, *Non-Profit Times*).
- costs for consultant services contracted to assist with the organization's fundraising efforts.
- salaries and benefits for those employees working specifically on fundraising efforts.
- registration costs associated with registering with the nonprofit agency's regulator (often the attorney general or secretary of state) in all states the organization plans on raising funds. Thirty-five states currently regulate fundraising and nonprofit organizations must register with the state, when applicable, to engage in any solicitation activity (National Council of Nonprofits, 2010a).

On the other hand, the indirect costs of the fundraising plan are expenses that are not readily identified but are nevertheless essential for the overall implementation and success of the fundraising campaign. Indirect costs are costs which are shared among programs, services, and functions such as fundraising efforts. Therefore, they are not necessarily identified for a particular project or event. Examples of indirect costs associated with fundraising include

- the portion of the executive director's salary, which is attributable to the fundraising campaign.
- the portion of staff and administrative time associated with the fundraising campaign.
- volunteer time connected to the fundraising campaign.
- use of facilities including utilities.
- the portion of utilities, postage, telephone, printing, and other shared expenses associated with the fundraising efforts.

Agencies must be realistic when estimating the costs of their fundraising plans. Organizations should use cost-efficient methods, so that costs do not exhaust all the fundraising profits. The cost of fundraising should not exceed 20 to 25% of the overall operating budget. This rate corresponds with the national average cost of 20 cents for each dollar raised.

Now that the components of the fundraising plan are in place, the case statement can be written. The case statement provides the rationale and justification for the fundraising endeavor. It is the key document to any successful fundraising campaign.

Writing the Case Statement

Individuals will give of their talent, time, and funds if they believe in the integrity and importance of the organization and its programs and services. When people are devoted to the organization's mission, they become dedicated and committed to the organization's cause. This passion leads to funding (Panas, n.d.). So how does an organization make known its mission and the importance and necessity of its services? Through a well-written case statement, that is how!

What Is a Case Statement and Whom Is It For?

> For the many potential donors who ask, "Why should I support your organization?" the case statement provides the answer in a succinct and convincing manner.

Every nonprofit organization seeking funding from individuals, corporations, or foundations, needs a well-written case statement. The case statement, also known as a case for support, is the heart of a quality fundraising campaign. It is the principal document that serves as the center of the fundraising plan and strategy. It is the detailed written justification for the fundraising campaign. It explains to donors and potential donors why the funds are needed, what the funds will be used for, and how the funds will advance the cause of the organization should the donor contribute. A case statement literally makes a case to potential donors for giving to one organization over another. For the many potential donors who ask, "Why should I support your organization?" the case statement provides the answer in a succinct and convincing manner.

Case statements, literally, make the argument for contributing. They are also used as the source for collateral materials such as pamphlets, brochures, letters, websites, and newsletters. The statements help keep the conversation about the organization clear, concise, and compelling. Without a well-written case statement, an organization's message may be lost.

Case statements can also serve as a helpful tool for evaluation purposes. The process of writing case statements forces agencies to carefully examine its programs and services in order to develop convincing arguments to support the need for their programs and services (National Consumer Supporter Technical Assistance Center, n.d.). Case statements can be used for any fundraising campaign but are particularly valuable for capital campaigns, major gift campaigns, and endowment campaigns. A persuasive case statement grabs the attention of the reader and never lets go.

Case statements are for both internal and external supporters. They appeal to a wide range of the agency's stakeholders. Therefore, case statements should be written in such a way that it is understandable to a broad range of agency constituents (Fritz, 2010i).

The statements are used to make a case to potential donors to gain their support for the organization. It lets prospective donors know what the agency intends to do with the funds.

How Is a Case Statement Used and What Should It Accomplish?

According to Panas (n.d.), a carefully created and well-developed case statement can be used to secure agreement, provide direction, inform leaders, enlist new leaders, cultivate potential donors, share the agency's vision, and provide a model for writing subsequent publications. Case statements are used to obtain agreement, understanding, and commitment among the organization's leaders and board members. They provide direction and strategies for how the organization can most effectively present its vision and case to its key constituencies. Case statements inform leaders and workers of the organization and demonstrate how the success of the effort will benefit those who are served. They are used to enlist new leaders to the organization and its cause. Case statements can be used to cultivate prospective major donors by providing them with a working document. They can endorse and share the organization's vision by accepting responsibility for identifying with the organization's mission and dreams. Lastly, case statements are used as a sourcebook and guide for writing subsequent publications such as foundation proposals and articles along with writing and producing videotaped presentations.

Ross and Segal (2009) assert that a quality case statement

- states the need and provides evidence that the need must be addressed immediately.
- states what sets the organization apart from other organizations.
- provides information on how the funds will benefit the agency.
- explains the consequences should the agency not obtain the necessary funds.
- describes the nature and extent of the agency's needs and details exactly what the need is and who will benefit once the need is met.
- illustrates that the need is reasonable so that contributors and supporters will feel that their contributions and support can make a difference.

In addition, a quality case statement presents evidence for the need for the organization's programs and services. Specifically, a strong case statement should

- make it obvious that there is an urgent need and that the need must be addressed swiftly.
- show that the programs and services are worth supporting.
- explain what the programs and services accomplish and what may happen if the programs and services were no longer provided. The case statement should include evidence to support this in the form of expert opinions, surveys, and statements from the beneficiaries.
- include statistics that are dramatic and demonstrative. Statistics should be displayed in a graph or other illustrative means to demonstrate the importance of the figures. Actual cases and real stories that can bring vitality (and dollars) to otherwise dull statistics should be incorporated into the case statement.
- show how the services and programs they provide differ from other agencies, which provide services to individuals with similar needs. For example, agencies

should disclose if they serve other populations, provide programs that are different from other programs, offer more cost-efficient services, or address different needs. The case statement should describe what is unique about the agency that makes it qualified to tackle this issue. It should explain what sets them apart from the others and why the organization is worthy of the support it is seeking.

- explain how the funds will help the organization become stronger and more effective. It should describe what the positive consequences of the agency's endeavors will be, both minor and major, should the agency be able to take immediate action. The case statement should state what is possible, what can be guaranteed, and explain how the organization will become stronger and more effective as a result of the funding. The statement should describe how the funds will help the organization to fulfill its mission and more effectively serve its clients and community.
- clearly spell out what the negative consequences will be, both minor and major, if the agency does not act. At times, this can be a powerful motivator for contributors.

Who Should Write the Case Statement?

A case statement is perhaps the single most powerful document that an organization ever prepares. Only the best talent and most responsible leaders of the organization should be involved in its production (Panas, n.d.). Although compelling case statements are rarely produced exclusively by a freelance author, a true collaboration between the organization and an outside writer can lead to an exceptional case statement. The following four steps provide a team approach to producing case statements:

1. Those most informed about the organization should furnish the basic material and data.
2. A competent writer, with an understanding of fundraising, should enhance the information, establish the concept, and put the material in written form.
3. Once the initial draft is completed, the draft should be reviewed by staff, board members, past donors, and volunteers and then edited so that the case statement "sounds like them." Figuring out what others think of the statement helps the agency to communicate more compellingly and clearly, which, in turn, helps the case statement to sound more like the organization (Mutz & Murray, 2010).
4. The professional writer should revise the case statement to incorporate the organization's changes and suggestions.

Agencies should ensure that the responsibility for the case statement is retained by the board of directors or a high-level committee with appropriate staff support and technical assistance. Although it can be beneficial to ask a wide range of agency supporters to review the draft of the case statement, organizations are cautioned to limit the number of people who are granted editing privileges (Panas, n.d.). Each person will have his or her own suggestions, and the more people involved, the more difficult it will be to reach consensus.

Types of Case Statements

There are two types of case statements, internal and external. Internal case statements are longer and more detailed than external statements. An internal case statement is typically 10 to 30 double-spaced pages in length. The size of the document is not as important as its quality. If the document is well-written, a prospect will read it. The statement serves as the basis for creating promotional marketing materials such as press releases, brochures, and external case statements. Public case statements are used by the fundraising staff and volunteers who make personal visits and for broader outreach such as targeted mailings (Schar, 2009). They also serve as the foundation for writing grant proposals. Internal case statements include talking points for prospects and donors. It specifies the organization's mission, vision, history, and rationale for seeking funds (Jones & Kasat, n.d.). It is rarely a printed piece and, therefore, does not need to look polished, slick, and expensive. It is more often typed and photocopied and used for limited distribution. There is no need to invest in fancy formatting and printing.

External case statements are usually no more than one page in length. External statements include information that is pulled from the internal case statement and tailored to fit its audience. They are typically used for proposals, letters, speeches, brochures, staff and board training, and reports (Jones & Kasat, n.d.).

Format for an internal case statement. In preparing the case statement, it is an excellent idea to gather all materials the agency has on its history, purpose, and programs. This information can be obtained from a previous case statement, direct mail letters, brochures, newsletters, and grant proposals (*e*How, 2010b). Once all of these materials have been collected, the writing can begin. Following is a framework for writing internal case statements:

- *Title.* The title develops the theme and tone for the case statement. Its function is to grab the reader's attention so that he or she will want to turn to the next page and start reading. Equate the title to a catchy newspaper headline.
- *Mission.* Following the title is the mission statement. The mission describes the organization's philosophy and focus and communicates what makes the agency invincible. It describes not only what the agency does but why the agency does what it does. The mission is the heart of the organization. It states the purpose for the organization's existence (Jones & Kasat, n.d.). It is essential to evaluate the mission statement prior to incorporating it into the case statement. The mission statement makes it possible for potential donors to determine if the work of the agency matches the donors' values (*e*How, 2010b).
- *Goals.* Goals should be based on the organization's mission. What does the organization hope to accomplish? What impact or outcome does the agency wish to achieve?
- *Objectives.* How does the organization plan to achieve its goals? What steps are in place to achieve the goals? What actions will be taken? How will the objectives be measured?
- *History.* What is the organization's track record? What objectives have already been accomplished? What successes has the organization had?

- *Structure.* How is the agency organized and governed? Who sits on its board?
- *Fundraising.* How has the organization planned for its future and how does it manage its finances? Let potential donors know how their support impacts the future of the organization. Provide statistics on the success of previous programs and services and show how the organization has made a situation better not just temporarily, but for years down the road (*e*How, 2010b).

Format for an external case statement. External case statements should address the history, challenges, characteristics, and achievements of the agency, and should include reasons for the appeal as well as contact information. Answering the following questions provides the necessary information for developing a solid external case statement.

- *History/the story.* What is the history of the organization? What makes the organization special?
- *Challenges/ramifications.* What are the challenges and threats facing the organization? What may happen if the challenges are not addressed? Emphasize the long-term effects of the agency's work. Let the potential donors understand that keeping the doors open is as important as fixing current problems (*e*How, 2010b). It is crucial to not come across as desperate; this may leave prospective donors questioning the financial management of the organization.
- *Who you are and what you do.* How did the organization begin? What is the organization's mission and vision? What makes the organization unique? How large is the organization and how many individuals are served? What programs and services are offered by the organization? How does the organization work to meet the challenges it faces (Jones & Kasat, n.d.)?
- *Results.* What results has the organization achieved so far? What are the organization's plans? What goals and values does the organization support? Agencies should create a sense of excitement about their work and make their commitment to the cause shine through in every sentence (*e*How, 2010b).
- *The ask/contact information.* Why is the organization asking for money? What will be the cost of the organization to do its work? If this is a special fundraising campaign, what is the organization's fundraising goal? How will the organization spend the money? What will be the long-term impact of the funds raised for the organization? How will the support make a difference (Jones & Kasat, n.d.)? How can people contact the organization?

Making a Strong Statement

The case statement should be written in a style that is unique to the agency. Paint images in the readers' minds. Visual words and action phrases activate the readers' imaginations and help them remember the organization's mission (Mutz & Murray, 2010). Sell the reader by stating the case in a way that propels the reader to contribute to the organization and its cause. The statement should be donor-oriented; it should be geared toward the prospect's area of interest. Demonstrate the organization's ability to solve problems that are relevant to donors. Whenever possible, tell the story with pictures and charts (National Consumer Supporter Technical Assistance Center, n.d.). Personalize statistics with case studies and real-life stories. When describing a program or service, speak of the opportunity the fundraising campaign presents to the prospective donor. Focus on the extraordinary work that has been performed with less than adequate resources. Be confident and convincing. All claims of agency success, whether grand or minute, must be supported by corresponding documentation (Panas, n.d.). Agencies should never present unsubstantiated and extravagant claims. Project the future instead of the past. Agencies should consider using the word *gift*, instead of *donation*. The word *gift* emits a positive, fun image that the word *donation* may not (Panas, n.d.). Finally, show the potential donor that the organization's wants and needs are an excellent investment (National Consumer Supporter Technical Assistance Center, n.d.).

What to Avoid

One of the biggest problems with case statements, according to Ross and Segal (2009), is that they are too internally focused, too long, and too rigid. Case statements should be written for contributors and supporters, not for the internal organization. Statements will be repeated and restated in a number of formats and forms; therefore, the core of the statement should be straightforward and easy to communicate. Case statements should not be written in stone as donors do not necessarily want to fund a completed plan. Major supporters want to be a part of its development. Space should be left for contributors and supporters to add their thoughts and ideas, thereby strengthening their engagement and participation (Bennett, 2009; Fritz, 2010i). There are pitfalls organizations should avoid when writing case statements. These include an undefined purpose, overstated emotionalism, excessive focus on financial needs, not focusing on the bottom line, vague plans, and exaggerated claims of success.

Some agencies make the mistake of not clearly describing the reasons the organization exists. The purpose of the agency should be defined in a compelling way. The purpose should be clear and concise and focused on the mission statement, goals, objectives, and program information (Mutz & Murray, 2010).

At times, the understated is more effective than the overstated. Although overstating the case may be an effective strategy when targeting those closest to the organization, a more understated approach is best for those outside the organization (Mutz & Murray, 2010). Agencies should not exaggerate. Pulling on heartstrings requires an even hand; it is best to refrain from gushing.

It is essential not to focus primarily on the organization's financial needs. It is better that organizations focus on existing opportunities, such as the promise of effective action and the answer to social problems. When agencies plead for resources, some outside the organization may question the agency's financial stability and management. Potential donors are interested in the financial stability of the organization, the cost of the proposed program or services, and how the program will be funded in the future (Panas, n.d.). Sometimes organizations will provide an overly lengthy history of the organization, as opposed to focusing on the bottom line.

The backbone of an organization's fundraising campaign is its case statement. The case statement outlines why the organization exists, who benefits from the organization, the needs of the organization, how the needs will be addressed, what makes the organization unique, how competent the organization is, and how others can help. Fuzzy plans do not inspire. Before the case statement is released, the organization's plan should address the five Ws: who, what, when, where, why, and how. A powerful case statement grabs the attention of potential donors and offers a sound basis for contributing to the agency. It lets donors know what the agency intends to do with the donations and how the donations will make a difference to the community.

A case statement serves as just one step, in a series of steps that lead to a winning fundraising campaign. Once it is written, it is time to develop the fundraising campaign timetable. In the realm of fundraising, timing is everything.

Planning Ahead: Timing Is Everything

The timetable serves as a road map to the design and implementation of the fundraising campaign. In some cases, the board of directors and executive director draft the timetable before choosing a leader for the fundraising committee. At other times, the first draft may be developed in collaboration with the fundraising leader and fundraising committee. Regardless of who develops the initial draft, as the campaign moves forward, it is essential that the entire fundraising team provides input into its revisions.

Effectively planning a successful fundraising campaign requires careful attention to the time it will take to prepare, cultivate, and implement the plan. The preparation, cultivation, and solicitation phases alone typically take anywhere from 3 to 18 months, whereas pledge payments may span between 2 and 5 years. Swift campaigns can realistically be completed in 6 months or fewer, whereas average campaigns require between 12 and 24 months. On the other hand, long-term campaigns can stretch over periods of 3 to 5 years.

> **Effectively planning a successful fundraising campaign requires careful attention to the time it will take to prepare, cultivate, and implement the plan.**

In addition to the timetable, a fundraising checklist can assist agencies in organizing the fundraising campaign. DoJiggy, LLC (2010), recommends that organizations begin planning months in advance by developing a checklist of tasks that must be completed. The checklist can be used as a guide when developing the fundraising timeline. The following is an example of an initial planning checklist:

- Recruit fundraising team members including committees, staff, and volunteers.
- Solicit in-kind donations and sponsorships.
- Create flyers, press releases, and various promotional materials.
- Determine dates and locations for events.
- Identify entertainment and refreshment needs for events.
- Implement a method for collecting contributions, handling money, and tracking campaign performance.

For many agencies, it becomes necessary to implement a number of fundraising activities throughout the year. If several fundraising activities take place within the year, it becomes necessary to plan the activities in a way to achieve maximum effectiveness while ensuring that the activities follow a reasonable sequence and do not conflict with one another.

Some fundraisers require a significant amount of time and careful planning. Among these are capital campaigns, special events, and gaming. Information regarding these types of fundraisers is covered in Chapter 6. The focus here is to provide information regarding the average timeframe for each of these activities. Capital campaigns may span 12 to 36 months. Sometimes it may be useful for organizations to establish a separate timetable and committee to plan and implement a capital campaign.

Special events may need to be sequenced with a major fundraising activity such as a capital campaign. They are usually a part of the overall fundraising plan and go hand in hand with a major campaign strategy. For example, an agency may hold an annual donor recognition dinner and use that occasion to promote the organization's capital campaign.

On the other hand, some major fundraisers may be more successful if scheduled at a time when they do not overlap with other major fundraising events. For example, gaming fundraisers such as a Monte Carlo Casino event may do better as a standalone fundraiser where they will not be competing with another major activity such as the launch of a capital campaign.

Another pertinent consideration is the timing of other fundraisers in the community. Competition for charitable resources among other community nonprofit organizations is a key component of philanthropy. The fundraising team has the challenge of vying with other agencies for area charitable dollars. Therefore, the scheduling of fundraising activities must be done in a way that best captures the attention and heart of the community. According to Hoffman (1992) only agencies with endowments large enough to generate their annual budgets can be categorized as non-competitors for funds.

> ### Administration
>
> Understanding and Mastery of . . . Planning and evaluating programs, services, and operational functions
>
> ---
>
> **Critical Thinking Question:** An effective fundraising campaign requires careful attention to the time it will take to prepare, cultivate, and implement the plan. What are the top five factors to consider when developing a fundraising timetable? Explain.

Developing a fundraising schedule or timetable, along with a fundraising checklist, is useful for planning and managing the entire fundraising campaign. It is essential to keep in mind that the schedule or timetable, and the checklist, will probably need to be tweaked and adjusted as the fundraising campaign unfolds. See Appendix C for a sample of a generic fundraising campaign timetable.

The final element of a well-organized fundraising plan is the evaluation process. Each component of the plan should be reviewed and assessed. It is astonishing what organizations may find.

Evaluating the Fundraising Plan

Evaluating the fundraising plan is an ongoing process that should be conducted throughout the development and implementation of the fundraising plan. It serves to improve the overall results of the fundraising campaign. Agencies should evaluate the overall fundraising plan by assessing each component of the plan, including the case statement, fundraising goals, fundraising objectives, the needs/problem statement, identification of existing resources, the estimated cost of the plan, and its timetable. Additionally, the National Consumer Supporter Technical Assistance Center (n.d.) suggests that organizations evaluate the performance of board members, volunteers, and staff; new leadership that was discovered; the practicality of the fundraising budget; and the variety of funding sources (i.e., were funds raised from a number of different sources or just a few?).

The evaluation should provide a detailed account of when and how the organization plans to monitor and evaluate its fundraising endeavors. The more precise the fundraising objectives, the easier it will be for the agency to evaluate them. For example, what was the actual cost of the fundraising plan compared to the estimated cost?

Organizations can use the results of the evaluations to determine what portions of the fundraising plan need to be revised or eliminated, and what needs to be added to a future fundraising plan. For example, how will the next set of fundraising goals and objectives differ? What fundraising budget items need to be modified? What could be done more effectively and efficiently (National Consumer Supporter Technical Assistance Center, n.d.)? With careful planning and attention to detail, the agency stands a greater chance of reaching its funding goals through a successful fundraising campaign.

Summary

A fundraising plan is the driving force behind a successful fundraising effort. Comprehensive fundraising plans include a number of key components. Fundraising goals emphasize the agency's needs and sets the organization's financial goals. Fundraising objectives are the means by which a fundraising plan is measured. Gift charts are useful tools that map the number of gifts and contributors needed to meet the agency's funding goals. Fundraising plans must also include a needs/problem statement. The needs/problem statement is connected to the organization's mission and addresses the need that will be focused on by the agency. Organizations must also identify existing resources while estimating the cost of the fundraising plan. Agencies will save time, energy, and money by identifying existing resources. This can lead to a cost-effective fundraising plan. When estimating the cost of implementing a fundraising plan, organizations must attend to both direct and indirect costs. The case statement provides the rationale for the fundraising endeavor by explaining the who, what, where, why, and how of the effort. The fundraising timetable serves as a guide to preparing and executing the fundraising plan and campaign. Finally, a winning fundraising plan requires ongoing attention to the evaluation process. Evaluations provide relevant information, which can be used to improve the overall outcome of the campaign as well as the overall results of future fundraising efforts.

The following questions will test your application and analysis of the content found within this chapter. For additional assessment, applying, analyzing, synthesizing, and evaluating chapter content with practice, visit **MySearchLab.com**

. . . .

1. This type of fund is used to fund the ongoing costs associated with running an organization:
   a. Annual fund
   b. Capital fund
   c. Restricted fund
   d. Unrestricted fund

2. According to Duggan and Jurgens (2007), when developing objectives, agencies should ensure that the objectives are
   a. meaningful, specific, and applicable.
   b. reasonable, time-limited, and relevant.
   c. measurable, action-oriented, and practical.
   d. comprehensive, inclusive, and reputable.

3. You are constructing two versions of a gift chart to illustrate the number of gifts and donors needed to raise $150,000 for your agency. The first version is the fundraising committees' working document and the second version will be presented to potential donors when meeting with them. The two documents differ, in that
   a. the first version contains the number of gifts received at each level but the second version does not.
   b. the second version contains the amount of donations needed but the first version does not.
   c. the first version contains the names of the prospects but the second version does not.
   d. the second version contains the amount of money raised but the first version does not.

4. You have been asked to proofread a funding plan that has been written by several of your colleagues. The needs/problem statement reads, "The problem is that there is no homeless shelter in town. Building a homeless shelter will solve the problem." You realize that the statement contains a flaw known as
   a. circular reasoning.
   b. cause and effect confusion.
   c. external analysis.
   d. universal deduction.

5. When estimating the cost of a fundraising plan, agencies must consider both direct and indirect costs. Identify three direct costs and three indirect costs associated with fundraising.

6. Effectively planning a successful fundraising campaign requires particular attention to the time it will take to prepare, foster, and implement the plan. What are some scheduling considerations when planning major fundraisers?

7. A case statement, also known as a case for support, is the fundamental document that serves as the center of the fundraising plan. It makes the case for giving to one organization. Who should write the case statement and why?

8. The evaluation of a fundraising plan is an ongoing process with an overall goal of improving the results of the fundraising campaign. What specific aspects of the fundraising campaign should be assessed?

CHAPTER 4

Developing and Implementing a Marketing Strategy

Tools and Techniques

Now that the team is in place, and the fundraising plan has been created, energy can be shifted toward marketing. Marketing can be a perplexing concept for many nonprofit agencies; however, with the right information and useful tools, marketing can be an exciting and enjoyable venture.

In the world of fundraising, an agency with the best programs and services around will not be able to raise funds to support its endeavors unless it take steps to ensure that everyone knows what it has to offer. Organizations should never assume that people will learn about their services through word of mouth. It does not happen this way. Nonprofits must "get the word out" through powerful marketing campaigns.

Most nonprofits are not known for their marketing prowess unless they have large budgets and are national in scope. Therefore, now more than ever, nonprofits must develop sound marketing competencies. However, marketing competencies cannot be developed without first understanding what marketing is.

What Is Marketing?

Due to strong competition for limited resources, many agencies are motivated to look for innovative ways to improve their fundraising capacities and better serve their communities. According to Hoffman (2002), an agency's fundraising efforts are directly related to its ability to connect to donors and convince them to contribute. Fundraising efforts are also closely tied to work that occurs well before the request for funds. Specifically, the level of satisfaction expressed by those served ties to the agency's fundraising efforts. When fundraising, an agency must position itself to compete for support, resources, and funds. Agencies do this by defining their constituents; assessing the needs of their constituents; developing programs and services to meet those needs; assessing the constituents' satisfaction with the programs and services; using the results of the assessments to improve the programs and services; and clearly communicating the above to potential donors, funders, and others. These methods describe marketing.

According to Andreasen and Kotler (2003), marketing involves the research, planning, implementation, and control of an organization's programs. These activities are meticulously designed to bring about voluntary exchanges of values with the target audiences for the purpose of meeting organizational objectives. Marketing involves fulfilling needs and wants through an exchange process. Only those customers with satisfied needs will exchange what they value, such as money. The greater the benefit provided, the higher the transactional value an agency can charge (Kotler & Armstrong, 2010). In a nutshell, marketing is the process of getting consumers interested in your product. For nonprofits, it is the process of getting clients, donors, prospective donors, and other agency constituents interested in its programs and services. In regard to fundraising, marketing involves everything the organization does to motivate potential donors about the organization's mission, programs, and services. The key word in this description of marketing is *process*. Marketing is the process of developing a marketing strategy, marketing plan, and choosing the best marketing techniques for "selling" the organization's mission, programs, and services. It is essential to understand the differences between marketing strategies and marketing plans, before addressing marketing techniques.

> ### Administration
>
> Understanding and Mastery of . . . Constituency building and other advocacy techniques such as lobbying, grassroots movements, and community development and organizing
>
> **Critical Thinking Question:** Marketing activities are designed to bring about voluntary exchanges of values with the target audiences for the purpose of meeting organizational objectives. In what ways can the marketing of an agency contribute to constituency building and advocacy?

Marketing Strategy

Before an organization can create a marketing plan, it must develop a marketing strategy. A marketing strategy answers the "what" question. What does the organization need to obtain? The marketing plan is a written plan that shapes the nonprofit's overall goals and mission. It describes the organization's services and target audience and defines the agency's role in the community in relation to other community agencies. The marketing strategy assesses the suitability and effectiveness of the marketing plan. A carefully planned marketing strategy provides ongoing benefits to the organization. By following the succeeding five steps, an organization can develop a sound marketing strategy.

1. Describe the organization's target market. Provide demographic information on the person likely to use the agency's programs and services, including age, gender, income, family composition, education, lifestyle, geographical location, and ethnicity.
2. Describe what sets the organization apart from other agencies in the area.
3. Explain the benefits of the agency's programs and services.
4. Create a complete marketing budget.
5. Describe ways the organization will position its programs and services in the community.

Following the completion of the aforementioned steps, organizations can begin to brainstorm marketing ideas. This is where the marketing plan comes into play.

Marketing Plan

A marketing plan answers the "how" question. How will the organization implement the marketing strategy? It is the practical application of the strategy. It involves creating a plan for the organization's marketing activities. These activities are often incorporated into the organization's strategic plan or mission. The goals and objectives of the plan depend on the overall goals and strategies of the agency. The plan usually includes the target audience the organization wants to reach, goals of the marketing plan, the marketing and advertising strategy, the features and benefits the organization wants to communicate to its target group, and how the information will be communicated. In addition, the marketing plan includes information on who will carry out the various activities, as well as the amount of money and resources budgeted for each activity.

Having a marketing plan helps the organization to focus on its target audience. Such plans can assist agencies in discovering gaps that may exist in the market and thereby provide new opportunities for agencies. The marketing plan also provides the organization with a way to determine how the fundraising campaign is progressing. This information can highlight the marketing techniques that are working and those that are not. Donors value a quality marketing plan because it provides them with confidence that the organization is knowledgeable about the market and knows how to achieve its objectives. The following five steps are useful in creating a marketing plan:

1. Analyze the organization's existing programs and services. Specifically, what programs and services do individuals expect the organization to provide? What will encourage individuals to continue to use the organization's programs and services? What might prevent people from wanting and using the organization's programs and services? Is it cost-effective to offer these programs and services?
2. Set realistic and measurable goals and objectives. Clearly define what the organization wants the marketing endeavors to accomplish and by when.
3. Select the marketing techniques. Agencies should select techniques that will most effectively promote the agencies' programs and services.
4. Develop an action plan. The action plan should specify the what, when, how, and who of the marketing plan.
5. Measure and evaluate the results. How will the organization measure success and what will the agency do with the results?

Simply put, the marketing plan and marketing strategy go hand in hand. An organization should not develop a marketing plan without also developing a marketing strategy. Marketing strategies identify the goals for the marketing plan, and the marketing plan serves as the blueprint for actions to be taken to meet those goals. Marketing for nonprofits is more than just securing a contribution. It is a way to reach potential donors and consumers and inform them of the organization's much-needed services.

Marketing Techniques

Marketing techniques vary depending on the organization's product, budget, and target audience or target market. Many marketing techniques for nonprofit, charitable organizations revolve around free and low-cost advertising. These can take the form of website links, online mailing lists, press releases, reasonably priced or low-cost newspaper ads, flyers, and advertising specialties such as customized pens, stickers, t-shirts, and cups. Marketing is unlimited by the imagination and can go well beyond traditional methods. So where does an organization start?

Branding

For some in the nonprofit sector, branding may seem like an unfamiliar concept. However, if one were to mention the American Red Cross, the United Way, the Salvation Army, the YWCA, Habitat for Humanity, or the American Cancer Society, chances are that the names alone conjure up a multitude of images, associations, and positive feelings. The reason?—branding! These easily recognized nonprofits are so well branded that the names alone elicit immediate impressions. According to Fritz (2010c), branding is neither advertising nor marketing (although these activities can help an agency's brand). Branding is about selling everything related to the organization. Checco (2005) states that branding is a method of making organizations more visible and persuading supporters of the value and importance of the agency. Successful branding can be accomplished by following a four-step plan: performing a SWOT analysis, reviewing the SWOT analysis for brand messaging opportunities, determining what messages are the perfect match for the agency's target audience, and creating a messaging package. Before getting into the four-step plan, one must know the meaning of a SWOT analysis.

> If one were to mention the American Red Cross, the United Way, the Salvation Army, the YWCA, Habitat for Humanity, or the American Cancer Society, chances are that the names alone conjure up a multitude of images, associations, and positive feelings. The reason?—branding!

A SWOT analysis is a strategic planning tool used to determine the Strengths, Weaknesses, Opportunities, and Threats embedded in a project, a program, or an organization. When conducting a SWOT analysis, representatives from every level of the organization should be included. The customary method of conducting a SWOT analysis is to create a blank matrix of four columns, one for each of the four SWOT categories: Strengths, Weaknesses, Opportunities, and Threats. Next, responses to relevant questions are listed beneath the appropriate heading. This matrix provides a way to summarize, and visually illustrate, the organization's internal strengths and weaknesses. In regard to branding, the SWOT analysis can help organizations determine what they do well and why. In addition, the analysis can highlight opportunities and identify changes that need to be made. Now that the SWOT analysis has been described, the four-step plan can ensue.

1. *Perform a SWOT analysis.* There are a number of questions that agencies can ask and answer during a SWOT analysis. The following table provides questions that can be asked to generate responses to the SWOT analysis.

Strengths	Weaknesses	Opportunities	Threats
1. What attributes of our organization are useful in achieving our goals and objectives? 2. What do we do best? 3. What differentiates us from other agencies? 4. How do we want our constituents to see us?	1. What attributes of our organization are detrimental to achieving our goals and objectives? 2. What services and programs can be improved? 3. What ways do we have trouble clearly explaining to individuals outside our discipline what we do? 4. What does our board know about branding? How well will the board be able to promote and protect our brand?	1. What external conditions are useful to our organization achieving our goals and objectives? 2. What is taking place in our community, which may offer our organization opportunities to provide support, advice, or additional programs and services? 3. How can we recognize and develop the market for our programs and services?	1. What external conditions can destroy our organization's ability to achieve our goals and objectives? 2. What external factors might prevent our organization from promoting its brand? 3. Who are our competitors? 4. What do we know about our competitors?

Information Management

Understanding and Mastery of . . . Utilizing research findings and other information for community education and public relations and using technology to create and manage spreadsheets and databases

Critical Thinking Question: A SWOT analysis is a strategic planning tool used to determine the Strengths, Weaknesses, Opportunities, and Threats of an agency. In what ways can an agency use the results of a SWOT analysis as a public relations (PR) tool?

2. *Review the SWOT analysis for brand messaging opportunities.* Once the SWOT analysis has been performed, agencies can review the results of the analysis in an effort to seek brand messaging opportunities. The following questions can serve as a starting point: What have we learned about our organization? Who are we, what do we do, and why should other people care?

3. *Determine what messages are a good match for the target audience.* What messages does the target audience want or need to learn? One of the best ways to complete this step is to examine a representative sample of the organization's target audience and conduct focus groups. This step is crucial as it provides insight into what the target audience wants to hear about the organization. This information may be quite different from what the organization may want to convey.

4. *Create a messaging package.* Once the agency determines what messages its target audience wants or needs to learn, the messaging package can be created. A messaging package is a collection of the key messages the agency wants its brand to communicate. It provides the words that help prospects and customers understand what the agency is all about. It helps to establish why the organization is valuable and what it believes in. It articulates the brand's promise and motivates desire for the agency and its services (Frederiksen & Taylor, 2010). Messaging packages include a tagline, mission statement, positioning statement, supporting statements, and a logo.

A tagline can establish a brand, maintain a brand, and allow a brand to differentiate itself from its competitors. Some popular taglines include "The mind is a terrible thing to waste," a tagline of the United Negro College Fund; "Friends don't let friends drive drunk," a tagline of the U.S. Department of Transportation; "This is your brain. This is your brain on drugs. Any questions?" a tagline of the Partnership for a Drug-Free America; and "Got milk," a tagline of the California Milk Processor Board. A tagline can have a profound effect on the organization. Therefore, agencies may want to invest in a branding or advertising firm. According to Blue Fountain Media (2010), organizations should keep the following rules in mind when developing a tagline: Keep it as short as reasonably possible, do not brag—it rarely works, do not be generic, and do not be afraid to create more than one tagline for different situations. Once the organization comes up with a tagline, it should be tried out. Agencies should run the tagline by its target audience. One way to do this is through focus groups. Getting input from the target audience is an essential step agencies should take before investing additional funds and resources into marketing it.

Put simply, a mission statement is a clear and concise statement of the organization's goals and primary role. It should include socially relevant and measurable criteria, the moral/ethical position of the organization, its target group, and its programs and services. It connects the agency to its constituents, the media, and others who may be using or requiring its services.

A positioning statement conveys what the organization does for whom in order to solve a pressing need. It requires the agency to determine and present, in one or two sentences, the distinct advantage of its programs and services in comparison to its competitors. The positioning statement becomes the underlying theme or belief for all the agency's marketing activities.

After developing a positioning statement, organizations need to expand and enhance the statement with three supporting statements. These supporting statements reinforce the importance, distinctiveness, and authenticity of the positioning statement. The supporting statements back up the positioning statement by answering the question, "How do we do it?"

The final component of the messaging package is the logo. Simply put, a logo is a visual symbol or mark used to promote and validate instant public awareness of the organization. It can be an icon or an image composed of the name of the organization. It builds the organization's recognition, tells people who the agency is and what it stands for, and can become instantly recognizable as is the case with the logos of the Girl Scouts of America, the United Way, and the YMCA, just to name a few. Airey (2008), a brand identity designer, states that a logo must be understandable, unforgettable, effective without color, and scalable (i.e., functional when it is merely an inch in size).

Before finalizing the message package, an agency must go back to its focus group. The message package should be tested by getting feedback and reactions from the typical consumer. The words and messages chosen should hold the same meaning to the organization's target group.

Branding is the chief marketing technique that lays the groundwork for all subsequent techniques. An organization's branding of its logo and message can be incorporated into all the following marketing methods.

Website Marketing

Website marketing, also referred to as Internet marketing, makes use of the Internet to advertise and promote an organization's programs and services. It uses websites and email to inform its customers about its services, to solicit their opinions and questions, and to accept donations through an electronic medium.

Website marketing is useful to nonprofit organizations in a number of ways. It can reach high volumes of people 24 hours a day, 7 days a week. It can provide visibility to the agency over those competitors without websites. It is a powerful and useful way to expand and promote the branding of the organization. It can reduce advertising and marketing costs. It is a cost-effective approach to soliciting donations. Website marketing offers a variety of marketing possibilities.

- *Search Engine Marketing (SEM).* Agencies can increase the number of visitors to their websites through search engine marketing (SEM). SEM can improve the organization's visibility by the use of paid placements in search engines, paid inclusion, search engine optimization, and contextual advertising or targeted advertising. The higher the rank of the website, the higher the probability of site visits.
- *Affiliate marketing.* Affiliate marketing is another way to use the Internet to promote nonprofits. It involves organizations advertising on websites other than their own site. Usually affiliate marketing rewards the affiliate for each customer or guest brought about as an outcome of the partner's marketing endeavors.
- *Banner advertising.* Banner advertising or web banner marketing. Banner or web banner marketing involves inserting an ad (banner) into a web page to attract traffic (the audience) to a website by linking the ad to the advertiser's website. Banners come in a variety of sizes, including full banners, medium rectangles, rectangles, leader boards, which span the width of the page, wide skyscrapers, and square buttons (Wilson, 2009b).
- *Email.* Agencies can use emails for marketing purposes. Email advertising is a form of direct marketing, which utilizes electronic mail as a means of communicating programs, services, and fundraising information to a targeted audience.
- *Writing articles.* An organization's visibility can dramatically increase by writing articles for others to publish on their websites or in e-newsletters. When articles written are in the author's areas of expertise, these articles can then be distributed to editors as free content for their websites and e-newsletters. In return, organizations can request that a description of the organization and a link to the organization's website be included with the article (Wilson, 2009a).
- *Directory listings.* Directory listing is another form of online marketing. Directory listings can market an organization when the agency advertises in web directories. Web directories consist of a series of web pages, which index links to other web pages. The collection of web pages makes up a web directory.
- *Advanced PR.* Another website marketing tool is the advanced PR option. According to Wilson (2009a), advanced PR describes marketing through press releases sent to web periodicals. When an organization includes the URL in online copies of the press release, traffic can be increased to the organization's website.

- *Mail linking.* Mail linking services provide a means to place the organization's website link onto thousands of targeted online "shopping malls," such as Charitymeter.com (2009). Mail linking services places the organization's website in front of targeted visitors who are true consumers of the types of organizations affiliated with the shopping mall.
- *Blogs.* Agencies can increase visits to their website by starting a blog and hosting it on their own domain. A blog is a part of a or a type of website. It consists of successive, chronological postings of thoughts, commentaries, and web links. People will likely visit the site if the organization offers excellent content and consistency. According to Wilson (2009a), this can increase the organization's web page ranking and visibility. Nonprofits can also use a charity badge on their blog. Charity badges can help get the organization's supporters to assist with fundraising efforts. Charity badges can be quickly set up and allow people to share the small graphic image the agency creates to make donations. ChipIn (2010) and Network for Good (2009b) have charity badges for a small fee. Blogging communities that work together can raise money by using charity badges.
- *Video blogging.* Video blogging, also referred to as vlogging or vidblogging, is a form of blogging. It utilizes embedded video or a video link and contains text or images that support the video. Organizations can use vlogging as a way to interact with their constituents.
- *Podcasts.* Podcasts offer another unique Internet marketing option. Podcasts are digital audio or video transmissions that can be downloaded to audio file formats such as MP3 players or listened to on computers. Agencies can use podcasts to provide updates on the organization's current activities and events; provide brief, informational pieces of information about current issues; transmit interviews and testimonials; broadcast segments of presentations and speeches made at conferences; and provide information on upcoming events and fundraisers.
- *Message boards.* Message boards are another means of website marketing. A message board or Internet forum, discussion board, bulletin board, or discussion group, is an online chat site. It permits individuals to post and respond to messages from other users and assess and examine the stream of a discussion. Message boards can be added to the organization's website, turning the website into a dynamic, social community. The boards can be used to enrich relationships with constituents, prospects, and donors. In addition, colleagues can use message boards to interact with each other and experts on topics related to the organization's mission.
- *Wikis.* Wikis can be useful website marketing methods for nonprofits. A wiki is a collaborative website that can be viewed and revised by an individual with a Web browser and access to the Internet. Wikis enable asynchronous communication and group collaboration even for those with limited technology skills. One of the most notable wikis is Wikipedia (2010), an online,

Information Management

Understanding and Mastery of . . . Disseminating routine and critical information to clients, colleagues, or other members of the related services system that is provided in written or oral form and in a timely manner

Critical Thinking Question: Internet marketing uses websites and email to inform its customers about its services, to solicit their opinions and questions, and to accept donations through an electronic medium. How can agencies best make use of their websites to disseminate vital information to their clients and to their communities?

free-of-charge encyclopedia that anyone can edit. Organizations can use wikis to create public communities of like-minded individuals who come together to solve a problem or discuss an issue. Private wikis can be created internally to record and manage projects.

As one can see, websites offer a number of ways for agencies to promote their programs and services. Developing a website is both an easy process and an affordable one. Following are some helpful tips to guide nonprofits in developing professional, affordable, and effective websites:

- In developing nonprofit websites, *e*How (2010a) recommends that agencies divide the organization into departments and services and have each department produce its own web page copy. Agencies can hold roundtable discussions, with agency administrators, to obtain their input in the content and setup of the website.
- Once the organization has the content for the website, professional assistance should be sought to setup the website. Agencies can contact the web design/graphic design departments at a local college or university and ask students if they would like to assist with the website development as a project to add to their portfolios. The agency should let them know that all the information and pictures will be given to them in an electronic format if they will create the organization's website. If this is not an option, agencies may need to hire someone to develop the website. As long as the agency provides information and pictures, the cost should be reasonable.
- After the website has been created, the site can be rolled out. The agency should write a press release informing the media and the public about its new website. The information can also be included in the agency's newsletter. Nonprofits should let the public know that they can visit the website for comprehensive information about the agency. This information can also be included on business cards, newsletters, letterheads, and other materials.

Developing a website is a cost-effective way to promote the organization. For agencies that have websites, the aforementioned tips can be used for enhancing existing sites.

Just as thought must be put into the content and setup of a website, agencies must also give attention to the organization of the website. If visitors cannot easily find what they are looking for, they can undoubtedly become frustrated and precipitately leave the site. Bluejay (2009) recommends that websites be designed to minimize clicking, limit screen-page length, allow visitors to easily return to the homepage, and reduce the time spent looking for website menus.

- Website pages should include a limited number of clicks on each page. Forcing visitors to click around the site in order to find the information they are seeking will likely result in their leaving the site.
- Websites should limit the length of the screen page. Normally, the length of each web page should not exceed two full screens unless it is an article. Articles should not exceed six to seven full screens.
- Each web page should include a mechanism, so visitors can easily return to the homepage. When visitors get lost in a website, they usually want to start over from

the beginning. Web pages should include a clickable "home" icon on the top of every page. This will make it easier for visitors to return to the homepage.

- Websites should include a menu on every page. Although websites should provide visitors with a quick way to get back to the homepage, visitors should not be forced to do so before they can visit another page. Menus should be placed on the top, left-hand side, of each page. Menus should not exclusively be placed on the bottom of the pages because visitors may not scroll all the way to the bottom to find it. If the page is long, menu bars should be placed at the top left and on the bottom of the page.

Along with the aforementioned suggestions for enhancing an organization's website, there are a number of common mistakes agencies must avoid to ensure their websites get noticed, but not for the wrong reasons:

- Including stock photos, amateur photos, or photos of people who are not affiliated with the organization (Harmon, 2010). Agencies should include attractive, eye-catching photos, and possibly video clips that create a warm first impression.
- Not including a "subscribe" button on the website. If the website does not include a way for individuals to provide their email address to subscribe to a newsletter, for example, it is difficult for the organization to cultivate prospective donors (Harmon, 2010). Subscribe buttons should be placed front and center on web pages.
- Placing too much text on their websites. For the most part, people scan websites; they do not read them word by word. Organizations can reduce the amount of text on their web pages by carefully choosing the text to include, and incorporating short phrases, video clips, 3-minute podcasts, and other snippets of information.
- Underlining words that are not links (Bluejay, 2009). On websites, underlined information denotes a link. Visitors to the site may become annoyed if web pages contain gratuitous links. To emphasize vital information on a web page, organizations should use boldface or italics.
- Not including something meaningful on each web page. Style is not all that matters. An organization's website exists to provide compelling and useful information (Bluejay, 2009). No amount of flashy formatting or fancy graphics is going to hold a visitor's attention if every web page is not helpful.
- Using Flash. Flash is a multimedia platform used to add animation, video, and interactivity to websites. Using Flash can take too much time for the site's homepage to load and many individuals are too busy to wait.
- Using scrolling or blinking text, animation, or auto-loading sounds. These gimmicks are distracting. According to Bluejay (2009), it is difficult for visitors to concentrate on reading what is on a website when there is blinking text, animation, and other distractions on the site. He compared it to trying to read the newspaper when someone is continually poking you on the shoulder. Readers bombarded by blinking text are likely to leave the site without clicking on anything. Scrolling text forces the reader to read the text in the speed delivered, and not at the rate preferred by the reader.
- Using image backgrounds and pop-up windows. Image backgrounds scream "amateur," because, for the most part, only amateur website creators use them.

Image backgrounds take long to load and do not look professional. Pop-up windows distract from the content of the website and the actual message the organization wants to deliver. Most visitors despise pop-ups when browsing websites.

- Creating websites using outdated templates and posting outdated content. Websites built on outdated templates are unsuitable for branding. They send a message that what the organization does is out of date. Agencies should archive outdated news. People are interested in learning about what the agency has been up to lately, not what it did several years ago.

Agency websites provide a wealth of marketing potential from member recruitment to generating support and funding. Related to the utilization of agency websites is the use of social networking sites in promoting an organization's mission, programs, and services.

Social Networking

Social networking is a popular and cost effective way of marketing for nonprofit agencies. There are two types of social networks. Commercial social networks are online communities, owned and operated by a corporation. Some well-known sites include Facebook, MySpace, and Twitter. House social networks are online communities built on a nonprofit's own website. More and more agencies are becoming aware of the value of social networking as a way to connect better with and motivate their supporters, while introducing new people to their organization. Social networks can be an agency's dream market with millions and millions of engaged users interconnected with millions and millions of other users. A survey conducted in 2010 examined the nonprofit industry's use of social networking (NTEN, Common Knowledge, & the Port, 2010). Over 1,000 nonprofit professionals completed a 50-item online survey. Specifically, individuals responded to questions about their agency's use of commercial social networking sites including their organizations' own hosted social networking communities. The majority of organizations completing the survey were human services organizations at 22.7%. The results of the study were quite revealing. Outcomes showed that Facebook was the most popular site, with 86% of nonprofits maintaining their presence. MySpace was the least used with 14.4% of nonprofits maintaining their presence. Ninety-two percent of organizations stated that they used commercial social networking sites primarily for marketing; 57% used their house social networks primarily for marketing. Forty percent indicated that fundraising played the second most central role in social networking, with 39% of nonprofits raising between $0 and $10,000 on their social networking sites, and 42% raising between $0 and $10,000 on their home networking sites. The average number of community members on organization's commercial social networking sites was 2,440. House social networking sites had an average of 3,520 community members.

Agencies considering utilizing social networks for fundraising purposes must plan their entry into this medium. DiJulio and Ruben (2007) and Fritz (2010h) recommend that agencies choose the right social networks that match their organization's cause. The size of the network should not be the only factor agencies consider. In addition to choosing the best network, organizations should locate an expert who is experienced in social networking; this way the organization will not have to start from scratch. In addition to social networking sites, agencies should consider professional networking sites such as LinkedIn, and issue-focused online networking sites such as Change.org.

Organizations should check to see if there are people on the social networking site who are acting as if they are representatives from the agency. There may be groups on the social networking sites who have set up informal profiles of your organization. Chances are they were created by enthusiastic supporters. These supporters may be willing to promote the agency's message.

Agencies should impress their audience from the start. They should control how they look on another individual's "friends" list. The agency's profile must be appealing. A striking picture and catchy title are excellent starting points. Social networks are the most effective when people pass around ideas. They will pass around messages only if the messages are inspiring. According to Fritz (2010h), agencies should post their edgiest and most viral content, use jazzy profile names, and incorporate video clips.

Organizations should search to see which of their supporters are already on social networking sites. When supporters are located, agencies can send them an email inviting them to join their group or become a "friend" of their group. Agencies should communicate to supporters, on a regular basis, critical issues and fundraising events. It is useful to assign staff time to communicating the social networking effort. Staff members can accept "friend" requests, post comments on other people's pages, and invite individuals to join the group or become a "friend." This is the purpose of social networking.

Eventually agencies will want to turn their social network friends into donors, volunteers, and activists. The nonprofit's social networking pages should contain opportunities to get involved and donate. People should also be informed about the outcome of a campaign or event. Even if they were not involved, they may be involved the next time. Social networking is an investment in the future. Many social network members are young. They may be the supporters and donors of the future.

Social networking presents some exciting marketing options for nonprofit agencies.

- Agencies can create their own profile or fan page on a social networking site and appeal to board members, committee members, volunteers, staff, donors, and other supporters to make the agency a "friend." Other users will see the associations and may be prompted to click on the agency's profile or fan page to learn more about the organization.

- Organizations can ask their volunteers to add information about their volunteer service into their profiles on the networking platforms they use. Having volunteers highlight their service on the profile page benefits agencies by providing exposure to potential new volunteers and prospective donors (Cravens, 2010). It may also lead to media contacts who see the listings when they use the site to network with others.

- Representatives of the agency can post questions and respond to questions in the discussion areas of the various sites. This opens up further opportunities for individuals to see the agency's name and attach it to an issue or topic. Agencies can pole current volunteers to find out what social networking sites the volunteers use. Organizations can encourage them to post updated information about their volunteer service with the organization. An agency can also encourage volunteers to post the agency's public events, watch for individuals commenting about the agency, and let the agency know what is being said, whether positive or negative (Cravens, 2010).

Just as there are advantages to promoting agencies through social networking sites, there are disadvantages that nonprofits need to be aware of. For example, volunteers may promote agencies on their social networking sites, but they may also engage in or promote activities for which the organization may oppose. Cravens (2010) recommends that agencies create a policy regarding why the agency may refuse to link to an individual's profile on a social networking site, and share the policy with the volunteers. It may be useful to have the volunteers assist in drafting the policy. This can create a sense of ownership of the policy among the volunteers.

With that said, agencies should not require staff and volunteers to link to the agency through a social networking site. Staff and volunteers may want to keep online social networking activities separate from their volunteer and professional activities. Staff and volunteers may be asked to accept other affiliates of the agency as "friends" on social networking sites; however, they may be uncomfortable linking with everyone. When a "friend" request is denied, feelings may be hurt, and the work environment may become uncomfortable. Organizations should encourage staff and volunteers to respect the fact that some individuals may want their social networking activities to remain private.

Many businesses and organizations block employee usage of online platforms. In addition, some of these platforms are not accessible for people using assistive technologies, or for individuals using older software and hardware. Therefore, agencies should not replace all of its outreach activities with social networking, as many people will not be able to access it.

Each time an agency creates a profile on a social networking platform, the agency has to re-type information that may already be available on its website. This can be time consuming. It is unrealistic to expect organizations to be on every social networking site. In addition, the popularity of networking sites changes with time. Organizations should ask staff and volunteers which sites they use, read news articles about the sites that appeal to the agency's demographics, and think strategically about what the agency wants to publicize about the organization. These tips can help organizations choose the top sites that match their needs.

With so many different ways for nonprofits to use social media, agencies should avoid making some common mistakes, such as providing only a one-way flow of information where it may appear that the agency is not listening to or interested in what visitors have to say (Chhabra, 2010). Keeping the following in mind can help ensure that other social networking faux pas are not made:

- If the agency is new to social networking and not sure of what to do, people will understand. Be honest about this and use the opportunity to seek advice and input.
- Tweets and posts should not be deleted. Someone has seen the post at one time or another, and there will probably be a backlash from removing them.

- Agencies must take responsibility for their words and actions. Executive directors or other influential individuals should not have other people write and post for them. When people find out, they do not appreciate this.
- Nonprofits should not sign up for a social media account just to have one. An inactive account is worse than not having an account.
- Agencies must be genuine. Being genuine adds credibility to the agency. It is difficult for others to respect an agency and its cause if the agency is not genuine.
- Agencies should not use social media as just another method for disseminating the same information distributed elsewhere. For example, social media should not be used as one more means to distribute a press release.
- Social networking sites should not be used solely for the purpose of promoting the organization. They should also be used to recognize others in the field, such as individuals, for-profits, and organizations that are doing exemplary work.

Social networking enables organizations to develop relationships with new consumers and engage with constituents. A viral marketing effect can be created with minimal effort by cultivating the online community.

> **A viral marketing effect can be created with minimal effort by cultivating the online community.**

Constant Contact, Inc.

Constant Contact (2011) is an organization that assists nonprofits, associations, and small businesses in connecting with their members, clients, and customers. It offers live personal coaching and support to assist organizations with event marketing and with creating email newsletters and online surveys. Over 100,000 nonprofits use Constant Contact for marketing purposes.

Constant Contact's event marketing feature guides agencies in setting up, promoting, managing, and even tracking and reporting events. The tools handle everything from event registration, to event ticketing, to online payment. The cost for event marketing ranges from $15 per month for up to five monthly events, to over $50 a month for over 20 events per month.

Its email marketing tools provide nonprofits with a step-by-step process for creating, editing, and emailing newsletters. Some of the features of the email marketing tools include ways to promote social media pages in emails by inserting links to blogs, Facebook, and LinkedIn, to name a few. The cost for email marketing ranges from $15 per month for up to 500 email addresses, to over $150 a month for more than 25,000 email addresses.

Constant Contact's online survey tools provide agencies with templates for creating and editing online surveys. There are also tools that organizations can use to invite individuals to participate in the surveys and to analyze the survey results. The cost for the online survey plans runs $15 a month for up to 5,000 survey responses, with an additional $.05 charge for each response over 5,000.

Nonprofits who prepay receive discounted prices for services. In addition, Constant Contact facilitates local seminars and provides resources, speakers, and small business professionals to assist nonprofits with their marketing efforts.

Foursquare

Foursquare (2011) is a web and mobile application that is a combination of a social city-guide, a friend locator, and a game that rewards people for doing certain things. Individuals "check in" to places when they are there, let their friends know where they are, and track the history of where they have been and with whom. Individuals earn points, mayorships, badges, and specials, by exploring their cities, trying new places, and revisiting old favorites. Foursquare is an app that is available for iPhone, iPod touch, Blackberry, Android, as well as other web and mobile devices.

Foursquare is increasingly utilized by nonprofit agencies for marketing and fundraising purposes. There are a number of creative ways to fundraise using Foursquare. One way to connect with constituents through Foursquare it to ask sponsors to donate $1 every time someone checks into their venue. Individuals simply show their Foursquare check-in to the manager, cashier, or other employee (Kapin, 2010).

If the agency is coordinating an event, attendees can be provided with an opportunity to earn a swarm badge. A swarm badge can be earned for being at the event with more than 50 people or for being at the event with more than 250 people (Network for Good, 2009c). These badges are hard to earn and considered a bonus.

A contest can be added, such as a random lottery drawing of everyone who checks in, or a reward for the person with the best "shout-out" (e.g., texting, tweeting friends) when he or she checks in (Kapin, 2010). Andrew Brockman (2010) adds a few additional ways to use Foursquare in fundraising. Specifically, he recommends that agencies use Foursquare for meet-ups using geolocation to promote the agency's cause, organizing volunteers in numerous locations, hosting runs/walks that request pledges for getting to various check-in points, and scavenger hunts.

Just as websites and social networks can inexpensively reach substantial numbers of people, emails provide another economical marketing strategy.

QR Codes

QR Codes, or "Quick Response" codes, are mobile phone–readable barcodes that have encoded web addresses (URLs), alphanumeric text, phone numbers, or other information. They can be read by QR Code scanners, including many camera-enabled mobile phones with QR Code-decoding software. A person points his or her mobile device at the QR Code and the mobile device fires up its browser and goes straight to that URL, makes a phone call, provides a geographic (GEO) coordinate, and more. Simply put, it's a print-based hypertext link.

QR Codes provide a number of marketing possibilities by linking offline information to online context. This can provide additional information and even multimedia files to an offline experience. For example, an agency can create print material and include a QR Code that will enable individuals to immediately go to the agency's web page without having to type in the agency's web address. Agencies can generate their own QR Codes by visiting one of the many QR Code–generating sites available, including QRstuff, smartytags, kimtag, i-nigma, and Unitag. Once the QR Code is created, there is a little wiggle room to play around with the image. For example, Photoshop can be used to work in the agency's logo or brand. It is important, however, to test the QR Code before printing and using it.

QR Codes offer many marketing possibilities for organizations. Agencies can print their QR Codes on business cards, advertising specialty items, t-shirts, stickers, and more. Agencies can also create mobile-friendly landing pages with Facebook "like" buttons or lead individuals to the organization's Twitter page for an easy way to "follow" the agency. In addition, agencies can create QR Codes to send people to the agency's email signup, allowing them to subscribe to the agency's email list.

Getting the Most out of Emails

With regard to staff and effort, emailing is one of the most cost-efficient methods for nonprofits to reach their donors, sister agencies, and volunteers. In addition, it can be a valuable recruitment tool. Email allows agencies to furnish information in a timely and professional manner.

Emails can be used to send an agency's weekly, bi-weekly, or monthly newsletters. Newsletters should be used to deliver informative and useful information. If the recipient finds the content useful, chances are he or she will forward the information to other prospects. These new prospects may then choose to join the organization's mailing list or visit the agency. The agency's email list can grow virally with little effort.

One basic, but sometimes overlooked, email marketing tool is the email signature. An email signature contains information which is automatically added to the end of an outgoing email. It lets people know who you are. Email signatures are powerful marketing tools for organizations. Each email signature is in essence a virtual business card; it indicates to the recipient that the email is from you and provides the context that reminds the person who you are and augments the person's perception of your message. The email signature informs the recipient of noteworthy news and makes it possible for the recipient to have direct access to the agency's website. In addition, recipients are also able to send email responses back with a simple click of a mouse. An email signature can contain the following information: name, title, name of organization, address, phone number, website URL, organization's tag line, and a graphical element such as a line of demarcation to differentiate the signature line from the rest of the email. Upcoming workshops, programs, services, and fundraising events can also be marketed through the use of signature lines (Schwartz, 2010).

Signature lines should be up to date and consistent throughout the agency. Each person in the organization should use the same signature line format, and the elements and sequence of the elements should be standardized on all staff signature lines. Consistency benefits the organizations by building a recognizable identity for the agency and enabling email recipients to make connections among the various emails received from different members of the organization. According to Schwartz (2010), a quality signature line is four to eight lines in length. She does not recommend including the email address in the signature line because the address is in the "from" field of the email and will be forwarded with the email. Instead, she encourages including the agency's website URL in the signature line, as this will lead the recipient directly to the agency's website for more contact information and details regarding the organization.

It is essential to note that, by law, emails sent to the organization's list must have an "unsubscribe" link or option so that recipients can unsubscribe from the list should they want to do so. It is illegal to send any bulk email without including this feature.

Email marketing can be a profitable and inexpensive marketing tool. When agencies consider the material from the recipient's point of view and dedicate email campaigns toward useful content, success is inevitable. Email campaigns can be used to recruit and maintain prospects, inform the public of the agency's programs, and solicit funds to support the organization's mission.

Press Releases

If used effectively, the media can provide nonprofits with a valuable avenue to promote their organization and their fundraising efforts. One way is through the use of press releases. A press release is essentially a narrative that may interest the public at large. Its design is a combination of an article and an ad. A press release is a fantastic way to promote an organization and its fundraising efforts. It not only attracts the agency's constituents but also attracts members of the community at large. It is relatively inexpensive, can boost the organization's visibility, can build the agency's donor base, and can establish the organization as an expert in its field.

> If used effectively, the media can provide nonprofits with a valuable avenue to promote their organization and their fundraising efforts.

If the organization takes appropriate steps to develop a quality press release, the fundraising benefits can be tremendous. Organizations mail, fax, or email press releases to editors of media distribution outlets, including newspapers, magazines, television stations, radio stations, and television networks with the hope that they will produce a feature story or request an interview. If a respected media outlet picks up the story and publishes it, the readers immediately feel that the organization is credible. Organizations can also post the press release on their websites to make a positive impression of the agency for visitors to the site.

According to Krupin (2010), the one-page press release needs to contain just enough detail and information to convince the editor that it can lead to a newsworthy feature story. Agencies must paint a word story that makes it effortless for the editor to visualize the final product and want it. The format of a press release typically looks like this:

- **Release instructions.** In the top left-hand section of the page, begin with "For Immediate Release" or "For Release on (date)" in bold uppercase.
- **Headline.** Using a large, bold font, place the title several lines under the "release line." When using a second headline, it should be in a smaller font. Make the headline clever. The headline should be an attention grabber.
- **Dateline.** Place the dateline just before the text of the release and include the city of the organization and the date of its release.
- **Body.** This is the main part of the press release. The initial paragraph should start out strong and attract the attention of the reader. Provide the basic details, with subsequent paragraphs providing additional information. Write the release in the third person, as if you are a journalist.

- **Media contact info.** A line or two following the body of the press release, provide the name, title, phone number, and, if applicable, email address, fax number, and website URL. Provide the email address only if the agency checks email regularly.
- **Signal end.** Two lines following the contact information, and in the center of the page, put "###" or "-30-" (omit quotes) to indicate that the press release is complete.

Press releases should address a number of questions, such as

- who is doing the fundraising?
- how will the funds be used?
- how much money does the agency need? Why is it vital?
- what's unique about the organization?
- how many people are involved?
- what organizations and community leaders are participating? How will the fundraisers be involved?
- what makes it especially urgent at this time? What is the emergency?
- who benefits and in what ways?
- how can people help?
- when and where is the event? How long will it LAST?
- how much is a donation and what incentives are available? What will happen when the agency meets its goal?
- what is the name, phone number, and email address of the person to contact for further information? What is the website URL?

According to Krupin (2010), editors are more likely to turn a press release into a feature story, when agencies respond to these types of questions.

The press release should focus on facts and circumstances that make the story newsworthy, such as

- experts, cultures, celebrities, and remarkable people.
- the involvement of children and individual case people in the effort.
- facts, figures, statistics, data, studies, and surveys.
- lists: Think of a list that ties to your organization (e.g., Top 10 Ways to Prevent Homelessness).
- narratives about a hero.
- key emotional and cultural hot buttons.
- news you can use.
- unusual legal restrictions that may be affecting fundraising activities.

In media releases regarding significant events, provide editors with information regarding whom the event is for and who will enjoy it the most. Include information regarding a call for action, but do not be too demanding of the editor's time, as this can have a negative impact on future press releases. Krupin (2010) also suggests that agencies include a statement indicating that high-quality photographs are available of fundraisers in action, the organizers, and persons receiving and experiencing the benefits and the emotional

Information Management

Understanding and Mastery of . . . Disseminating routine and critical information to clients, colleagues, or other members of the related services system that is provided in written or oral form and in a timely manner

Critical Thinking Question: A press release is a narrative used to promote an organization. What can an organization do to enhance the possibility of a media outlet picking up the story and publishing it?

impact of the organization's efforts. Offer editors more samples, data, information, and interviews. Send invitations to editors inviting them to attend and cover special events. News conferences and presentations can be scheduled for the benefit of the editors. Offer editors unique photo opportunities and interviews with agency constituents. Provide editors with concrete dates, times, and places to receive detailed information. Treat editors well and give them special attention, for example, stage an event or a demonstration can be staged for their benefit.

People make judgments about the overall image of an organization based on the quality of its marketing materials; this holds true of web-based marketing materials, press releases, as well as printed materials. Although the web and press have become more and more popular in marketing organizations, at times, printed materials are necessary.

Marketing Through Printed Materials

Business cards, brochures, newsletters, annual reports, and flyers are examples of tangible printed materials that can be placed directly into the hands of constituents and prospects. These materials convey the agency's brand, mission, and strengths. Whether a business card, poster, leaflet, brochure, or an event program, the printed material may be the first piece of information a prospective client or funder sees about the organization. Remember, first impressions are lasting, so presenting a professional image is essential. People do tend to judge a book by its cover. What the agency produces for marketing purposes tells its constituents a lot about the organization, including its management, reputation, and how individuals are likely to be cared for. Following is some helpful information agencies should be aware of when producing printed marketing materials.

According to Small Fuel Marketing (2009), if the agency outsources the production of the printed materials, design is extra. In other words, design is not included in the price of the printing. Some printers have their own design staff, but the cost of using the printer's design staff is usually more than finding an experienced graphic designer on your own. Printers specialize in different services. For example, online printing may provide quality service on straightforward projects such as pre-designed business cards. If the printing project is more difficult, the agency may be better off visiting a printer in person in order to discuss the agency's individual needs. For most nonprofit agencies, budget is a concern. Building a solid relationship with a local printer may save the agency printing costs. Smaller print shops tend to have more flexibility in making deals.

Typos, along with contextual and grammatical errors, stand out. Do not simply rely on the word processing program's spell checking capabilities. Computers cannot guess what the writer means. Organizations should check the telephone number, address, website address, and other significant information. If there is information that changes frequently such as dates of annual events, agencies should refer to the information without explicitly stating it on the printed material, as this will soon outdate the document. It is better to refer individuals to the agency's website.

Material printed in color adds a touch of professionalism and shows the organization's commitment to its business. In actuality, printing in two colors is not much more expensive than printing in black and white. Printing in four colors may be possible even for agencies with smaller budgets. For the most part, the biggest printing expenses are the set-up fees, time on the press, and the paper (Jacobs, 2009). Agencies can save on additional set-up fees, by ordering a large number of copies at once.

Because print material allows only a certain amount of space, agencies should include only the most significant points. Information regarding what makes the agency unique, why someone should visit the organization, and why someone should contribute to the organization is significant to include (Jacobs, 2009). Organizations should concentrate on the benefits to the community and the people it serves. Contact information should always be included. Materials that are well developed will attract the attention of others and will convince them to go online, send an email, or make a phone call to find out more.

Too many photos can clutter up the space and may result in losing the interest of a potential consumer. White space should be used effectively. If it is difficult to read the message, the marketing costs may be wasted. The brightness and weight of the paper can make a tremendous difference in how the printed materials turn out. It is essential to know, ahead of time, the color and style of paper preferred. As stated by Small Fuel Marketing (2009), changing the materials at any point can modify the budget and can change what the printer or designer needs to do to create a quality product.

Make certain that all printed materials are consistent. For example, all business cards from the same agency should look the same. Information should be formatted in the same way. In addition, Small Fuel Marketing (2009) recommends that different materials match each product. For example, brochures should match the organization's fliers, letterhead, and other marketing materials. Agencies should keep an eye out for marketing materials that are exciting. What is it about the material that is attention grabbing? Learn from what other agencies have done and seek input from others before spending money on printing.

Printed material can be distributed at conferences, visitors' bureaus, chambers of commerce, and through direct mailings. It can also be used to advertise in magazines, newspapers, telephone books, and on television. There are many options for printed materials. Getting them into the hands of the right people is one more crucial aspect of a winning marketing campaign.

Both online and offline marketing is key. It is necessary to keep in mind that online marketing can benefit from traditional offline marketing and vice versa. The goal is to have all marketing efforts support one another. Including the agency's URL on all letterhead, business cards, printed promotional materials, and printed ads will provide another avenue for name recognition. It is imperative that all information is up to date and that both online and offline materials are consistent and complement each other. When rolling out a new fundraising campaign or promoting a new fundraising event, organizations should roll out online and offline campaigns simultaneously. AllBusiness.com, Inc. (2010), suggests that organizations plan a date for the launch of the campaign and ensure that all is ready on both fronts. One helpful piece of advice is to "tease" consumers about an upcoming event or campaign through print materials that direct them to the organization's website for further information. Agencies can get the most out of their marketing campaigns by using an integrated strategy.

Advertising Specialties and Promotional Products

Advertising specialties and promotional products are useful items imprinted with the organization's logo or advertisement and given to prospective and present contributors to the organization. Examples of advertising specialties are notepads, calendars, baseball caps, pens, pencils, key rings, tote bags, cups, t-shirts, flash drives, memo cubes, magnets, and calculators.

Promotional products come in a wide range of prices, from a few cents to several dollars. Therefore, even agencies with meager budgets may be able to afford advertising specialties. Unlike mass-marketing techniques such as websites and press releases, advertising specialties are products aimed specifically at the agency's target group. Because the products are useful, to some degree, they are often kept and used by the recipients. Whenever an individual uses the product, the agency's name and its message get exposure.

Along with the advantages of advertising specialties, there are some disadvantages. For example, the space available on the product limits the size of the advertisement. On a pencil, for instance, there may be enough room to include only the agency's name and address. Another limitation is that the production time and delivery of the product may take 4 to 8 weeks. If an event is just around the corner, the organization may not receive the items in time for the event. One additional downside is that it can be difficult to determine whether the promotional product was successful in securing donors or prospective donors.

Tips for Strengthening the Success of the Marketing Efforts

Marketing techniques are the tools used to make the community aware of the mission of an agency and the benefits of the agency's programs and services to the community as a whole. The more knowledgeable individuals are of the central role an agency plays in the community, the more individuals will contribute to the agency. According to Leduc (2010), marketing efforts can be more effective when organizations keep adding something new, become valuable resources, separate themselves from other organizations, promote the end result, and anticipate change.

> **Marketing materials become obsolete if they are not updated with new information, new photos, and new graphics. Changes to marketing materials create another opportunity to attract new prospects and donors to the organization.**

Marketing materials become obsolete if they are not updated with new information, new photos, and new graphics. Changes to marketing materials create another opportunity to attract new prospects and donors to the organization. Adding new information can enhance fundraising efforts by attracting new donors and prospects who previously were not interested in the agency or its programs and services. It can generate additional contributions from existing donors, who are interested in newly offered programs and can generate contributions for existing services or programs of which the donors were unaware.

Agencies can look for ways that the organization can be a resource to the community. They can supply groups, organizations, schools, universities, and individuals with free information and offer to present to groups on a topic related to the organization's services.

Agencies must find creative ways to inform the community of what separates them from other organizations, which offer similar services or serve similar populations. For example, does the agency provide programs during weekends when other agencies do not? What unique advantages does the agency provide that other organizations do not provide? Promote these unique advantages in all the agency's marketing materials. Give potential donors another reason to contribute to your organization. Most potential donors will probably never use the programs or services that an agency provides. Therefore, it is necessary to promote how the agency has made a difference in the community by offering its programs and services. Make sure that the organization's marketing materials are promoting its end results.

Expect that the economy will change, that fewer resources will be available, and that funding opportunities will become scarcer. Expect change and prepare for it by developing the habit of looking for early signs of change and then confronting it before it is too late. Begin increasing and modifying the programs and services offered. Utilize a variety of different marketing techniques. When agencies remain one step ahead of the game, only a small segment of the organization is negatively impacted when change occurs.

Summary

Nonprofit organizations have an extraordinary opportunity to help countless numbers of people. By connecting consumers to beneficial programs and services, organizations can bring individuals from the depths of despair to greatness. Regardless of how impressive an organization's mission is, if the agency spends all of its time and energy focused solely on running the organization, no one will know about it, not the prospective clients, the community, or prospective donors. Marketing a nonprofit organization puts the agency and its mission into the hearts and minds of the community, and sometimes the country and the world. A well thought-out marketing strategy and plan are essential. Innovative marketing techniques, such as branding, website marketing, social networking, Foursquare, emails, press releases, printed materials, and advertising specialties, can place an agency on the map, literally. Regardless of the marketing strategies, plans, and techniques organizations adopt, any marketing effort can be more effective when the agency provides the public with updated information, becomes a significant resource, separates themselves from other agencies, markets the end result, and prepares for change.

The following questions will test your application and analysis of the content found within this chapter. For additional assessment, applying, analyzing, synthesizing, and evaluating chapter content with practice, visit **MySearchLab.com**

1. This marketing technique is about selling everything related to the organization. It is a method of creating a messaging package that makes the organization more visible and persuades supporters of the value and importance of the agency.
   a. A press release
   b. Branding
   c. A tag line
   d. Website marketing

2. When performing a SWOT analysis, which of the following questions can be asked to generate information regarding possible threats to an agency?
   a. How can we recognize and develop the market for our programs and services?
   b. What services and programs can be improved?
   c. How do we want our constituents to see us?
   d. What do we know about our competitors?

3. Email marketing can be an inexpensive and profitable marketing tool. It is one of the most cost-efficient methods for nonprofit organizations to reach donors, volunteers, and sister agencies. Regardless of how important and beneficial email campaigns may be, agencies must carefully understand the law as it pertains to sending emails to their email lists. Particularly, laws prohibit agencies from sending emails
   a. without a signature line.
   b. more than four times a month to the same recipient.
   c. to nonprofit agencies.
   d. without an "unsubscribe" link or option.

4. You have been asked to develop a new website for Sticks and Homes, a nonprofit agency that provides building materials to homes that are in need of repair. You create a homepage and review it with the director of the agency. She is pleased with your work but asks you to underline some of the text to make it stand out more. You are hesitant to do so because underlining text on a web page can
   a. signify a link and may annoy visitors to the site if the web page contains faux links.
   b. be distracting because they will not understand why the information is emphasized.
   c. look unprofessional because only amateur website creators underline text.
   d. look outdated and send a message that what the agency does is out of date.

5. A marketing plan involves creating a plan for the organization's marketing activities. It describes how the organization will implement its marketing strategy. What components should be included in a marketing plan?

6. Due to a variety of reasons, one of which is budget costs, some agencies may be tempted to replace all of their outreach activities with social networking. What are some reasons why this is not recommended?

7. Quick Response (QR) Codes are mobile phone–readable barcodes that provide a number of marketing possibilities by linking offline information to online context. In what ways can QR Codes be used for marketing purposes?

8. Marketing campaigns can be more successful when agencies look for ways in which they can be resources to the community. In what ways can agencies be resources to the community?

CHAPTER 5

Identifying and Managing Funding Sources

The majority of a nonprofit agency's programs and services are funded by external donations made possible by soliciting individuals, businesses, government agencies, and other funding sources. Identifying and managing funding sources can seem like a daunting task. However, with the right information coupled with practical skills, agencies can easily become proficient in this essential stage of the fundraising process.

Developing an Initial Donor and Prospect List

A donor and prospect list sustains the organization's fundraising efforts and serves as the response to the question, "Who may want to donate to our agency?" Donors are individuals who have already contributed to the agency or cause. They are likely to give again, as past behavior is a strong predictor of future behavior. Prospects are individuals who have not previously donated to the organization. Developing the initial donor and prospect list requires dedication and vigilance, but the potential benefit to the organization is worth the commitment.

One of the most fundamental principles related to developing the agency's initial donor and prospect list is that the closer one is to the prospective donor, the more likely that person is to donate to the organization. For example, if you ask your best friend to give, he or she most likely will give. If you ask your colleagues to donate, they probably will (Garecht, 2010).

The second principle, according to Garecht (2010), is affinity. In other words, who would likely be empathic for the mission of the agency? A person who is moved by the mission of the organization is likely to give. For instance, if your best friend participates in Relay for Life, he or she may be more likely to donate to your cancer research fundraising effort.

Learning Objectives
- Describe ways to build a donors list.
- Identify target markets that match agency needs.
- Locate and reach target markets.
- Employ suggestions for diversifying funding sources.
- Apply methods for storing and managing donor information.

· ·

A donor and prospect list sustains the organization's fundraising efforts and serves as the response to the question, "Who may want to donate to our agency?"

Members of the fundraising team should begin building their donor and prospect lists by expanding on these two principles, specifically,

- they should start with their family and friends and then contact current and former work associates; personal vendors (i.e., accountants, doctors, attorneys, etc.); neighborhood contacts; church or synagogue members; connections from school; associates from organizations, clubs, and leisure activities; current and former classmates; and individuals associated with businesses frequented. Other names may come from various group memberships.
- each team member should list individuals they "kind of know" but who have an affinity for the mission of the agency. It is important not to limit the prospect list to those individuals known to the fundraising committee members. There are many people who may give money based on a number of different reasons for wanting to give. Individuals give at different levels and through various kinds of fundraising initiatives. It is impossible to know just who will and who will not give. The fundraising team should not simply write down those they "think" will give; they should list their entire network.

Developing an initial donor and prospect list is the first step in identifying potential funding sources. Once agencies develop this initial list, they can expand their reach by identifying a wider range of target markets.

Target Markets

In order for a nonprofit to be successful, it must know its niche. Specifically, an agency must know who comprises its target market and how the target market is served. Why is this necessary? The number of nonprofits is increasing every year, yet there are fewer and fewer dollars to go around. Therefore, agencies must know whom they are serving, and the benefits they provide to their target (Siege, n.d.). Target marketing involves giving thought and time to identifying the most probable donors. It is an essential and necessary step to successful fundraising. Through target marketing, nonprofits can identify individuals, corporations, and other prospective groups who are likely to contribute to the agency. It involves breaking down a market into portions so that marketing efforts can be focused on just a few of the segments. When an organization targets its fundraising efforts on the segment of the market that is most likely to be interested in the agency's mission, promoting the organization's services and programs becomes easier and more economical.

Identifying Target Markets

Each organization is different and its target markets vary. However, there are common target markets that many agencies tend to pursue. An article on *eHow* authored by weazelgrl (2010) states that common target markets for nonprofits include donors, membership organizations, employees, and volunteers. These, along with other common target markets, can provide agencies with a base to start from when developing their individual lists of target groups. The following points capture some of the best and most important target markets agencies should consider:

- *Donors.* For most organizations, donors are typically the target that agencies want to reach the most. The marketing efforts should focus on both current donors and potential donors. The majority of donors and potential donors are moved by the mission of the organization. In other words, the agency's mission resonates with donors and prospective donors, even though the agency's work may never benefit the donors directly. High-end donors produce the greatest part of donor contributions. During tough economic times, many donors decrease the size of their contributions, which makes it even more essential that nonprofits intensify their pursuit of current and prospective donors.

- *Members.* Nonprofits must not forget those closest to the operations of the nonprofit, the members. Organizations with memberships are required, by law, to inform their members of annual meetings, as members have the right to attend and vote. In order to have a large number of members in attendance, nonprofits should promote annual meetings in a positive way by offering incentives for attending the event, such as door prizes. The annual meetings can serve as another platform for fundraising, as asking for donations face-to-face is more successful than soliciting donations through the mail. Members of nonprofits are perhaps the most passionate about the organization's success. They donate because the mission is essential to their everyday lives and is something from which they collectively benefit.

- *Clients/customers.* Even if an agency's programs and services are offered for free or at a low cost, it is vital that nonprofits know who is using and who will use their programs and services. By including those being served and those who will potentially be served in the list of target groups, individuals become aware of the programs and services available. Educating current and potential clients, about the programs and services offered, can help agencies remain competitive. In addition, some agencies need to target prospective clients for revenue purposes. For example, if an agency charges fees or solicits donations from clients for programs and services, attracting more clients can increase revenue to support and expand such services.

Client-Related Values and Attitudes

Understanding and Mastery of . . . Confidentiality of information

Critical Thinking Question: In many cases clients and customers are included as a target group. How can agencies ensure that such information remains confidential in cases where clients and customers are identified as a target group?

- *Volunteers.* Targeting volunteers can be an ambitious undertaking, especially when there are a number of other nonprofits in the area vying for the same volunteers. The volunteer market is unique and should not be overlooked or neglected. The work of volunteers attracts additional supporters, which can lead to more contributions.

- *Other nonprofits.* At times, nonprofit organizations are interested in joining forces with other nonprofits. For example, smaller agencies can collaborate with larger agencies to put on a major fundraising event. By working with other agencies, each nonprofit can showcase its causes, share the work involved in putting the fundraising event together, and potentially raise more money. Larger events also reach a greater audience. In addition to collaborating on fundraising events, agencies can also join forces in applying for grants. For example, governmental funders may request that organizations collaborate on a project in order to receive funds. In such cases, duties can be split between the nonprofits. Including other nonprofits as a target group may provide additional funding opportunities.

- *For profits.* Cause-related marketing is becoming more and more popular, as an increased number of consumers are making buying choices based on altruistic reasons. Nonprofits can target for profits that share their cause-related mission. More and more businesses recognize the benefits and opportunities of working with nonprofit agencies. One of the reasons agencies may attract sizeable donations from for-profit organizations is that corporations often view relationship as an entrepreneurial venture. Businesses and nonprofits can often find common ground that connects business interests with community needs. Corporations may see that a specific problem can be solved with a huge donation. Nonprofits that hook up with specific for-profit companies can place their names and missions into a larger spotlight while also receiving a donation in the process.

- *Legislators and policymakers.* Reaching out to legislators and policymakers can aid policies related to the agency's mission. Legislators and policymakers help ensure the continued viability of the nonprofit. Getting the attention of legislators and policymakers requires creativity. For example, an agency can lobby the government for support by convincing the government that the agency can provide more economical and effective solutions for existing programs and services. Agencies can include a link on their websites to provide individuals with the resources needed to contact their local representatives.

- *Employees.* Employees are the "people-power" of nonprofit organizations. They create and deliver the agency's programs and services and, therefore, are a critical part of the marketing mix.

Nonprofits find themselves competing for top-notch employees. Attracting the best employees to an organization requires time and effort. These recruiting efforts result in marketing the agency to individuals in the field.

Nonprofits seeking funding need to know their target markets. Target markets are necessary both for receiving funds and for helping. Without target markets, agencies are truly lost. Once target markets are identified, agencies can shift their energy toward locating and tapping into these markets.

Administration

Understanding and Mastery of . . . Constituency building and other advocacy techniques such as lobbying, grassroots movements, and community development and organizing

Critical Thinking Question: There are a variety of groups that make up target markets. How might an agency identify target markets through grassroots movements and lobbying efforts?

Locating Target Markets

The importance of identifying target markets is evident, but agencies must also know how to reach their target markets.

The importance of identifying target markets is evident, but agencies must also know how to reach their target markets. Hawkins (2009) recommends speaking to media outlets, tapping into publications, and planning public relations (PR) blitzes, to name a few. Both Hawkins (2009) and Masters (2003) tout the benefits of utilizing agency staff to assist in locating target markets. The following tips can aid nonprofits in locating target markets:

- *Rally staff.* Agencies should work from the inside out by rallying their staff. Employees are a nonprofit's greatest endorsers. Through word of mouth, the influence of staff cannot be beat. Organizations should speak to everyone and anyone at the agency to find out the best way to identify its target markets.

- *Seek interviews.* Locating the nonprofit's target markets means getting the word out that the agency is looking for them. Organizations should seek interviews through a number of media outlets, including community papers, radio, and television. Agencies can also take part in podcast sessions on the web with those who share the organization's mission. This will allow the agency to reach a worldwide audience.
- *Search for publications.* Searching for specialty publications that speak to the agency's mission is another way to locate target markets. Organizations can tap into these publications for contacts, get in touch with editors, and ask for their assistance. Agencies can also check business and trade publication directories. Trade directories provide listings of thousands of local, state, and regional nonprofits and charity institutions throughout the United States. Some of the information available in the directories includes contact information; descriptions of services; publications and newsletters; conferences, meetings, and conventions; staff and membership size; annual budget; year founded; and nonprofit or for-profit status.
- *Check governmental resources.* Governmental resources can also be tapped. Agencies should check with state and federal offices of human services and social work for information on resources, services, and consumers served both locally and nationwide.

> **Information Management**
>
> Understanding and Mastery of . . . Utilizing research findings and other information for community education and public relations and using technology to create and manage spreadsheets and databases
>
> **Critical Thinking Question:** In what ways can an organization's target market be used for public relations purposes?

As previously stated, an agency's target market is often the agency's best funding source. The next section illustrates how various target markets make for valuable funding sources, especially when such funding sources are diversified.

Identifying and Tapping Into Funding Sources

Credible financial planners will recommend to their clients that they diversify their portfolios. Why diversify? Diversifying helps clients reduce risks by spreading money among various types of investments. By doing so, positive performance of some funds will counteract the potentially poor performance of others. This same premise holds true in regard to agencies and their funding sources. Relying too heavily on one source of funding can spell disaster should the funding source dry up. Nonprofits need to diversify their funding sources. The more diverse the funding sources, the more apt the agency will be able to ride out any unexpected storms. The next section offers a sundry of funding sources to assist agencies in diversifying.

> **Nonprofits need to diversify their funding sources. The more diverse the funding sources, the more apt the agency will be able to ride out any unexpected storms.**

Individuals

Individuals comprise the largest funding source of nonprofits. In a study conducted by the Giving USA Foundation (2006), of the $260 billion donated to charitable organizations in 2005, individuals donated $199.07 billion. A popular saying in fundraising is, "People give to people!" People like to help others for a variety of reasons. They may be motivated due to cause-related reasons, community pride, a need to belong to an organization, altruistic reasons, a potential tax break, or just being asked to give. One of the most likely reasons is that as human beings we have a tremendous tendency to simply "do good." Giving to others leaves the giver with a feeling of self-enlightenment, mental peace, and happiness. According to Russell Clark (2008), individuals are particularly concerned with social responsibility. Donating to something, in which they believe in, leaves them with a feeling that they are making a difference. The perception that you are leaving the world a better place than you found it is quite appealing.

The premise that people donate primarily for altruistic reasons was the finding of a telling study conducted by Fisher, Vandenbosch, and Antia (2007). Fisher et al. examined viewers' responses to four separate fundraising drives by a public television station over a 2-year period. They examined 584 pledge breaks that contained 4,868 individual appeals. The appeals were divided into two fundamental dimensions based on the empathy-helping hypothesis: the appeal beneficiary (self versus other) and emotional valence (positive versus negative). The findings revealed that most effective fundraising appeals were those which communicated the benefits to others, rather than to the self, and induced negative emotions rather than positive emotions. Fundraising appeals that emphasized benefits to the self resulted in significantly fewer calls, especially when the appeals induced positive emotions. The practical application of this research may assist agencies in guiding their fundraising activities with regard to soliciting donations from individuals.

With the aforementioned insight into what motivates individuals to give, agencies can establish winning fundraising appeals. Barker (2010) recommends that agencies develop compelling requests for donations, clearly state what an individual will get in return, provide donors with a means to track donations, and acknowledge donations.

Agencies must develop compelling requests for donations. When individuals believe in the mission of the organization, and also trust that the agency will be a good steward of their contributions, they will be more likely to give. It is also essential that organizations clearly state what individuals will get back from donating to the agency. For example, donors will get satisfaction from knowing that a family will have food for the month.

Individuals want to be reassured that their contributions are going to the programs, services, or causes for which their donations were designated. Therefore, agencies should provide individuals with information on how donations can be tracked.

Boards

One of the most fundamental and significant funding source is the nonprofit's board of directors. When board members give, it can signal the board's commitment and gives its members a sense of investment in the agency. Some ask, "Should board members be required to give?" There is no perfect and correct answer to this question. The question is a complex one, and therefore, the answer is just as complex. Having a giving requirement for one agency may work, whereas the same requirement may not work for another agency.

Although some agencies require board members to give, nearly half of the agencies do not have such a requirement. Some funders believe it is unrealistic to expect anyone, whether a relative, friend, corporation, or foundation, to donate money to an agency that does not have the board's financial support. Because one of the major responsibilities of the board is to raise funds, giving money may be viewed as an expectation.

In a national study conducted by BoardSource (2007), only 27% of nonprofit agencies had minimum giving requirements of their boards. Another 28% required boards to contribute, but did not specify an amount. Nearly 45% did not have any giving requirement. For those agencies with minimum giving requirements, the average requirement was $150 a year.

Even more fascinating were the results of a study conducted by Marts and Lundy (2008). It surveyed 51 organizations to look at trends in board fundraising involvement, expectations for board contributions, and board giving patterns. Their findings revealed no obvious differences in board member unrestricted annual fund giving between those organizations with specific giving requirements and those without. In other words, there was no significant difference in giving between board members who had a specified giving requirement and those who did not.

Although the organizations in both the BoardSource and Marts & Lundy studies were weighted more toward larger nonprofits than smaller, community-based nonprofits, the percentage of board members giving is worth noting. BoardSource (2007) found that human services board members gave 63% compared to arts and culture at 80%, health at 58%, and educational institutions at 57%. The giving capability of board members typically differs based on the type of nonprofit. For example, the board of a community-based nonprofit would likely give less than board members of a major not-for-profit research hospital. In addition, smaller boards will likely have board members of significant varying means (Ford, 2010).

According to Masaoka (2009), policies that require board giving can limit board participation to individuals of economic means. These policies can therefore exclude, from the board, perspectives and voices of lower-income members of the community. He also argues that there may be board members who have lost their jobs, savings, or both and may no longer be able to give or may not be able to give at the same level to which they previously gave. Another case in opposition to specified giving amounts is that board members tend to give at the minimum obligatory level; yet if specified amounts were not given, some members would give more.

Boards should value a diverse perspective and welcome members from varying income levels and backgrounds. They should appreciate the $10 gift as much as the $10,000 gift. Each gift is significant to the giver and the $10 contribution may be all that a board member can afford. In other words, a $10 gift from one member may be a greater stretch than a $10,000 from another member.

Nonprofits are more likely to meet a goal of 100% board giving by clearly communicating any giving expectations to prospective board members. If an agency has giving requirements, and the board member is uncomfortable with the requirement, board members should be given an opportunity to back out. Lastly, if the board has giving expectations, members should be offered alternative ways to contribute. For example, boards can provide members with an option of donating or raising money.

Clients/Customers

Some nonprofits are compensated for the programs and services that they provide to their clients and customers. However, the total cost of delivering the programs and services are not covered by the fees. As a result, nonprofits may also rely on additional donations from people who have benefited in the past from such programs and services. Foster, Kim, and Christiansen (2009) refer to this funding model as the Beneficiary Builder. Examples of this nonprofit funding model can be found at many universities and hospitals. Organizations seek supplemental support by building long-term relationships with individuals who have benefited from their programs and services. Clients and customers are inspired to contribute because they believe that the programs and services they received changed their lives in a positive way. According to Foster et al. (2009), nonprofits contemplating this funding model must create a mission that reflects individual and social benefits, design programs and services that promote customer and client loyalty, and develop an infrastructure able to reach out to its clients and customers.

Members

Another fundraising source is a nonprofit's membership. Members donate money because the cause and mission of the organization is central to the members' everyday life, and it is something from which the members benefit. Examples of nonprofits that often have a membership are environmental, religious, and cultural organizations, which link with their members by offering programs, services, and activities that the members are seeking. According to Foster et al. (2009), organizations that rely on members as funding sources must take measures to ensure that their membership feels that the endeavors of the organization are benefiting them. In addition, organizations must have the capacity to involve their membership in fundraising activities, commit to fundraising endeavors that resonate well with their membership, and turn down those opportunities that are not well supported by their members.

Foundations

Private foundations are nonprofit, nongovernmental organizations that maintain principal funds to serve the common good. They typically award grants to nonprofit, charitable organizations. There are literally thousands of foundations interested in supporting nonprofit agencies.

The Foundation Center (2010) documents grant-making patterns of a sample of the largest community and private foundations, and tracks differences in funding trends by foundation, region, and type. According to The Foundation Center (2010), human services captured the largest share of grant dollars awarded in 2008, with 26.4% of grants conferred. There are several types of foundations, including private or family, community, and corporate. They differ according to quantity, features, flexibility, and type (David, 2008).

Funding opportunities from private or family foundations are usually based on a match between the personal philosophies of the foundation and the mission of the nonprofit. They often provide start-up funds only, and the application process may be difficult and lengthy.

Community foundations offer funding opportunities to agencies within a specific community or region. Community foundations are often made up of a host of foundations within a foundation. Their monies are frequently earmarked for specific projects.

Corporate foundations provide funding to organizations that address cause-related issues for which the corporation would like to be identified with. They are also more likely to fund programs or services that benefit a particular group such as the corporation's employees and their dependents. Corporate foundations can be a source of large money, but smaller amounts of money may be ongoing.

Corporations

Corporations and industries often direct their giving to programs and services that benefit employees and communities where their employees live. Funding can come from corporate giving programs and company-sponsored foundations. One of the best sources of funding comes from companies with national headquarters in the agency's local community. According to the Giving USA Foundation (2006), corporate donations grew by 22.5% to a total of $13.77 billion. Corporations are an especially good source of funding for new projects, programs, and services. They are more prone to contribute to nonprofits that have cause-related missions to which the corporation would like to be attached. Corporations, for the most part, want to gain something while giving. For example, corporations are likely to want a return on their investment.

One way in which corporations and businesses can provide support is through in-kind donations. In-kind donations are donations in the form of goods and services, as opposed to donations in the form of monetary support. Corporations may be motivated to provide in-kind donations because the goods they are donating may otherwise go to waste. They may also donate in-kind goods because the cost of their production is low. Examples of in-kind donations are food, medication, and clothing. In-kind donations are distributed at a number of centers, including soup kitchens, food pantries, senior centers, homeless shelters, and daycare centers.

Another way in which corporations can support nonprofit agencies is through sponsorships. Agencies can set up sponsorship levels. Levels provide corporations with an opportunity to choose levels which match their corporate giving budget while providing the level of exposure they seek. Examples of sponsorship options are sponsorships of cause-related events and sponsorships of programs. Corporations provide monetary or in-kind support, and in return, nonprofits give corporations exposure. For example, nonprofits can print corporate sponsor names and logos on specialty advertising items such as t-shirts, include corporate information on promotional materials, and display corporate signs in prominent areas.

Churches and Civic Groups

Churches and civic groups are another valuable funding source. Churches and civic groups often look for service-related group projects within their community. Contributions are usually in the form of in-kind services and goods but can also include monetary contributions. For example, some churches have benevolence programs to help those with legitimate financial needs. Benevolence programs may be managed by benevolence committees who meet and evaluate requests for funding that have been presented to the church. Many civic groups have giving programs devoted to health projects and community service. Examples are Rotary Clubs, Lions Clubs, American Legions, and Kiwanis Clubs. The most effective method for identifying potential funding sources of local chapters of civic groups is to contact their national organizations.

Government Sources

Many nonprofits can benefit from funding from all levels of government: federal, state, and local. The government provides funds for a variety of cause-related programs and services, especially in areas of healthcare and social services. Some government agencies set aside funds for community projects with clear benefits. Federal funding sources typically look for projects with evidence of strong community support and projects that can serve as models for other communities. State funding is sometimes generated through taxes and fees from drivers' licenses, vehicle registrations, and speeding tickets. Local funding may be available through town, city, and county governments.

Government sources provide funding to nonprofits through various grants and endowments. The amount of funds possible can be quite large, and the process for applying for the funds tends to be clear and firm. Government funds can sometimes provide ongoing money but, at times, only pay by unit of service. The application process is sometimes long and tedious, and the record keeping can be difficult. Depending on the features of the fund, unspent monies may need to be returned. Applying for local funds may not be as involved as the process for applying for federal and state funds. Depending on the locale, nonprofits may be able to obtain local funds simply by making presentations at town meetings.

Federated Funds

A federated fund, also known as a community fund, is a cooperative enterprise which is owned and managed by the nonprofit members. Federated funds are often state- or community-wide. The purpose of federated funds is to raise capital for nonprofits by serving as contribution vehicles, where donors can direct their dollars to charities for which they care. Contributions are distributed to all the member organizations, or donors can target their contributions to specific charities in the federation. Many federated funds partner with employers and implement giving plans that feature payroll deduction options. Federated funds typically provide nonprofits with a relatively large sum of money. They are usually available only to well-established nonprofits, and as a result, smaller, newer, and more unique nonprofits may be at a disadvantage. Federated funds often provide steady sources of funding. One of the most recognizable federated funds is the United Way. The United Way is a worldwide network of 45 countries and territories with approximately 1,300 organizations in the United States. The United Way focuses on three key building blocks of education, income, and health by addressing the underlying problems that prevent progress in those areas (United Way, 2010).

Agencies should always be on the lookout for potential funding sources. Nonprofits should monitor newspapers and the local Chamber of Commerce for new businesses opening up in the area. These organizations are often excellent prospects. They should visit professional organizations, civic organizations, and networking groups. Organizations should also be sure to add individuals who express an interest in getting involved with the organization, as well as those who contact the organization. By collecting business cards, agencies can add potential donors to their lists. The possibilities are endless. By employing these tips, organizations will have a solid foundation for their fundraising efforts (Garecht, 2010).

Once funding sources have been identified, agencies must have a plan in place to manage the donor information. The final section in this chapter will examine ways to manage such critical data.

Managing Donor Information

Effectively managing funding and donor records is critical in the overall success of a nonprofit's fundraising endeavors. An agency's ability to reach its fundraising goals is dramatically affected by the way funding information is stored and managed.

> **An agency's ability to reach its fundraising goals is dramatically affected by the way funding information is stored and managed.**

Managing Donor Lists

Once an agency begins to identify its potential funding sources, it must effectively manage this critical information. In order to manage this information, it must first be organized. It is imperative to keep an organized database of former and prospective funding sources. This way the agency will have the needed contact information on hand each time a fundraising initiative begins. Whenever a new funding source or prospective source is identified, the individual or organization should be added to the database as soon as possible. Agencies must clean up their organization's database on a regular basis. For example, anytime mail is returned due to an invalid address or due to forwarding instructions, which have expired, a note of the issue should be made in the database. Organizations should try to locate updated addresses, and if unavailable, the name or business should be removed from the database. This will save money in the long run as it will keep the organization from costs associated with sending mail to undeliverable addresses. By continually developing and updating the database, agencies will be ready to roll each time a new fundraising initiative begins.

Donor Management Systems

Another tool for agencies is the donor management system, also known as constituent management software or fundraising software. Donor management systems can do everything from managing a fundraising campaign to profiling donors. The software varies considerably in regard to cost, ranging from free to tens of thousands of dollars. An important point to consider regarding donor management systems is that agencies should be extremely careful about the information they put into the system. Every comment and note put

Information Management

Understanding and Mastery of . . . Recording, organizing, and assessing the relevance, adequacy, accuracy, and validity of information provided by others

Critical Thinking Question: Donor management systems can be used to profile donors. What information should be included and what information should be excluded in an agency's donor management system? Explain.

into the system should be one that the agency would not mind having the person about whom the comment was made, read. If a donor requests to see what is in his or her profile, the agency needs to be ready to show it. Therefore, there is no place for comments expressing displeasure over the size of the donation. The organization needs to operate in a manner that respects the funding source and donor confidence (Poderis, 2009c).

Managing donor lists is one of the most critical administrative responsibilities of an agency. Mishandling donor information can be the downfall of a fundraising campaign. On the other hand, donor information, which is organized, updated, and secure, can serve as the impetus to a winning fundraising initiative.

Summary

Identifying, locating, and managing funding sources is perhaps one of the most critical tasks of a nonprofit's fundraising initiative. Nonprofits' programs and services are funded by external sources ranging from individual contributors to governmental support. Each agency has unique needs, and therefore, their target markets and funding sources will differ. Knowing how to identify and locate target markets is a necessary step toward identifying and tapping into funding sources. Agencies that rely too heavily on one source of funding risk problems should the funding source disappear. To reduce such risks, nonprofits should diversify their funding sources. Donors, prospects, and funding sources are the heart of every fundraising campaign, and agencies must take extraordinary care to ensure this critical information is managed effectively.

The following questions will test your application and analysis of the content found within this chapter. For additional assessment, applying, analyzing, synthesizing, and evaluating chapter content with practice, visit **MySearchLab.com**

1. This target market includes those individuals who are being served or will potentially be served by the agency.
   a. Members
   b. Clients/customers
   c. Donors
   d. Volunteers

2. Working from within the organization by rallying staff is one way agencies can
   a. manage donor lists.
   b. manage donor information.
   c. tap into funding sources.
   d. locate target markets.

3. Donor management systems, also known as constituent management software or fundraising software, are used to profile donors and manage fundraising campaigns. When using these systems, you should
   a. input detailed information into the system including personal comments and notes to ensure that the information is comprehensive and that nothing is left out.
   b. keep the information confidential and not make it available to anyone.
   c. be extremely careful about the information you put into the system and include only information you wouldn't mind the donor reading.
   d. hire a donor management system specialist to manage the system so that staff at the agency do not have access to it.

4. You are the director of a small nonprofit organization. For the past 5 years you have secured funding, from a local business, to fund a summer camp for children who have suffered a loss. Two weeks before this year's camp, the business contacts you to let you know that it is unable to fund the camp due to economic reasons. You are at a loss as to what to do. You know the children will be devastated. You have been counting on the money and have no other means to finance the camp. The error you likely made was
   a. not diversifying the funding sources.
   b. not sending the business a "thank-you" card the year before.
   c. getting the children's hopes up about the camp.
   d. not sharing with the business how its donation would make a difference.

5. When developing an agency's initial donor and prospect list, the agency must know its target market and how the target market is served. Why is this necessary?

6. Although each agency has different target markets, there are common target markets that the majority of nonprofit agencies tend to pursue. Describe three common target markets that nonprofits are inclined to pursue.

7. It is critical that nonprofits diversify their funding sources. Explain why diversification of funding sources is so important.

8. Effectively managing donor information is critical to ensure that the information is up to date, organized, and ready when a fundraising initiative begins. What steps can an agency take to manage donor lists?

CHAPTER 6

Selecting the Best Fundraisers

Learning Objectives

- Describe and plan easy fundraisers, fundraising events, and online fundraising.
- Explain the differences between inbound and outbound telephone fundraising campaigns.
- Distinguish among capital campaigns and corporate, foundation, and legacy fundraising.
- Explain giving circles and how they benefit agencies and circles.
- Define planned giving and describe the most common planned gifts.

Agencies realize more and more that their survival depends on their ability to tap into both public and private resources. Unfortunately, some organizations may rely on a single, substantial revenue source. Although large donations are fantastic, their longevity is difficult to predict. By depending on a single stream of revenue, nonprofits may find it difficult to meet their goals and satisfy their missions. Tapping into an ever-dwindling number of resources requires creativity and diversification. Therefore, agencies are increasing the number and types of fundraisers. This chapter presents a variety of fundraisers to meet the funding needs of any organization.

Fundraisers make it possible for organizations to foster community involvement while raising funds. Profitable fundraising endeavors result in obtaining donations from individuals at all income levels as well as from massive corporations. The scope of funding opportunities is as varied as the types of fundraisers available. When organizing fundraisers, three fundamental questions must be answered. First, what is the size of the fundraising team? Small teams may want to consider fundraisers that can quickly bring in funds such as direct-sale fundraisers. Larger fundraising teams may put their energies toward a variety of fundraisers such as turnkey fundraisers coupled with capital campaigns. Second, how much money does the agency need to make? Small profits can easily be made through catalog sales, where large profits require more sophisticated fundraising initiatives such as planned giving. Finally, where does the nonprofit plan to fundraise? Agencies must consider the prospective donors. Knowing the agency's target market can assist in answering this question.

Regardless of the funding needs of an organization, there are fundraising options to meet those needs. Following is a catalog of fundraisers beginning with easy fundraisers and ending with the more complex.

Easy Fundraisers

Easy fundraisers allow nonprofits to raise funds quickly and with minimal expense. They require little administrative support and investment and bring in unrestricted funds that can help support the daily operations of an organization. This section covers a number of easy fundraisers, including direct sales, discount cards and coupon books, scratch cards, spinners, brochure sales, and ongoing fundraisers. Scores of companies on the Internet offer easy fundraising items, products, and information.

Direct-Sale Fundraisers

Direct-sale fundraisers require agencies to purchase items up front. They typically result in sizeable profits. After the initial investment, money made afterward goes directly to the cause. Direct-sale fundraisers work particularly well for nonprofits that have available funds to invest. Some popular direct-sale items include Smencils (scented pencils), candy bars, gourmet lollipops, meat snacks, healthy snacks, popcorn, and bracelets.

Discount Cards and Coupon Books

Discount cards are cards that are purchased and then sold for anywhere from 40 to 90% above their costs. Cards can be purchased readymade or customized. Readymade cards offer discounts on general restaurants or services, whereas customized discount cards feature discounts from local merchants who are approached by the nonprofit organization and asked for their support. In exchange for the discounts, merchants receive free advertising on the cards. Discount coupon books provide a variety of coupons, including discounts to restaurants and discounts on entertainment, merchandise, travel, and services. One of the most popular discount coupon books is the Entertainment Book fundraiser.

Scratch Cards

There are a variety of scratch card options including personalized cards. The concept is straightforward. Agencies purchase the scratch cards for a nominal amount, usually $5 or $10 per card. Organizations can earn up to 95% on each card. Each fundraising member receives a card filled with scratch dots, usually 50 dots. Members approach family, friends, coworkers, and other acquaintances asking them to scratch dots on the card to reveal donation amounts. Players pay the revealed donation amount and, depending on the scratch card, may receive something in return, usually coupons.

Spinners

Spinners are the size of a DVD case and contain a spinning arrow. They are reusable and can be personalized with the nonprofit's name and logo. Spinner fundraising involves fundraising members' approaching family, friends, neighbors, and coworkers and asking them to spin the arrow to determine their donation amount. Donation amounts typically range from $1 to $4. As a "thank you" for the donation, participants receive a coupon sheet.

Brochure Sales

Brochure fundraisers are popular fundraisers because they usually do not require any up-front money. The fundraising team collects money when orders are placed, and the items are shipped to the organization or to the purchaser. There is a wealth of items available for sale. Examples are flower bulbs, candles, gourmet cookie dough, desserts, popcorn, magazine subscriptions, jewelry, nuts and snacks, frozen pizza, toys, kitchen accessories, fruit, paper products, holiday items, calendars, eco-friendly products, salsa, coffees and teas, gift wrap, cheese, and beauty products.

Ongoing Fundraisers

Ongoing fundraisers virtually run themselves. Essentially all that is required to get started is to register the organization and share information. Once registered, ongoing fundraisers entail a planned endeavor to collect, redeem, and claim funds. In some cases, the sponsors take care of most of this. There are a variety of ongoing fundraisers ranging from collecting labels to recycling products. A number of large companies and domestic manufacturers offer fundraising opportunities for schools and agencies that collect or redeem coupons from product packages in exchange for money or goods. One example is the General Mill's Box Tops for Education (2010) program where schools receive earnings by collecting box tops. Since 1996, Box Tops for Education has helped America's schools make over 430 million.

There are various "Green" fundraising options available to nonprofits. Recycling cell phones and ink cartridges keeps hundreds of thousands of used cell phones and cartridges out of landfills. Depending on the recycling company and the unit model number, agencies can earn between .10 and 60.00 for each cell phone and between .20 and 10.00 for each ink cartridge. Implementing a recycling fundraiser is easy. First, agencies contact participating companies to obtain a list of accepted cartridges and cell phones. Next, agencies distribute the lists to their supporters and area businesses asking them to donate their used cell phones and ink cartridges. Collection boxes are then setup throughout the community and at local businesses.

Once the cell phones and cartridges are collected, organizations sort through the items and weed out broken units that are beyond repair. The units are then packed up and shipped to the participating companies following each company's redemption and payment schedule.

The loyalty program is another type of ongoing fundraiser. Loyalty programs are offered by some retailers and service providers who volunteer to donate a percentage of their profits to agencies whose supporters patronize their businesses. Patrons are often required to register in order to be designated as a participant of the loyalty program. They are often given a card to identify themselves as a supporter of the agency. When the patron makes a purchase or uses the service of the business, the patron shows his or her card and the nonprofit earns cash. Loyalty programs are a win-win for businesses and agencies.

Information Management

Understanding and Mastery of . . . Disseminating routine and critical information to clients, colleagues or other members of the related services system that is provided in written or oral form and in a timely manner

Critical Thinking Question: Ongoing fundraisers require agencies to register their organization and share information. What information must an agency share and to whom should the agency share the information with to guarantee a successful ongoing fundraiser?

Easy fundraisers require minimal planning with little investment on the part of the agency. When easy fundraisers are well planned and organized, the potential for raising substantial funds is great. Fundraising should be fun, and easy fundraisers, when carefully planned and organized, can be an enjoyable and profitable experience.

> **Fundraising should be fun, and easy fundraisers, when carefully planned and organized, can be an enjoyable and profitable experience.**

Next, fundraising events will be explored. Fundraising events require more planning, effort, and sometimes more up-front costs than easy fundraisers; however, the income potential is typically greater.

Fundraising Events

Only one's imagination limits the variety of fundraising events possible. Fundraising events bring organizations, businesses, families, and communities together. They easily motivate and excite fundraising members to actively participate in the event in order to generate the finances needed by the organization. This portion covers a number of fundraising events, ranging from festivals to "don't come events." Let's start with calendar celebrations.

Calendar Celebrations

The calendar presents all sorts of holidays and festive days that can serve as the inspiration for a number of fantastic charity events. Organizations can use their imagination to essentially turn any day into a fundraising festival. Examples are a Scarecrow Festival, Hot Chili Fiesta, Valentine's Day Festival, Mardi Gras, Wild West Day, Rainbow Festival, Mutt Show, Chocolate Festival, and Summer Solstice Festival. Nonprofits must secure a suitable venue and plan the event well in advance. Depending on the nature of the festival, offering classes, demonstrations, and competitions can help increase festival participation. Renting vendor space can bring in additional money. By holding the event annually, the festival can become a regular fixture on a community's event calendar.

Art Raffles

Art raffles can be an enjoyable and exciting way to fundraise. Nonprofits essentially host an event where local artists donate art pieces. The art is raffled off through the sale of a select number of high-dollar raffle tickets. Tickets are randomly drawn during a gallery-style event. The winning ticket holders choose their selections right off the walls and displays. Artists are more inclined to donate their work because it can provide them with exposure to potential buyers. Inviting artists to the event is a nice approach to securing items as they can mingle with art patrons and make potential sale contacts (Fundraiser Help: Fundraising Ideas & Resources, 2009).

Rubber Duck Races

Rubber duck races are a unique, exciting, family-oriented fundraiser. The event involves racing rubber ducks down a flowing river, stream, or other waterway. The waterway must be long enough to hold the event but not too long where it would take too much time for ducks to reach the finish line. Participants adopt ducks for $5 or $10 each for a chance to win monetary or donated prizes. Each ticket's number corresponds to a number written, with a waterproof pen, on a rubber duck. There are typically 3,000 rubber ducks in a race, but the amount can be adjusted to match the number of supporters. There is an initial outlay for the rubber ducks, but the investment can easily be recouped in ticket sales and then negligible in ensuing years. At the starting line, large containers or plastic bags of ducks are simultaneously dropped into the water. The winning duck is the one that crosses the finish line first. A net placed below the finish line is used to catch the floating ducks. Organizations can make the competition even more profitable by selling chances to predict the time the winning duck will cross the finish line, setting up concession stands at the event, and/or organizing the race around another event such as a local festival. A spin on the rubber duck race is the "message in a bottle" option. Here names of the supporters are written on cards and placed in plastic bottles. The bottles are then dropped into the water and the bottle that crosses the finish line first is the winner.

Flamingo Flocking

Flamingo flocking has become more and more popular over the past few years. It is a fantastic and entertaining fundraiser. There are a number of options for flamingo flocking; the most common approach begins with the organization announcing that it will be holding a "Flamingo Flocking Fundraiser." Organizations purchase or rent a flock of plastic pink flamingos. Next, volunteers secretly go to a "victim's" home and plant the large flock of pink flamingos in the "victim's" yard along with a sign that reads "You've been flamingoed!" It is helpful to put an explanation note around the neck of one of the flamingos. This will let the victim know who did this and why. Laminating the explanation note or placing it in plastic bags will safeguard the note from moisture. The "victim" must make a donation to the organization to have the flamingoes removed from the yard. The donation can be a set amount, such as $25, or can be an amount set by the "victims" that may generate larger profits. The "victim" then chooses the next house for the flock to visit. The volunteers then move the flamingos to the next "victim's" home and the process starts all over again. There are a number of variations on this theme. One common variation is to offer "Anti-Flocking Insurance" at the time the fundraiser is announced. The price of the insurance can be set by the organization, and the insurance safeguards that the flock will never visit the insurance recipient's yard. Organizations can even make insurance certificates for the insured to display in their windows. Other variations include having multiple flocks visiting "victims' " homes simultaneously; communicating "flock sightings" through emails, newsletters, and agency websites; taking orders and having people pay in advance to have the flock land in someone's yard; decorating the flocks; and accepting freewill donations.

Holiday Shops

Holiday shops are seasonal fundraising stores, typically held at schools, where students can purchase inexpensive gifts sold on consignment by the sponsoring organization. The most successful holiday shops offer a wide range of items and price ranges to suit the needs of the shoppers. This type of fundraising event works for a wide range of holidays, including Christmas, Valentine's Day, Easter, Mother's Day, and Father's Day.

Talent Shows

Hidden talent can be found in almost every community. With the onslaught of televised talent competitions, community-based talent shows are becoming more and more popular. It is a terrific time for nonprofits to take advantage of the popularity of talent shows by organizing their own talent competition and selling tickets to the event. There are a number of possible talent categories, including singing, comedy, rock band, acting, dancing, choir, stepping, gymnastics, magic, cheerleading, and poetry. Hosting a talent show pulls the whole community together in a fun and entertaining way.

QR Codes Scavenger Hunts

As discussed in Chapter 4, Quick Response (QR) Codes have opened the door to a number of creative marketing possibilities. QR Codes also provide unique fundraising possibilities. For example, organizations can create fun and exciting scavenger hunts using QR Codes. For this event, individuals or teams register and pay a fee to participate. The QR codes reveal a sequential order of clues ultimately leading to a final destination. On the day of the event, and at a designated time, agencies tweet the start location for the scavenger hunt. When participants arrive at the start location, they scan a QR Code to get the clue for the next location. When they arrive at each subsequent location, they scan additional codes. A time limit should be set for participants to complete the hunt. Prizes can be awarded throughout the hunt, with a grand prize awarded to the first person or first team who makes it to the final destination. Agencies can add to the fun by having participants dress in costumes and awarding a prize for the best costume. For additional information of QR Codes, refer to Chapter 4.

Murder Mystery Dinners

Hosting a murder mystery dinner is a wonderful, interactive fundraising option. Organizations select a storyline tailored to the number of attendees. Agencies can purchase murder mystery kits or can create their own. With murder mystery dinners, every guest participates. Guests purchasing tickets receive costume suggestions and ideas. Along with the costume suggestions, guests receive a summary of the party's storyline and the setting. The decorations and menu are tailored around the theme. At the actual event, attendees receive clues in between each course and spend 15 to 20 minutes per scene revealing the necessary information to one another, while staying in character. Guests use this information to decipher the murderer's identity, motive, weapon, and opportunity. Basing the number of scenarios on the number of courses in the meal is effective. Including a cocktail hour in the mix can provide time for even more scenes. After ample investigation has taken place, guests write down who they feel committed the crime and which characters hold vital clues. The dinner host tallies the results and awards prizes to the winners.

Casino Nights

Casino nights and other games of chance, such as bingos, raffles, and poker tournaments, are subject to regulations at both the state and federal levels. They may be banned altogether in some areas, and other areas may limit the means and types of gambling permitted. Therefore, before conducting games of chance, agencies must refer to their state's local government for applicable laws, mandates, protocols, and licenses.

Casino nights offer dozens of ways for nonprofits to raise significant amounts of money. This fundraising event combines a number of gaming options such as poker and blackjack tournaments, roulette, and craps. Casino nights can be themed to add an additional ambiance to the evening. Decorations and props can match the theme. Examples of themes are Hollywood, Monte Carlo, Las Vegas, Wild West, and Gangster casino nights. For an added twist, guests can be asked to dress in theme-inspired outfits. Casino equipment such as gaming tables, roulette wheels, and chips are usually rented but can be purchased. Professional staff should be hired to run the gaming tables. Fundraising members solicit prizes from area businesses. Popular prizes include complimentary dinners, spa services, limousine rentals, and hotel stays. Casino participants want to win something, so securing as many gifts as possible increases their chances of walking away with a prize.

Ticket purchases entitle guests to a set amount of play money that they receive when they arrive at the event. The play money is then exchanged for chips. Depending on the event and function, the gaming can be coupled with a sit-down dinner, food stations, or buffet. Meals are typically served before the casino play, and the casino play usually lasts for 2 to 4 hours. When guests run out of chips, they can obtain additional play money for a token donation.

Agencies profit through ticket sales, table sponsorships, and food and beverage sales. The cost of table sponsorship should cover the expense of renting the equipment and hiring staff. Nonprofits can increase their profits by combining casino nights with other fundraisers such as silent auctions, pull tab tickets, and 50/50 raffles.

Golf Ball Drops

A golf ball drop fundraising event entails selling numbered raffle tickets that correspond to numbered golf balls. Golf balls are dropped onto a target and the person whose golf ball lands closet to the target's center is declared the winner. A prize can also be awarded for the ball that rolls the furthest from the center of the target. This event can provide even more spectator appeal by dropping the golf balls from a tethered hot-air balloon or from a helicopter hovering above the target. Prize money and/or non-cash prizes are awarded. The more prizes available, the better the ticket sales, as individuals tend to buy more tickets if they believe there is a high probability of winning a prize. Golf ball drops can be even more profitable when held in conjunction with a festival or other local event. Combining the drop with a hot-air balloon festival, for example, is a natural fit.

Marathons

Although running and walking marathons are common, unique marathon fundraisers are becoming more and more popular. Marathons from the past, such as sock hops and disco parties, can be trendy today. Still other kinds of marathons can be pulled from pop culture, such as *Glee* episode marathons. The possibilities are endless. Funds are typically raised when marathon participants solicit pledges. For example, a donor might pledge $5 for each *Glee* episode watched during a designated period of time.

Game-Day Competitions

Game-day competitions are entertaining fundraisers for people of all ages. Agencies collect a variety of both board and video games, and participants are charged a donation to compete. Participants must at least attempt to play each game during the competition. The champion is the person who wins the most games. A prize is awarded to the champion. Additional prizes can be awarded for a number of categories such as "most video games won," "youngest player," "oldest player," and "sorest loser."

Movie Nights

Movie nights can be tailored around any age group or theme. For example, family night, date night, and girls' night out make popular movie night themes. Movies are shown on a large-screen television or projected onto a screen. A host can facilitate discussions following the film. Typically, admission is charged for watching the movie, but organizations can raise additional revenue by setting up refreshment stands and selling popcorn, hotdogs, candy, drinks, and other snack items. Movie nights are an enjoyable and profitable fundraising event.

Auctions

Auctions offer a variety of formats and have the potential of bringing in thousands of dollars. According to Carson (2010), approximately 200,000 to 300,000 fundraising auctions are held each year raising $14.6 billion. There are a number of different auction formats (i.e., live, silent, blind, and online), but regardless of the format, all auctions begin the same way, by soliciting auction items. The best auctions have a wide variety of items, including service items, gift certificates, and auction themed items. Examples of service items are spa services, restaurant gift certificates, photo sessions, car repair vouchers, art lessons, guitar lessons, dance lessons, and swimming lessons. Themed items, if applicable, tend to attract bidders. Some of the more popular items include gift certificates, jewelry, trips, weekend getaways to local hotels, gift-of-the-month clubs, tickets to sporting or cultural events, and adventure experiences such as hot-air balloon rides. From the smallest to the more exclusive, bidders appreciate a wide variety of items. Once items are secured, a master list is created. The master list contains the donor's name, address, and phone number, along with the item number, item description, value, with space left to record who won the item, the person's phone number, and how much the person paid for the item. Following is an overview of live, silent, and blind auctions. The online auction is discussed in the "Online Fundraising" section.

Live auctions can be exciting and entertaining fundraisers when attention is given to these important details:

- Auction items should match the auction time frame. For example, it would not make sense to hold a 70-minute auction with only 10 auction items.
- A professional auctioneer must be employed. A trained charity auctioneer can substantially contribute to a fun, lively, and successful event. Professional auctioneers know how to build anticipation, encourage bidding wars, and effectively close the bidding. They are also able to sell more items in a given time frame than an untrained auctioneer.

- A local celebrity should be asked to serve as the master or mistress of ceremonies. Local celebrities can help increase interest and attendance at the auction.
- Seating should be arranged so that guests sit next to friends and acquaintances, so they feel more comfortable during the bidding process.

Silent auctions are auctions held without an auctioneer. Instead, participants place their bids on sheets of paper. Silent auctions can begin and end in an hour, a day, a weekend, or longer. The beginning and ending times can also be staggered. For example, auction items can be placed on different-colored tables, with each table beginning and ending at different times. Setting up a silent auction takes time, but the time can pay off in the amount of money raised. Running a silent auction involves a few steps:

1. *Label items.* Label each auction item with a number.
2. *Create bidding sheets.* Create a separate bidding sheet for each item. The bidding sheet should include the name of the item, a brief description of the item, its value, the donor's name, a minimum bid (usually 20% of the value), and the minimum bidding increments. Space should be left for the bidder's number or name, phone number, and bid.
3. *Assign numbers to bidders.* Some organizations assign numbers to bidders to help maintain anonymity. When doing so, bidders fill out registration cards and are given a bidding number that they use on the bidding sheets in lieu of their name.
4. *Place auction items.* Place auction items, and their corresponding sheets, on tables, on walls, and/or on easels.
5. *Monitor tables.* Once the auction begins, volunteers should monitor the tables to make sure the bid sheets are in place and that participants adhere to the minimum bid and minimum bidding increment requirements.
6. *Make announcements.* Announcements should be made at least 10 and then 5 minutes before the auction ends.
7. *Collect bidding sheets.* Once the auction ends, all the bidding sheets should be collected, the winning bids circled, and lines drawn through the empty spaces on the bidding sheets.
8. *Sort bidding sheets.* Sheets are then sorted by the last name of the winning bidders.
9. *Collect payments.* After all the sheets are sorted, the winning bidders pay for, and pick up, their items.

Planning and Evaluation

Understanding and Mastery of . . . Program design, implementation, and evaluation

Critical Thinking Question: Auctions have the potential of bringing in thousands of funding dollars. When planning an auction, what steps would you take to ensure successful implementation of the event?

. . . .

An innovative spin on the live auction is the blind auction. Here, people bring wrapped items or items are solicited from businesses and wrapped by the auction coordinators. Each wrapped gift contains a nice, usable item to be auctioned off. The wrapped items are placed on display so that people can examine them, weigh them, and guess what might be in the packages. To mix it up, large boxes can be used to conceal small presents, and packages can be weighed down to make it more difficult for bidders to guess the contents. When the auction begins, bidders are asked to wait until the last item has been auctioned off before opening their packages. Once the last item is sold, winners simultaneously open their packages and show the group what they have won.

Combining a live auction with a silent auction can be an incredibly effective method. People may find silent auctions boring, and live auctions may force people to sit around and wait until the auction item of their choice is up for bid. By combining auction formats, bidders will be more entertained and more likely to give.

Jail and Bail Events

Jail and bail events raise money by donors paying to have someone arrested and by having the arrested "prisoner" raise money in order to be released from jail. The reason for the arrest can be anything from leaving dirty clothes on the floor to not washing the dishes—any reason works. Once the donation is made, a warrant is issued for the arrest of the suspect. A volunteer police officer picks up the suspect, cuffs him or her, and takes the person to jail. The person must be willing to be arrested. The jail can be set up anywhere: a local restaurant, a school, or the nonprofit agency that is holding the event. A mug shot is taken of the "prisoner" wearing prison attire, and the individual then goes before a judge. The judge sets bail based on severity of the crime. The prisoner is then given a cell phone to make calls to raise the amount necessary to be released from jail. Once the bail is raised, the prisoner is released.

Don't Come Events

Don't come events are perfect fundraisers for busy people who do not have time to attend yet another fundraising event, and who would appreciate a creative way to support an organization. Planning and implementing a "Don't Come Event" is as amusing as the concept itself. The nonprofit sends out a humorous invitation to an event that will never take place. Invitations should be appealing and display worthy; some invitees may want to keep it as a conversation piece. Because the event will never take place, organizations can use their imagination and hold the event anywhere and at anytime. For example, invitations can say something like this:

XYZ organization is holding its fifth annual Black Tie Non-Event. The event will NOT take place on July 4, 2012. Refreshments and hor'devours will NOT be served at 5 p.m. and dinner will NOT take place at 6 p.m. There will NOT be famous keynote speaker at 8 p.m.

Another non-event concept is the "Stay at Home" event where donors purchase tickets entitling them to stay home and relax. This is a terrific event for people who are always on the go and could use a quiet night at home. On the invitation, outline the mission of the organization, how donations are used to support the mission, and invite donors to stay at home in honor of the organization and its cause. Donations are made when invitees purchase tickets to the "non-event." One of the major advantages of this fundraising event or "non-event" is that agencies are free to invite anyone, including media personalities, celebrities, and politicians.

A final non-event idea is the "Bakeless Bake Sale." Invite donors NOT to bake. Explain the mission and cause of the agency and how donations will be used. Describe the amount of time saved by NOT having to bake and by just helping out with a donation. Consider asking for a donation equal to the amount of time saved by not having to bake and/or equal to the amount of money saved by not having to buy ingredients.

Following a "non-event" fundraiser, "non-attendees" should be thanked. One suggestion is to mail thank-you certificates to the supporters for not attending or participating in the fundraising event that never happened.

Event fundraisers offer a multitude of options that can be combined with other fundraisers. For example, a talent show can be combined with a silent auction. A game-day competition can be coupled with a gourmet bake sale. The possibilities are endless.

Next, online fundraising will be covered. Online fundraising is unique, in that it offers fundraising options with absolutely no geographical or time constraints: Websites can be viewed worldwide, 24-hours a day, 7-days a week.

> Event fundraisers offer a multitude of options that can be combined with other fundraisers. For example, a talent show can be combined with a silent auction. A game-day competition can be coupled with a gourmet bake sale. The possibilities are endless.

Online Fundraising

The Internet has transformed fundraising. Increased donations and reduced expenditures have led to more and more agencies wanting to learn how they can benefit from online fundraising. Although access to websites is amazing and affordable, nonprofits are subject to various jurisdictions that regulate fundraising endeavors. Therefore, organizations using the Internet to solicit funds must first register their organization in each state that requires such registration and registrations must be renewed annually. As discussed in Chapter 1, the majority of states utilize a uniform registration form through the Unified Registration System (DeMartinis, 2005). It is necessary to understand that the author is not an attorney and is not providing legal advice. Before soliciting donations online, nonprofits should seek the advice of a lawyer familiar with out-of-state fundraising concerns. With that said, the variety of online fundraisers will now be discussed beginning with selling web space for advertising.

Selling Web Space for Advertising

One way of using the Internet to raise funds is through the sale of advertising space on the agency's website. Some of the options include flat-rate ads, pay-per-view ads, and selling an advertiser's homepage. Flat-rate ads are often associated with banner ads or limited-time sponsorships. Banner ads are purchased by advertisers for a flat rate and placed on the agency's website. Once there, visitors click on the ad to reach the advertiser's website. Pay-per-view ads are banner ads that pay a small amount each time a visitor clicks on the ad to view the advertiser's website. Selling an advertiser's home page involves inviting visitors to use the advertiser's website as their "homepage" or to frequently visit the advertiser's website. Agencies earn money based on the number of visitors who use the advertiser's website as their homepage and the number of visits to the advertiser's website (Mercer, 2005).

Online Auctions

Online auctions remove the barriers of geography and time. Bidders can live miles away and participate in the auction 24 hours a day, 7 days a week. Online auctions perform best when they run for 1 to 3 weeks. This time frame expands the nonprofit's marketing efforts. Online auctions are also incredibly measurable. They produce useful information about the types and categories of items that receive bids. When the auction is over, the information generated from the progress reports can be used to plan future auctions and fundraisers.

Nonprofits benefit from online auctions because they are easier to organize and manage than live auctions, and organizations can raise more money than they might earn in a live auction. Not only can nonprofits raise money from the auction items themselves, they can sell sponsorship on their websites. This provides an advertising alternative for businesses that would like to support a charitable cause while receiving online exposure. Agencies can create their own online auction or auction items off on an existing site, such as eBay. For agencies wanting to create their own online auction site, the following steps may be helpful:

1. *Build an auction website.* Check out what is available. There are a number of software programs available for building and managing online auction sites. Some programs even provide items for organizations to auction off (Whole Auction Fundraising Solutions, 2010). IDonateToCharity.org (2009) is a charitable auction website that charges an annual fee of about $500 but does not charge organizations a percentage of the proceeds from each auction, like most auction sites. For agencies without the expertise or time to create and manage their own online auction website, a professional website developer can be helpful. The website developer can be employed to create the site, post pictures of the auction items, and manage the bidding and payment process.

2. *Solicit items.* Solicit items from businesses in the community. Businesses that donate items can reach new clients. Offer businesses a clickable link and logo so they can check the bidding activity of their items. Almost any service, product, or item can be put up for auction. According to Carson (2010), the majority of online bidders tend to be women, at 71%. It is crucial to keep this demographic in mind when soliciting auction items.

3. *Customize site pages.* Customize the auction website so that it contains information about the nonprofit. This provides the nonprofit with an opportunity to educate the public about the agency's mission, programs, and services. It is essential to assure bidders that the cause is meaningful and that every dollar raised will support the nonprofit's mission.

4. *Promote the auction and reach your audience.* Get the word out: Market the auction through newsletters, emails, ads in local papers, radio spots, local media, word of mouth, press releases, websites, social networking, and other channels.

5. *Manage the auction.* Monitor the daily activity of the auction to determine whether changes need to be made. Use progress reports to determine what needs to be done to help promote items that do not have enough bids. Monitoring and evaluating the auction while it's in progress can ensure that the fundraising goals are met. To improve the success of an online auction, agencies can use email and website traffic to expand the bidding pool to a broader audience.

Some agencies may choose to auction items off on preexisting auction sites, such as eBay. Auction websites have different fee structures. eBay, for example, has a number of possible fees based on the category of the item, number of items, final value of the item, and listing upgrades, just to name a few (eBay, 2010). However, some online auction sites waive fees or offer reduced fees to nonprofits using their sites to fundraise.

Commercial Co-Venture Programs

Another online fundraising option is the commercial co-venture program. There are several types of commercial co-venture programs. One type is when a business donates a portion of its sales to a nonprofit organization. Another type is when a nonprofit promotes merchandise on its website and includes a hyperlink that takes visitors to the business where the merchandise can be purchased.

Through collaborations with commercial businesses, nonprofits can increase their ability to promote their organization's cause through the larger financial resources of businesses. Co-ventures also allow nonprofits to reach potential donors through the business's customer database. Not only can nonprofits benefit from commercial co-ventures, "for profits" can benefit as well. According to HighBeam Research, Inc. (2009), co-ventures can promote a business by inducing positive public relations, providing additional marketing opportunities, and enhancing customer relations.

To protect consumers against deception and fraud, commercial co-venture relationships are regulated (Perlman & Chang, 2007). Before an organization enters into a commercial co-venture program, it is recommended that the arrangement be reviewed by an attorney or accountant.

Selling Merchandise

Nonprofits can fundraise by establishing online storefronts. Normally this is done by selling promotional items, such as coffee mugs, t-shirts, and hats that bear the agency's logo and/or name. Organizations can also sell donated items online. There are three typical methods of payment for merchandise purchased on online storefronts: printable order forms that can be mailed or faxed to the agency, merchandise displays with a phone number to call in orders, and web-based forms that can be submitted online.

Messaging Mechanisms

Message-based communication mechanisms are an effective method of online fundraising. Examples of online message-based communication are Usenet, social networking, and email. Usenet is a universally disseminated discussion system that consists of hierarchically classified newsgroups (Usenet.com, 2009). Usenet provides nonprofits with unique fundraising options. Nonprofits can choose newsgroups devoted to topics related to the agency's cause, and post messages to those groups. The tone of the messages should be straightforward, concise, and free from catchy slogans and desperate language. Usenet.com (2009) encourages experts in the field to consider becoming regular contributors to newsgroups that are committed to the individuals' topics of expertise. Nonprofits can take advantage of this medium by regularly posting information, answering questions, and appealing for donations. Including contact information with each posting places the agency front and center of people who might otherwise not be familiar with the agency's mission and its funding needs.

Social networking presents another effective messaging mechanism. Nowadays almost everyone is online and involved in social networking. Nonprofits that do not use social media are missing out on massive fundraising potential. Social networking is a quicker and more efficient way to fundraise when compared to some alternatives such as direct mailing. It introduces potential and current donors to others who share a common passion for the mission of the organization. Raising money is as easy as making the public aware of the nonprofit's needs and keeping the public's attention. The first step to fundraising through social networking is to explore what other organizations are using and how well it is working for them. The next step involves choosing the best social networks. The right networks are not necessarily the largest; smaller networks may be more effective. Next, social networking sites are created. Using staff members or volunteers experienced with social networking can save time, as the organization will not have to start from scratch. Agencies should use a mass marketing approach and set up more than one profile. For example, nonprofits should consider creating group sites and event sites, whenever possible. After developing the social networking sites, fundraising efforts should be targeted to the right people. Before soliciting donations, agencies should cultivate relationships with the potential donors. Cultivating relationships entails informing the public of the agency's activities, publicizing events, and posting pictures of sponsors and members involved in the work of the agency.

Email fundraising is a form of messaging mechanism that allows nonprofits to build relationships with their members, donors, and potential donors. Agencies can make funding appeals directly through email and can include funding requests in email attachments, such as newsletters. However, email fundraising works only when agencies have the email addresses of both donors and prospective donors. A great way to start collecting email addresses is by advertising the agency's email newsletter. Nonprofits can mention their newsletters in articles, on their websites, on FAQ pages, at fundraising events, and on social networking sites. Once agencies have secured email addresses, they should take steps to increase the likelihood that their email funding appeals do not end up in the readers' "trash" folders. First, agencies should place the name of the organization in the "from" line and the recipient's name in the "to" line. The name of the publication, or a current related headline, should be placed in the "subject" line. By personalizing the email, readers are more likely to see that the correspondence is from a trusted source. Second, the email should inspire the reader to visit the agency's website. By including a link to the organization's website, readers will be motivated to go online to learn more about the agency. Third, the email should make it easy for email recipients to share the information with friends, family, and colleagues. Include a "Forward-this-to-a-Friend" button in emails. By making emails as interactive as possible, the fundraising potential of emails increases.

Nonprofits can raise sizeable funds and reach more donors through online fundraising. The more agencies get their messages online, the greater the benefits. Online

> ## Information Management
>
> Understanding and Mastery of . . . Using technology for word processing, sending email, and locating and evaluating information
>
> **Critical Thinking Question:** Technology provides agencies with numerous fundraising possibilities. In what ways can email be utilized in fundraising endeavors?

fundraising efforts can augment more conventional approaches, reach thousands of potential donors, and deepen relationships with existing contributors.

Next, telephone campaigns are addressed. Although telephone fundraising may be an unpopular method of fundraising for some people, it can be immensely profitable in certain situations.

Telephone Campaigns

Telephone campaigns can be an effective way to fundraise. They usually produce a higher rate of return than direct mail campaigns and tend to be more cost-effective. There are two types of telephone campaigns: inbound and outbound. Inbound calls are typically responses to some form of agency solicitation made through the mail or through various media channels. An example of a well-known inbound telephone campaign is the Jerry Lewis MDA (Muscular Dystrophy Association) Telethon that raises millions of dollars annually.

Outbound telephone campaigns take place when callers work from a list of current or prospective donors, calling them to talk about the work and needs of the organization in hopes of convincing them to contribute. Although some agencies make cold calls in an effort to get the agency's foot in the door; most calls are targeted and may be follow-ups to a direct-mail campaign. According to CharityFacts (2010), telephone fundraising is an effective way to fundraise when there are emergency appeals that require agencies to quickly reach their supporters, when the message is complicated and needs an explanation, and in situations where the supporters prefer to be contacted by phone instead of by mail.

Most telephone campaigns work off a telephone fundraising script. According to Mal Warwick Associates (n.d.), the most effective scripts are respectful, build rapport, are straightforward, simulate a real conversation, communicate enthusiasm, speak to donor benefits, are written in natural language, seek commitment from the donor, and clearly explain the payment procedures.

Some organizations have staff who make the fundraising calls or train and use volunteers. However, the majority of organizations hire independent contractors to make the calls for them. Outside contractors hire and train staff to solicit funds by working off a script.

As with most fundraisers, telephone fundraising is governed by laws that tend to vary coming directly by state. Some states require organizations to disclose whether the calls are directly coming from the agency itself or from an outside contractor. If coming from an outside contractor, organizations must also disclose an estimate of the amount of funds raised that will be paid to the contractor. According to Nonprofit Hub.com (n.d.), it is deemed unethical for outside fundraising contractors to keep a set percentage of funds raised; instead, most agencies pay a flat fee per donor contacted or per contribution collected.

Although telephone fundraising is one of the most intimate forms of fundraising, it can be the least trusted form. Telephone campaigns work as long as they are executed properly. When done correctly, telephone fundraising is a cost-effective fundraising communication method.

The next section addresses capital campaigns. The goal of a capital campaign is to raise money for a major purchase, such as a building or a high-priced piece of equipment.

Capital Campaigns

A capital campaign is a time-limited effort to raise significant dollars for a specific project. Since the effort is time-limited, the funds are considered restricted. Capital campaigns have a beginning and an end that typically span over several years. The funds are generally used to finance a new building or an expensive piece of equipment. Capital campaigns use all the standard methods of fundraising, such as email marketing and direct solicitations; however, they necessitate exceptional planning and skillful implementation (Fritz, 2010a). The following steps provide guidelines for running a successful capital campaign:

> **Capital campaigns use all the standard methods of fundraising, such as email marketing and direct solicitations; however, they necessitate exceptional planning and skillful implementation.**

1. *Develop a timeline.* Before implementing a capital campaign, it is essential to lay the groundwork. Planning is a vital component. Agencies must plan for the campaign months in advance, sometimes even a year in advance. It is crucial to establish a time frame for the campaign. Capital campaigns that drag on and on can prove to be a disaster. Because the purchase of the new building or piece of equipment is presumably vital to the nonprofit's ability to achieve its goals and fulfill its mission, the longer the campaign lasts, the more the donors are likely to believe that the capital purchase is unnecessary. According to Gaebler Ventures (2010), selecting and adhering to a capital campaign deadline is likely to avoid this trap.

2. *Develop a budget.* Once the timeline is established, a budget should be developed. It is necessary to solicit input and bids from all parties involved. For example, if the goal of the campaign is to fund a new building, then the architect, contractor, project manager, and other tradespeople should provide estimates (Poderis, 2009a). Real-world costs should be researched. Chances are the project will cost more than the agency's initial estimate. Agencies should obtain several estimates and add 10% for unexpected overruns (Gaebler Ventures, 2010). It is also useful to identify other organizations, which have had similar capital construction budgets. Much can be learned from their building undertakings (Poderis, 2009a).

> ▶ **Administration**
>
> Understanding and Mastery of . . . Developing budgets and monitoring expenditures
>
> **Critical Thinking Question:** A successful capital campaign requires careful planning and skillful implementation. If the capital campaign is established to fund an expensive piece of equipment, whom should the agency solicit input from when developing the budget?

3. *Solicit pledges.* After the budget has been determined, organizations can solicit pledges. As discussed in Chapter 2, gift charts are an essential planning tool for illustrating the number of gifts and the number of donors needed to raise a specified amount of funds. They are especially helpful in charting the fundraising needs of a capital campaign.

4. *Market the capital campaign.* Once a gift chart is created, the capital campaign can be marketed. Market the campaign through events such as luncheons, dinners, kickoff events, groundbreaking events, dedications, and open houses.

5. *Tell the story.* The agency's case statement should be used to tell the story. Enlighten and inform current and prospective donors on the reasoning behind the needed building, or piece of equipment (Gaebler Ventures, 2010). For example, a separate domestic violence shelter may be needed to provide a safe haven for victims of intimate partner violence who are also struggling with chemical dependency issues. Educate donors on the importance of having a separate shelter to provide treatment for the individuals' chemical dependency concerns. A testimonial by someone who has benefitted from the agency's services can also inspire people to give. Whatever the method, make sure that the funders understand the importance of the capital purchase and the impact it will have on the community.

6. *Communicate progress.* Throughout the capital campaign, nonprofits must diligently communicate their progress to their donors. Donors need to be kept in the loop about the progress of the agency in reaching its goal.

7. *Send pledge reminders.* For those who have pledged a specified amount, friendly reminders along the way will help keep the amount the agency receives close to the amount the donors have pledged.

One of the major advantages of a successful capital campaign is that the agency is left in a much better place than it was before the campaign. The effort required to raise considerable funds justifies the amount of planning and resources necessary to run a successful capital campaign.

Corporate fundraising will now be discussed. Corporate fundraising is unique in that companies are able to not only provide funds, but may also offer goods and services. In addition, this is one of the few fundraisers where the donor may contribute as a means to gain exposure and community respect.

Corporate Fundraising

Corporations offer a number of funding possibilities to nonprofits. Potential sources of funding include event or program sponsorship, corporate membership, corporate partnerships, and corporate support. Because companies operate worldwide, corporate fundraising can be conducted anywhere. Nonprofits must consider the number of staff or amount of volunteer time required to develop strong corporate relationships. Corporate fundraising may present a challenge for agencies with limited resources.

It is essential to note that corporate/nonprofit partnerships may not be viewed by the corporation as a charitable contribution as one generally refers to charitable contributions. For many corporations, the partnership infers that they will get something in return for their support. In other words, corporations may give in order to gain exposure, community respect, and publicity. This may take the form of name and product recognition through the placement of their logo on collateral material or an opportunity to distribute their products at an event. Corporate funding tends to be more episodic and revolve around specific events and campaigns.

There are a number of resources that can be useful in assisting nonprofits in creating a list of potential corporate partners. Some of the sources include chamber of commerce directories and business journals; Kiwanis, Rotaries, and Lions Clubs; corporate donors' lists available from other nonprofit agencies; association groups; management companies; magazines; and top lists. Many of these sources have lists that are readily available, such as the chamber of commerce directories.

Creating healthy relationships with corporations will assure successful partnerships that will provide nonprofits with the needed funding. Cultivating relationships with corporations begins with relationship building with the right corporate decision-makers. Bulk mailings to corporations are impersonal and can be viewed as insulting. Face-to-face communication works best. Corporations are more prone to providing funding to an organization when solid, close relationships exist between the company and the agency. When reflecting on the qualities valued most in a friend, one is likely to include honesty, integrity, loyalty, trustworthiness, and reliability. These hold true for qualities corporations look for in the relationships they form with nonprofits.

There are a number of unique, face-to-face methods nonprofits can employ in order to develop corporate relationships. For example, agencies can do the following:

- *Invite representatives to present.* Invite corporate decision-makers to present corporate information to the nonprofit's board, when appropriate.
- *Schedule meetings.* Schedule one-on-one meetings with a corporate representative to discuss agency services and programs and ask for feedback; when suitable, attend corporate meetings.
- *Invite representatives to events.* Invite corporate representatives to attend agency events, as guests.
- *Host forums.* Host a corporate forum of supporters and advisors.

The more personal and meaningful the connection is with the corporate decision-makers, the greater the likelihood that a partnership will form.

Although the funding possibilities are limitless, organizations are cautioned to carefully examine businesses from which they seek funding. Nonprofits should avoid engaging with companies whose public reputations may damage the nonprofit's credibility. The optimal partnerships are those that provide natural links between the corporation and the agency's mission, programs, and services. These links can lead agencies to corporate dollars and corporations to greater name and product recognition.

The next section addresses foundation fundraising. Foundation fundraising involves pursuing and securing funds from private funding organizations such as a foundation or trust.

Foundation Fundraising

Private foundations are nongovernmental, tax-exempt nonprofit organizations, with funds usually donated by high net-worth donors such as a single individual, family, or a corporation. According to Fritz (2010b), there are approximately 80,000 private foundations. Some of the foundations are large and well known, such as the Bill and Melinda Gates Foundation, but about two thirds of the foundations have assets totaling less than

$1 million. They are established to provide grants to nonprofit charitable organizations and causes, and are typically managed by their own trustees or directors. Foundations adhere to the desires of the families and donors and must disburse at least 5% of their endowment income each year.

Community foundations are public foundations, which pool the assets from numerous donors. The goal of community foundations is to improve their local community by awarding scholarships and grants and by providing services to donors. Community foundations have become more and more active in providing donor-advised funds to donors wanting to become more focused in their giving but not wanting to set up their own private foundations (Fritz, 2010d).

Information on both large and small foundations is available from a number of organizations. The following organizations provide a variety of resources to foundations, grant makers, and grantees:

Association of Small Foundations

The Association of Small Foundations (2010) is a membership organization for donors, trustees, employees, and consultants of foundations with few or no staff.

Council on Foundations

The Council on Foundations (2010) is a nonprofit association of 2,100 grant-making corporations and foundations. The council serves community foundations, corporate grant makers, family philanthropy, global philanthropy, and private foundations. It provides a Community Foundation Locator, which is a national database of community foundations across the United States.

Foundation Center

The Foundation Center (2011a) is a national, nonprofit service organization that connects nonprofits and grant makers to useful tools and information. The center maintains an inclusive database of U.S. grant makers and their grants.

Fundsnet Online

Fundsnet Online (2010) provides nonprofits with an extensive list of links to funding resources.

Grantmakers for Effective Organizations

Grantmakers for Effective Organizations (2009) is a community of over 350 grant makers who come together to promote strategies and practices that contribute to grantee success.

National Center for Family Philanthropy

The National Center for Family Philanthropy (2010) is a charitable organization that promotes humanitarian values, vision, and excellence across donors and their families. It assists family donors with governance and management needs to help donors achieve their charitable missions.

Philanthropy Roundtable

Philanthropy Roundtable (2006) is an association of corporate giving officers, individual donors, and foundation trustees and staff. Its purpose is to help philanthropists achieve their charitable objectives by offering expert advice and guidance.

Because foundations are available worldwide, foundation fundraising depends more on the focus of the program or project that the funds are being raised for than on the location of the foundation. The key to successful foundation fundraising is to carefully research the foundations and write quality proposals. Part 2 of this text provides detailed information on grant writing.

Next, giving circles will be covered. Giving circles have become more and more popular over the years. They are driven by a common desire to help communities through shared giving.

Giving Circles

Giving circles, also referred to as shared giving, are comprised of like-minded people who pool their resources, time, and money to jointly support charitable organizations. They can be small and informal, or large, formally staffed organizations. Circles form when individuals come together, combine their money into a shared fund, learn about their community and philanthropy, and collectively decide where to give their money. They meet in community centers, in living rooms, and rely on volunteers. Their mission is to improve the world (Forum of Regional Associations of Grantmakers, 2007).

Giving circles can provide nonprofits with an alternative source of funding. In a 2006 national survey conducted by the New Ventures in Philanthropy Initiative at the Forum of Regional Associations of Grantmakers (2007), 400 giving circles across the United States were documented. A sample survey of 160 of these circles revealed that nearly 12,000 people participated in the 160 giving circles and raised approximately $100 million since 2000. One third of the surveyed circles went through five rounds of grant making. Although once considered a women's philanthropy phenomenon, approximately half of the circles surveyed had male members. Giving circles are also becoming more common among people of color and people of minority sexual orientation.

Giving circles make grants to both large and small nonprofit organizations, as well as to community groups and individuals. Shared giving appeals to a wide range of donors. Some giving circles create low levels of giving that can appeal to donors without a lot of extra cash. Other circles have higher levels of giving. The majority of giving circles request between $500 and $1,000 annually from each of their members (Forum of Regional Associations of Grantmakers, 2007).

Many nonprofits find that giving circles are an excellent way to increase visibility of the organization in the community while introducing donors to philanthropy using a shared-giving model. Nonprofits can benefit from giving circles by

- starting, hosting, or supporting circles.
- becoming actively involved with giving circles.
- engaging existing donors in an atypical and novel way.
- reaching potential donors.

- developing community leaders.
- building grant-making programs.
- building larger endowments.
- providing different or additional services to their consumers.
- promoting a culture of giving.

Not only do organizations benefit from hosting giving circles, the circles benefit from their hosts. Hosting organizations

- provide credence to a new giving circle.
- inspire confidence in the circle's sound money management practices.
- provide administrative support during the circle's start-up phase.
- can hold the circle's pooled donations.

The host organization is a safe, tax-deductible steward of the circle's funds (Forum of Regional Associations of Grantmakers, 2008).

> The ultimate benefit of giving circles is the empowerment of donors through collaborative decision-making and shared giving.

The ultimate benefit of giving circles is the empowerment of donors through collaborative decision-making and shared giving. Shared giving provides both the hosts and the giving circles with opportunities for highly productive and mutually beneficial partnerships that increase community philanthropy (Forum of Regional Associations of Grantmakers, 2007).

Next, the spotlight will shine on legacy fundraising. A legacy is a gift left to a charity in the form of an item, a cash sum or money, or a shared value of an estate.

Legacy Fundraising

Legacy fundraising is a significant source of funding for many agencies. Legacy fundraising involves a nonprofit asking its supporters to consider leaving a bequest gift. Legacy gifts are often the single largest donation a supporter will ever make. There are two types of legacies: pecuniary and residuary.

- *Pecuniary legacies.* Pecuniary legacies are when the person stipulates in his or her will that a specific amount of money should be left to an organization.
- *Residuary legacies.* Residuary legacies are when all the pecuniary legacies have been paid, and the rest of the person's estate goes to the organization. Residuary legacies tend to be more valuable but are more difficult to obtain.

Legacy fundraising typically involves approaching supporters and asking them to consider incorporating a legacy bequest into a will or making a change to an existing will. Changes to existing wills are often in the form of a codicil. A codicil is a brief, straightforward document that can be affixed to an existing will to add that a set contribution is to be given to the nonprofit. Some agencies provide freewill service to donors wishing to leave a contribution to the agency. Other agencies offer to pay for all or a portion of the legal costs associated with a codicil.

When beginning legacy fundraising, agencies should promote the legacies by creating brochures and marketing packs and including information about legacies in various marketing materials. Nonprofits should start with existing supporters and encourage them to consider a legacy bequest. In some instances, it may be appropriate to seek legacy bequests from existing consumers of the agency's services. For example, an agency that provides shelter and adoption services for abandoned animals may choose to approach its consumers about the agency's legacy fundraising efforts. All potential donors should be informed of how their legacy will be used.

Potential donors should be informed that if they choose to pledge to the legacy fund, they should notify the agency so that the agency can properly thank them and update them on the nonprofit's work. To maintain strong relationships, legacy donors should be invited to a small reception where they can learn about the work of the nonprofit in a more personal and intimate way.

When money is left to an agency, KnowHow NonProfit (2009) suggests using this as a way to promote additional legacy income. Sometimes money is left, and the reasons for the bequest are unknown. Agencies should research who donated and the reasons behind the contribution. Friends and family members can be contacted to see if they know the reason behind the bequest. Sometimes the executor of the estate may be able to help. This information can be used to direct marketing efforts to people similar to those who have left legacy money.

In order for agencies to benefit from bequests, they must regularly and openly discuss legacy fundraising and back up their discussions with ongoing marketing efforts. Such agencies are more likely to come across supporters inclined to remember the nonprofits in their wills.

Lastly, planned giving/gift planning will be addressed. Through planned giving, individuals support nonprofits by making large gifts, some of which can return income to the donors.

Planned Giving/Gift Planning

Planned giving, also referred to as gift planning, is a method of supporting nonprofits through the giving of gifts that maximize the gift while minimizing the impact of the gift on the donor's estate. Most planned gifts pay an income to the donor for life. Therefore, organizations invest the gift to produce an income stream to the donors (Jordan & Quynn, 2009). Organizations do not use the principle of the gift until the contributor dies. This unique arrangement allows nonprofits to build their futures and their endowments through strong relationships with their donors.

A successful gift planning program balances and stabilizes an organization's development plan. It focuses on gifts that will be realized during a 50-year period, with most gifts materializing over shorter, 5- to 10-year, periods of time. There are three categories of planned gifts:

1. Gifts that use appreciated assets as a substitute for cash.
2. Gifts that return financial benefits to the donor in exchange for the contribution (e.g., gift annuities that make fixed payments or deferred payments).
3. Gifts payable upon the donor's death (Jordan & Quynn, 2009).

The most common planned gifts are bequests, charitable annuities, charitable gift annuities, charitable remainder unitrusts, charity remainder annuity trusts, charitable lead trust, and retirement plans. Following are descriptions of each of these planned gifts:

Bequest

A stipulation included in a will stating that a gift is to be paid to an organization after the donor's death or after the death of the donor's survivors.

Charitable Gift Annuity

A gift made to the nonprofit in exchange for an irrevocable transfer of money or property. Upon the death of the donor, the residual balance of the annuity is used by the nonprofit for the purpose specified by the donor (BusinessDictionary.com, 2010).

Charitable Remainder Unitrust

A trust that pays income to the donor or a beneficiary for a period of time and then pays the balance to the nonprofit. The income is paid as a fixed percentage of the annual value of the unitrust (PlannedGiving.com, 2010).

Charitable Remainder Annuity Trust

A charitable remainder trust pays income to the donor or other beneficiary for life or for a period of time. The remainder of the balance is paid to the nonprofit (Investment Dictionary, 2010). This trust differs from the charitable remainder unitrust, in that payments do not change during the term of the trust.

Charitable Lead Trust

A charitable lead trust pays income to the nonprofit for a stated period of time or for the life of the contributor; when the trust expires, the balance is returned to the donor or to the donor's beneficiaries (InvestorWords.com, 2010).

Retirement Plans

The nonprofit is named as the beneficiary of all or a portion of the donor's IRA, 401(k), or other retirement account.

Planned giving offers several tax benefits to donors. First, donors, who contribute appreciated property such as real estate or securities, receive a charitable deduction for the entire market value of the property. In addition, there is no capital gains tax on the transfer. Second, donors who set up life-income gifts receive tax deductions for the full market value of the contributed assets minus the present value of the income interest retained. Third, donors, who fund gifts with appreciated property, pay no up-front capital gains taxes on the transfers. Fourth, gifts payable to charity upon the donor's death are exempt from estate tax. Jordan and Quynn (2009) recommend that charities offer planned gift options that commensurate with the nonprofit staff members' experience and the potential donors' anticipated level of interest and financial complexity. Organizations should wait until a successful annual fund program is in place before implementing a planned giving program.

Planned giving offers rewards not only to the nonprofit but also to the donor. Donors are honored throughout their lives for what they are doing and leave behind a legacy of humanitarian support.

All fundraising campaigns take time and effort, but the sustainability of the organization is well worth the endeavor. A successful fundraising campaign not only achieves an agency's financial goals but also helps communicate the agency's mission.

Summary

Fundraising ensures that nonprofits have the resources necessary to improve the quality of life for countless people. Billions of dollars are raised each year through fundraising. Gone are the days that organizations can rely on a single source of revenue. Therefore, meeting funding needs requires inspiration, ingenuity, and resourcefulness. There are countless fundraising options, all of which fall under one of the following categories: easy fundraisers, fundraising events, online fundraising, telephone campaigns, capital campaigns, corporate fundraising, foundation fundraising, giving circles, legacy fundraising, and planned giving/gift planning. When deciding on the types of fundraisers to incorporate into the fundraising campaign, nonprofits must consider the size of their fundraising team, the amount of money they need to raise, and where they plan to raise the money. From the simple to the more elaborate there are fundraisers available to meet the needs of any agency.

The following questions will test your application and analysis of the content found within this chapter. For additional assessment, applying, analyzing, synthesizing, and evaluating chapter content with practice, visit **MySearchLab.com**

1. For nonprofits needing to raise unrestricted funds quickly and with minimal expense, this type of fundraiser requires little administrative support and investment:
   a. Giving circles
   b. Online fundraising
   c. Telephone campaigns
   d. Easy fundraisers

2. You have been asked to coordinate an annual fundraising event. A local business has donated $4,000 toward the initial costs of funding a "Rubber Duck Race." The best use of this seed money would be to
   a. put toward monetary prizes.
   b. print tickets.
   c. purchase the rubber ducks.
   d. pay for advertising the event.

3. One of the main benefits of an online auction is that
   a. geography and time barriers are removed.
   b. you can set up online auctions in less than an hour.
   c. there is no work involved once the website has been created.
   d. there are no costs associated with online auctions.

4. Outbound telephone campaigns are most successful when
   a. agencies make cold calls.
   b. there are emergency appeals that require agencies to quickly reach their funders.
   c. the reason for calling does not need an explanation.
   d. the organization has extra time to call supporters.

5. You are coordinating a QR Code scavenger hunt fundraiser for a local community center and want to collaborate with local businesses. In what ways can local businesses provide support for the fundraiser?

6. Corporate fundraising offers a variety of funding possibilities. Creating healthy relationships with corporations can ensure successful partnerships. Describe three ways in which agencies can develop relationships with corporations?

7. Giving circles are comprised of like-minded individuals who combine their time, money, and resources to support charitable nonprofit organizations. List three ways in which nonprofits can benefit from giving circles.

8. Legacy fundraising involves a nonprofit asking its supporters to consider leaving a bequest gift. There are two types of legacies: pecuniary and residuary. Explain the differences between these two types of legacies.

CHAPTER 7

Fundraising Tips for Success

. . . .

A successful fundraising campaign entails a strong fundraising team, a comprehensive fundraising plan, a creative marketing strategy, skill in identifying and managing fundraising sources, and an excellent mix of fundraisers. Profitable fundraisers also necessitate that nonprofits focus energy on a few additional fundraising tips. Passive philanthropy is no longer effective. Nonprofits must pay attention to detail throughout their fundraising efforts. Creating conditions that motivate potential donors and cultivate relationships with these prospects will lead to donor excitement. This excitement can encourage a prospective donor to invest in services and programs, which can lead to an organization meeting its fundraising goals.

Motivating Prospects and Cultivating Relationships

Fundraising can be summed up in just one word—relationships. Relationships are fundamental. At its heart, fundraising is about an organization's leadership and staff developing and cultivating relationships with individuals and corporations able to provide support. Building and cultivating relationships with donors and prospects is an agency-wide responsibility and process. It takes the commitment and involvement of the entire organization. It is a process that involves learning more about each donor's interests, professional and social contacts, lifestyles, and philanthropic desires. Cultivation is carefully planned and strategic. It is not a haphazard process. The more time and energy organizations devote to learning about prospects, the better able they will be to initiate contact with and respond to the donors more effectively (Poderis, 2009c). But first, nonprofits must identify the motivation behind giving.

What Motivates Someone to Give?

Many donors are either personally affected by the mission, values, and vision of the agency, or they are passionate about the agency's cause. Many universities and colleges, for example, understand this, and

Learning Objectives
- Describe and apply ways to motivate and cultivate prospective donors.
- List various ways to show appreciation to donors and volunteers.
- Share ways to repair damaged relationships.
- Identify ways to manage and process donations.
- Explain ways to organize and manage fundraising documents.

. . . .

Fundraising can be summed up in just one word—relationships.

therefore, they appeal to their alumni for donations knowing that countless alumni feel an immense sense of gratitude and appreciation to their universities and colleges for the role the school played in preparing them for the future (X Factor Consulting, LLC, 2010).

Donors often contribute to human service organizations because a family member or a close friend was a recipient of the organization's services. Therefore, the donors want to show their gratitude by ensuring that the organization has the funds to continue to provide programs and services that will help others. Some donors give to organizations for personal reasons, such as the loss of a loved one due to a personal tragedy or due to illness or disease (X Factor Consulting, LLC, 2010). The reasons for giving vary, but it usually comes down to a strong personal connection between the donor's passion and the organization's mission. When prospective donors are identified based on solid connections, developing and cultivating these relationships becomes an enjoyable and fulfilling process.

How to Motivate People to Give

As previously stated, people contribute because they believe in the mission and cause of the organization. Nonprofits are likely competing with other nonprofits for donations. Therefore, it is key that agencies connect with potential donors and make it clear what donors will get in return for their gifts. For example, donors may gain satisfaction from learning that a victim of intimate partner violence will be protected in a haven. The following list provides additional suggestions on ways to motivate people to give:

- Recognize donors during an event or on the agency's website.
- Build the agency's reputation so individuals want to give. Document the organization's charity work through newsletters, websites, photos, videos, emails, and flyers.
- Advertise through inspiring and appealing advertisements that promote the agency's mission while providing a list of upcoming events. Not only will this help motivate people to give, it may also motivate people to volunteer.
- Provide a free service or event. People who receive something for nothing may be encouraged to contribute.
- Make the giving process easy. Potential donors are more likely to give if the agency makes the process trouble free. The simpler the process, the more apt people are to donate. Walking around collecting money, including donation buttons on websites, placing donation bins in high-traffic areas, and distributing self-addressed postage-paid envelopes, are several ways that make donating a straightforward and effortless process.
- Ensure donors that their gifts will go toward the purpose for which they were designated. Providing donors with a way to track their gifts will enable them to know that the organization is accountable, transparent, and trustworthy.

Nonprofits are involved in critical work that helps resolve serious social problems. Their budgets are dependent on the contributions made by individuals, businesses, corporations, and philanthropic foundations. Motivating people to give is one of the most fundamental duties of every nonprofit's work.

Tips on Cultivating Prospective Donors

Cultivating prospective donors sets the stage for profitable "asks." It encompasses all the communication and contacts agencies have with potential donors, including email, newsletters, special presentations, events, and annual reports. It is a carefully planned and strategic process. Following are a number of suggestions for cultivating prospective donors:

- Involve all members of the organization; it must be a coordinated effort. Cultivating donors is a collaborative effort that must involve board members, staff, volunteers, and donors. Staff members set up and participate in events where board members and other volunteers meet with and communicate with prospective donors. Current donors are included as well; they are exceptional advocates for the agency and its mission (Sprinkel Grace, 2006). All interactions with prospective donors should be reported to a key person such as the executive director or the chair of the board. In addition, the names of potential donors should be regularly added to the organization's database.
- Develop a strategic plan and include a follow-up plan. According to Sprinkel Grace (2006), cultivating donors is a two-part process: general and specific. General cultivation entails regularly scheduling events for prospective donors, such as presentations, tours, and lunch get-togethers. On the other hand, cultivation is also designed for specific prospects who may or may not also attend regularly scheduled events. Not only should the cultivation process be strategic, it must have a follow-up plan. For example, agencies should follow up by sending thank-you letters to prospective donors after every event.

> ### Planning and Evaluation
>
> Understanding and Mastery of ... Skills to develop goals, and design and implement a plan of action
>
> **Critical Thinking Question:** Cultivating relationships requires strategic planning. What elements should go into a strategic plan aimed at cultivating prospective donors?

- Throw the net wide. Organizations should not limit cultivation to major gift prospects. Limiting cultivation to large gift prospects can negatively impact the overall amount of funds an agency secures. Everyone who attends an event should leave with additional information about the organization. This can be in the form of a packet, a brochure, or a brief presentation.
- Take advantage of the various modes of communication. Cultivation takes place anytime an agency communicates with a prospect, regardless of the mode of communication. Cultivation is not limited to personal interactions with potential contributors. It can occur through a newsletter, email, or website. Cultivation can be unanticipated. A nonprofit may receive positive press coverage, which can bring potential donors directly to the organization.
- Know when to ask for support. Agencies need to be aware of when to ask for support. Knowing when to ask requires knowing when the potential donor is ready to be asked. The goal of cultivating, after all, is to ensure the success of the solicitation.

Cultivation takes time, and as a result, it may be difficult for agencies to make the case that cultivation activities are necessary and costs money and time. According to Sprinkel Grace (2006), having narratives at hand about prospects who became donors as a direct result of cultivation activities can help plea the case for funding for such activities.

Tapping into Corporate Philanthropy

The process of cultivating foundations and corporations differs from the process of cultivating individuals. When cultivating foundations and corporations, there is usually a precise process, and a set deadline. With individuals, a timeline usually does not exist. In both cases, cultivation must be planned, systematic, and coordinated. Most companies receive hundreds of contribution requests each year, so it is imperative that agencies accurately follow the company guidelines, and if agencies have questions, they should get them clarified. Nonprofits must research corporations for information on their contribution policies, giving calendar, applications, and forms required for donation requests (Kronberger, 2010).

Agencies should look for corporations whose mission is related to the agency's mission. In addition, board members can be asked to introduce the nonprofit to representatives of companies with which they do business and who may be passionate about the mission of the agency.

Nonprofits can tap into corporate philanthropy in a number of ways, but regardless of the method, cultivating these relationships takes time. According to Kronberger (2010), it is not often that corporations contribute the first time they are asked. Nonprofits should not give up with one try; they should take the long-term approach. Inviting representatives from the corporation to visit the organization is an effective way to familiarize corporations to the agency's work.

In-kind support is just as valuable as money. Corporations are more and more interested in giving in other ways beyond money. Examples are volunteering their expertise or supplying products and services to improve the community. Solidifying a sound relationship with the corporation can be a tremendous benefit for the agency's future fundraising endeavors.

Lastly, corporations want and need to know how their contributions were used; how programs, services, and projects progressed; and what the organization is planning for the future (Kronberger, 2010). This information is vital to maintaining a sound, long-term, and mutually beneficial relationship.

Cultivating Donor Loyalty

The vast majority of donations, approximately 85%, come from private individuals (Poderis, 2009c). Therefore, it is imperative that organizations build lasting relationships with each prospect and donor so that when the time comes, agencies can aptly solicit and secure donations. When an agency loses a repeat donor, it loses in a couple of ways. First, a lost donor is a loss to the organization for many years and perhaps forever. Second, every lost donor will need to be replaced with a new donor and usually the exchange is not equivalent. This is because, in general, the longer an individual donates to an organization, the more frequent and greater the gifts become.

According to X Factor Consulting, LLC (2010), cultivating donor loyalty goes far beyond basic fundraising. It embraces the entire process of actively engaging donors in the cause and keeping donors interested and pleased with their investment and their relationship with the organization. Donor loyalty is attained by responding to donors with vigorous cultivation, thoughtful consideration, and kind appreciation.

Fundraising strategies should address every component of cultivation in every step of the fundraising campaign.

Respectful appreciation is not limited solely to donors. Respectful appreciation expands to the countless fundraising volunteers who contribute their time and expertise to ensure the success of the fundraising effort.

Showing Appreciation to Donors and Volunteers

Showing appreciation to donors and volunteers can make all the difference in whether or not donors and volunteers are enthusiastic about future contributions to the agency. Too many times, agencies neglect to send thoughtful thank-you notes, show donors the significance of their gifts, or recognize donors and volunteers for their support. The way agencies treat their donors and volunteers can determine whether or not the donors and volunteers will provide support in the future or simply vanish, never to be heard from again.

> **The way agencies treat their donors and volunteers can determine whether or not the donors and volunteers will provide support in the future or simply vanish, never to be heard from again.**

Showing Appreciation to Donors

One of the kindest demonstrations of appreciation a donor can receive from a nonprofit is a thoughtful, well-written, personal letter of thanks that does *not* ask for money. A "non-ask" communication to donors shows donors that their gift is truly appreciated and that there is no hidden agenda tied to the letter of gratitude. According to Poderis (2009h), letters should praise the donor's generosity, and, if applicable, show appreciation for the regularity of the donor's contributions. Other suggestions for writing thank-you letters include the following:

- Keep the letter or note a bit informal. Overly formal letters and notes can appear stiff.
- Personalize each letter. The opening sentence or two should clearly reveal the letter was written on a specific day, by a particular person, and for a distinct purpose. The letter should contain details that make the letter personal and not generic. Donors want to be recognized by a human being, not by a computer.
- Indicate that the donor's gift arrived in the morning mail or acknowledge the gift as soon as possible.
- Show how the donor's gift promotes awareness of the organization and raises the morale of the staff and other individuals working for the organization.
- State how the gift will be put to use today, making a positive difference in the lives of others.
- Let the donor know that others are also responding as the donor has and that the donor's gift, added to other contributions, is having a significant and positive impact.
- Give an example of a recent, positive and uplifting, outcome of one of the agency's programs or services.
- Share with the donor a story of a person who has benefitted from the agency's programs and services. Do not underestimate the power of facts and statistics. Communicate the progress that has been made.

- Report on a recent event hosted by the organization.
- Announce an upcoming event that is possible as a result of the donor's generous gift.
- Discuss a societal trend or current event that illustrates the need for your organization's work and their continued support.
- Report on the growth of the agency's membership.

In addition to letters of thanks, thank-you calls are powerful tools of gratitude. Few agencies recognize gifts through personal phone calls, but doing so shows the donor that the agency took the time to pick up the phone and personally thank the donor. Each phone call typically takes only a few minutes. The following script makes the process easy:

1. State the donor's name and identify the name of the organization and the caller's name.
2. Inform the donor of the reason for the call. For example, the caller can explain to the donor that the donor's check arrived and that the call is to thank the donor.
3. Invite the donor to ask questions and to share information that the donor would like to have passed on to a board member, the executive director, or another agency representative.
4. Before ending the call, thank the donor again.

Letters and phone calls of appreciation foster strong relationships, boost donor loyalty, and increase chances of receiving additional gifts in the future. Showing donors the significance of their gifts is one of the greatest ways to demonstrate appreciation to donors.

Showing Donors the Significance of Their Gifts

One of the best ways to show appreciation to donors is to show them what their gifts allowed the organization to accomplish. What an agency does with the gift is just as important as what the agency did to secure the gift. Nonprofits must use the contributions the way they stated the money would be used.

Sharing facts and accounts of how their contribution changed the lives of real people in need is one of the greatest ways to acknowledge donors. Doing so shows donors exactly how their money was put to the best use in the agency's programs and services (Fritz, 2010g).

Agencies should not wait until donors ask how their gifts were used; agencies should share this information with their contributors as soon as feasible. One of the best ways to share this information, according to Mutz and Murray (2010), is to show the donors photos of the programs they helped to support and let them see the fantastic work that their gifts made possible. Donors love to see the significant difference their support made. The earlier an agency provides this information, the better.

At times, the art of appreciating donors extends to recognizing donors. The following section provides several options for recognizing donors.

Recognizing Donors

Almost every nonprofit organization wants to recognize its donors in some way, shape, or form. Recognition can be a retention issue for organizations. Therefore, organizations are putting more and more passion into recognizing their donors in hopes of keeping their existing donors while attracting new ones. It goes without saying that organizations should respect the privacy of donors who request anonymity. For those who do not request anonymity, well-planned donor recognition can motivate donors to give more. The recognition program should be integrated into the fundraising campaign from the very beginning, as this can show donors how they will leave their mark. For example, the agency can show an illustration of a gift wall or a sample of a plaque with space for names of annual donors to encourage future gifts. Some of the tried and true means to recognize donors include the following:

- *Recognition plaques.* Typically a bronze plaque highlighting individual or corporate contributions to a fundraising project.
- *Gift trees.* A three-dimensional sculpture of a tree with burnished metal leaves, each engraved with the donor's message. The tree is fixed on a wooden backdrop and mounted on a wall.
- *Donor bricks.* Donor bricks are personalized or engraved bricks that are often used to pave a sidewalk or entryway, or used in an artistic display, in a garden or landscape.
- *Donor walls.* Using the personalized or engraved brick but instead of using them in a horizontal display, using them vertically by constructing a wall.

With budget cuts and a rough economy, nonprofits look for creative and affordable means to recognize their donors. Acknowledging donors on the organization's website, in annual reports, newsletters, and during agency events are economical ways to recognize donors.

Acknowledging Volunteers

It is important to recognize all the volunteers who have assisted with the fundraising campaign. Organizations should plan well in advance how they will acknowledge and thank their volunteers. This will show the volunteers that the plan for thanking them was well coordinated and thought out. Waiting until the last minute to throw something together often appears insincere. Recognition of volunteers does not have to be in the form of an expensive gift, but personal recognition that their role in the fundraising campaign was vital to the organization. For example, agencies can celebrate an achievement by acknowledging the role of the volunteers in making it happen. Volunteers should be recognized often and sincerely. Volunteers who feel appreciated are likely to continue to volunteer and may even recruit new volunteers for the agency. There are countless ways to show volunteers appreciation for their countless hours of hard work and unwavering dedication to the organization and its fundraising efforts. Here are a few examples:

- Invite volunteers to lunch, to a movie, or to get a snack.
- Acknowledge volunteers in the local newspaper.
- Write an article of appreciation in the organization's newsletter.
- Thank volunteers when other people are around to hear.
- Have a "Volunteer of the Month" award.
- Acknowledge volunteers on the agency's website.
- Award each volunteer with a plaque of recognition.

- Ask staff to adopt a volunteer as a "secret friend."
- Hold a volunteer get-together or party.
- Greet volunteers with appreciation, enthusiasm, and a smile.
- Give service pins to volunteers.
- Give volunteers a book of inspirational quotes, poems, or stories.
- Tell others of volunteers' contributions.
- Give each volunteer a certificate of appreciation.
- Send a "thought you would like to know" letter of appreciation to the volunteer's employer.
- Have a picnic or barbecue for volunteers.
- Acknowledge volunteers at a recognition dinner or event.
- Send volunteers personal thank-you notes, birthday cards, holiday cards, and anniversary cards highlighting their years of service.
- Dedicate an event to volunteers.
- Give volunteers personalized token gifts, such as a candle with the note, "No one holds a candle to you."
- Ask volunteers to serve on advisory committees.
- Send Hershey's Kisses to volunteers with a note, "You deserve a kiss for all your hard work." Or send peppermint patties to volunteers with a note, "Your hard work is worth a mint!"
- Nominate volunteers for awards.
- Reimburse volunteers for any out-of-pocket expenses they incur.
- Have a volunteer "Wall of Fame" and post pictures and names of all volunteers.
- Celebrate National Volunteer Week.
- Give a small, inexpensive gift that is related to volunteers' interests.
- When volunteers have been away, let them know that they were missed.
- Provide scholarships to volunteers to attend conferences or workshops.
- Collect money from a group to give bigger gifts such as personalized gift baskets.

The key point is that any acknowledgment of gratitude should be personalized to each volunteer. In other words, volunteers should not receive form letters addressed to "Dear Volunteer."

When agencies do not show gratitude toward their volunteers and donors, relationships can become strained. Strained relationships can lead to terminated relationships. The next section provides helpful advice for repairing damaged relationships.

Repairing Damaged Relationships

No matter how large or small the contribution is, not acknowledging a donor's gift or a volunteer's time will likely lead to a relationship that cannot be repaired.

There are various reasons why donors and volunteers may become disenchanted with an organization that they have supported. Some include misspelling names, acknowledging the wrong amount of a gift, and one of the worse mistakes, not acknowledging the gift, or volunteer time, at all. A gesture of appreciation is often forgotten. No matter how large or small the contribution is, not acknowledging a donor's gift or a volunteer's time will likely lead to a relationship that cannot be repaired.

There is absolutely no excuse for not acknowledging a contribution. How can an agency expect to prosper off the generosity of others when a simple thank-you note, or any communication for that matter, appears to be too much to ask? Not thanking, not thanking quickly enough, or sending the donor or volunteer a form letter with a scanned signature will likely alienate a supporter.

How an agency treats a first-time donor or volunteer is vital for securing the supporter's long-term relationship with the agency. The donor or volunteer's first contribution is the most important contribution an organization will receive. Supporters tend to measure the level of involvement as a signal of the organization's interest and gratitude for their contribution. No engagement equals no future contribution and no long-term relationship.

If a relationship with a contributor is damaged, there are a number of ways that nonprofits may regain the faith and confidence of their supporter. Here are a few:

- Extend a sincere and honest apology for the transgression. A sincere apology is an apology made without excuses. The apology should be made by the executive director or another leader of the organization even if the leader was not involved in the perceived blunder.
- Plan private meetings with key supporters to repair the damaged relationship. Private meetings provide agencies with opportunities to listen to their supporters, gather suggestions, and make changes when appropriate. Reconnecting with supporters demonstrates the agency's sincerity in restoring relationships that have been damaged.
- Talk to other leaders of other nonprofits who may have experienced similar setbacks. Other organizations may be able to share success stories on how they mended damaged relationships with their donors. By consulting with other nonprofits, some helpful suggestions may be revealed.

> ## Interpersonal Communication
>
> Understanding and Mastery of . . . Developing and sustaining behaviors that are congruent with the values and ethics of the profession
>
> **Critical Thinking Question:** Not acknowledging contributions from donors can alienate donors. In what ways can interviewing disillusioned donors help repair damaged relationships?

The issues behind strained relationships can be serious and sometimes difficult to fix. However, choosing to ignore damaged relationships and the causes that lead to them will only result in fewer contributions and an agency in jeopardy.

As is apparent, donor and volunteer relationships are extremely important and, at times, complex. Cultivating, acknowledging, and repairing damaged relationships require careful management of information. The following section provides ways to manage donor information and process donations.

Managing Donor Information and Processing Donations

Successfully managing and processing donations is an important goal most nonprofits seek to obtain. Organizations are on a continual search for improved solutions to effectively and efficiently manage these activities. This section begins with an overview of donor management systems and concludes with a synopsis of ways to accept and process donations.

Donor Management Systems

Collecting, storing, and retrieving information necessitate a clear understanding of donor management systems. One of the most efficient and economical ways to manage donor information is through specialized software. Over the years, tools for managing donor information have become increasingly available. Donor management systems, or computerized donor databases, have been gaining popularity for a couple of decades. Although donor profiles can be placed in file cabinets or on index cards, computerized donor databases provide a more efficient and secure means to manage information. According to Poderis (2009h), computerized donor databases provide greater data accessibility, easier data collection, and enhanced means to organize, manipulate, and use the data. There are a number of donor management systems available, ranging from the basic and simple systems to the more complex ones that offer all sorts of features. Depending on the database, there is a wide array of information that can be added and stored, including

- contact information, including name, address, phone numbers, email address.
- tags that allow organizations to attach donors to a number of categories that allow organizations to generate targeted communication lists. For example, a donor can be tagged as a newsletter recipient and as a board member.
- customized fields that allow agencies to track information specific to the organizations needs.
- profiles used for fundraising purposes that provide snapshots of donors' contribution history, including number of years as a donor, pledges, most recent and largest donation, and annual totals.
- personal involvement with the agency.
- communication history that tracks communication the agency has had with the donor through newsletters, annual reports, and magazines.
- miscellaneous parameters that can provide agencies with additional donor information, such as whether a donor has requested an annual receipt or whether a donor wishes to remain anonymous.
- appreciation the organization has shown for the donors through acknowledgments of gratitude and recognition.

Donors are the lifeline of nonprofits; nonprofits cannot survive without them. Donor management systems are indispensable for tracking information and maintaining strong relationships.

Options for accepting and processing donations are as varied as the types of information that can be stored in donor management systems. The more ways an agency can accept and process donations, the more donations an agency will receive. The next section provides a variety of ways nonprofits can manage donations.

Accepting and Processing Donations

For nonprofit organizations, accepting donations online can be a convenient and a cost-effective way to generate funds. Individuals are more apt to donate if there is a quick, secure, and convenient way to do so. The majority of online donations are completed by means of credit cards. Therefore, it is critical to configure a website to accept credit card donations in a secure environment. There are a variety of ways for an organization to accept online donations securely, but first it is necessary to consider what types of transactions the agency will have.

Some agencies accept one-time donations, whereas others take recurring donations. The types of transactions an agency will have can profoundly influence which processing option is the best choice. If an agency handles recurring donations, it is best to process these donations through a merchant account because this can automate the process based on payment schedules and payment amounts. Following are some online options, especially useful for processing recurring donations:

- Build donation processing functionality directly into the organization's website. Agencies that employ, or are able to contract, a web specialist can add the ability to accept online donations, directly to their website. This feature allows donors to carry out the transaction without leaving the agency's website. When building an in-house functionality feature, agencies must establish an SSL (secure socket layer) technology for secure commerce, create a donation form, authorize credit card acceptance by setting up a merchant account, and decide how to process the donations. Processing of donations can be entirely automated or done manually. Manual processing requires that the organization receive the donation information, complete a paper receipt, and call the toll-free credit card company number (or use a dial-up terminal) to process the donation (Corporation for National and Community Service, 2010).
- Outsource online donation features by outsourcing to a company that specializes in these services. These companies, also known as application service providers (ASPs), charge fees but are a nice option for organizations that are unable to build in-house functionality directly into their own website. Two examples of ASPs that provide this service for nonprofit organizations are Acceptiva (2010) and Network for Good (2010).
- Utilize charity portals. Charity portals are directories of nonprofit organizations that have built-in donation processing capabilities. Organizations list themselves at the charity portal and pay a fee for the donation processing service. Agencies are able to add a donation information page to their website. This page allows agencies to summarize their mission and include a link to the charity portal. The charity portal displays the organization's profile and ensures that the online transactions are secure. GreaterGood.org (2010) and Network for Good (2010) are two such charity portals.
- Use a third-party processor. There are some benefits of using a third-party processor. They are usually easier and may be slightly cheaper than in-house payment services. In addition, some third-party processors, such as PayPal (2010), have unique options for nonprofits. However, there are some disadvantages as well. When a third-party processor is used, it is the processor's name that appears on the donor's credit card statement, instead of the agency's name. Because the donor may not recognize the

Information Management

Understanding and Mastery of . . . Utilizing research findings and other information for community education and public relations and using technology to create and manage spreadsheets and databases

Critical Thinking Question: In what ways can the Internet be used to process donations?
. . . .

An organization's ability to achieve its mission is directly related to its ability to raise funds, successfully manage donor information, and efficiently process donations.

processor's name, the possibility of chargebacks, or the return of funds back to the consumer, is increased, which can be costly. In addition, because a third party is processing the donations using its merchant account, there is typically a lag in time before the agency receives the donation (TransFS, 2009).

- Agencies that rarely take donations but prefer the option of accepting online donations may want to consider a service such as Square (2010). This service allows the iPhone, iPad, and Android to be used as a terminal without the agency having to sign up for a merchant account. According to TransFS (2009), the fees for Square tend to be higher, but it is a nice option for agencies with occasional transactions.

With hundreds of funding sources and methods to raise money, it is no surprise that keeping track of all of this information is no easy task. An organization's ability to achieve its mission is directly related to its ability to raise funds, successfully manage donor information, and efficiently process donations. Not only are these elements crucial, managing fundraising documents, through the fundraising campaign, assures that future campaigns are winning campaigns. Therefore, the final fundraising tip for success is in regard to appropriate management of the fundraising documents. Many organizations have fundraising committee positions that last for only a year. As a result, each year new members are recruited and trained. Having a number of helpful documents available can make the transition from former members to new members a smoother process.

Managing Fundraising Documents

When a fundraising campaign is first initiated, it is necessary to begin to organize documents associated with the campaign. Organizing and managing these documents will enhance future fundraising activities. Some typical documents are meeting minutes and financial reports. However, there are other documents that are critical to current and future fundraising campaigns. Some of the fundamental fundraising documents that need to be retained and kept in a safe place include

- names, addresses, phone numbers, email addresses, and job descriptions of all team members including staff and volunteers.
- updated records on funding sources, including names of prospects and donors, their funding interests, community contacts, and their history with the agency.
- annual reports.
- Internal Revenue Service 501(c)(3) determination letter.
- copies of the mission statement, case statement, letters of support, and testimonials from persons served.
- a list of the most frequently requested proposals for unrestricted grants and program grants, proposal cover letters, and requests for proposals (RFP).
- examples of thank-you letters, letters of inquiry, and door-opener letters.

- information on fundraising product suppliers that the team used or were considering using and notes of the types of services and products offered by the suppliers (FastTrack Fundraising Tips and Articles, 2009).
- documents regarding the distribution of products and storage records.
- financial ledgers with fundraising account details, receipts, check and credit card statements, and income and expenditure records.
- planning documents, including the fundraising timetable, fundraising checklist, committee meeting schedule, and volunteer training information.
- documents on fundraising and money management policies and procedures including budgets.
- documents on fundraising committee meetings, including discussions, decisions, actions, and reviews.
- separate folders for each fundraising event, with documentation on each activity.
- copies of awards letters and any accounting materials.
- lists of any donor requirements, including donor reporting, required activities, and publicity.
- copies of press clippings and articles highlighting the organization and its accomplishments.

> ### Administration
>
> Understanding and Mastery of . . . Planning and evaluating programs, services, and operational functions
>
> ---
>
> **Critical Thinking Question:** Organizing fundraising documents is a critical step in planning for future fundraising campaigns. How can agencies effectively organize fundraising documents to make the work of future fundraising committees more manageable?

With essential documentation that is well written, catalogued, retained, and well managed, the work of fundraising newcomers will be simplified. New team members are better able to learn from their predecessors when detailed records of the previous committee's work are organized and easily accessible.

Summary

Relationships are the most fundamental component of fundraising. Fundraising is about an agency's ability to motivate individuals and corporations to give. People give for different reasons but at the core of most contributions is the potential donor's passion for the cause and mission of the agency. Prospective donors are more prone to donate when agencies make donating an easy process, and when potential donors are reassured that contributions will go toward the purpose for which they were intended. Cultivating potential donors must be a synchronized effort and involve all members of the agency. Cultivating individuals differs from the way foundations and corporations are cultivated. When cultivating individuals, a specific process and set timeline usually do not exist, whereas when cultivating foundations and corporations, there is usually a particular process and a set deadline. Cultivating relationships does not end when a donation is secured; agencies must show their appreciation to donors and volunteers and show the significance of their gifts. At times, relationships with donors may become damaged due to a variety of reasons. Agencies that address these issues head on may repair strained relationships and pave the way to healthy, strong, and positive relationships in the future. Managing donor information, effectively processing donations, and organizing fundraising documents can ease the work and eliminate many problems for current and future fundraising efforts.

The following questions will test your application and analysis of the content found within this chapter. For additional assessment, applying, analyzing, synthesizing, and evaluating chapter content with practice, visit **MySearchLab.com**

1. Successfully cultivating relationships with prospective donors necessitates that agencies
   a. understand what motivates someone to give.
   b. leave the job to the executive director.
   c. limit the cultivation to large gift prospects.
   d. limit the cultivation to personal interactions with potential donors.

2. You are the assistant director of an agency that provides support services to military families. You are in the process of writing thank-you notes to individuals who provided monetary support to the agency. After completing the letter, your director looks it over and asks you to remove the sentence that
   a. reports on a recent event hosted by the agency.
   b. describes how the donor's gift promotes awareness of the agency.
   c. asks for continued support.
   d. states how the gift will be used.

3. One of the greatest causes of damaged relationships between an agency and a first-time supporter is the agency
   a. acknowledging the wrong amount of a gift.
   b. misspelling the name of a donor.
   c. not sending a thank-you note to the supporter within 48 hours from the receipt of the gift.
   d. not acknowledging the donor.

4. Application service providers (ASPs) are a nice option for agencies that are unable to process their online donations. One example of an ASP includes
   a. charity portal
   b. Acceptiva
   c. PayPal
   d. Square

5. When a nonprofit loses a loyal donor, the effect to the organization can be detrimental. Explain the potential impact, to an agency, of losing a repeat donor.

6. There are many creative ways that agencies can recognize their donors. Describe three creative ways that donors can be recognized.

7. When recognizing volunteers, it is important to personalize the acknowledgment. Describe three ways in which agencies can personalize the way they recognize volunteers.

8. Managing fundraising documents is essential to strengthen future fundraising campaigns. What are the five fundraising documents that should be retained to simplify future campaigns?

CHAPTER 8

Setting the Stage

Grant Writing Considerations

Before the first section of a grant proposal is written, organizations must take time to ponder some key grant writing considerations. One such consideration is the role that collaboration plays in the grant writing process.

Grant Writing: A Collaborative Effort?

Grant writing can be a perplexing, time-consuming process. Collaborating on writing a grant can enhance or complicate the experience. The following section describes the benefits and problems associated with collaborative relationships and provides tips on making collaborations work.

Collaborating With Colleagues

Getting a group of busy colleagues together to write a grant proposal may appear to be more work than it is worth. In fact, collaborating with colleagues on grant writing may require more time than writing the grant alone. This does not mean that collaboration is a terrible idea; it just means that attention must be paid to taking time putting together a quality team. Team members who are compatible and self-motivated should be chosen. Roles should be assigned that suit the team members' talents, skills, interests, and abilities. According to Henson (2003), time should be taken, from the onset, to clarify the roles of all participants: the principal investigator (PI), the co-PI, the researcher, and so on.

Teaming Up With Other Organizations

With today's fiscal environment, many organizations, especially small-sized to medium-sized agencies, will need to be open to pursuing funding streams, which require them to collaborate with other entities. Teaming up with other organizations can be a productive and practical way to seek funding. Collaboration provides organizations

Learning Objectives
- Provide ways to collaborate with colleagues on grant writing.
- Offer ways to team up with other organizations on grant writing.
- Discuss the three phases of a grant proposal timeline.
- Provide alternatives for proposal submissions when deadlines cannot be met.
- Identify pros and cons of hiring a professional grant writer.

Information Management

Understanding and Mastery of ... Obtain information through interviewing, active listening, consultation with others, library or other research, and the observation of clients and systems

Critical Thinking Question: When working with colleagues on producing a grant proposal, how can an agency ensure that individual roles match each team members' skills, talents, abilities, and interests?

> Teaming up with other organizations can be a productive and practical way to seek funding. Collaboration provides organizations the opportunity to pool their efforts, allowing for the probability of better proposals and higher grant amounts.

Information Management

Understanding and Mastery of ... Obtain information through interviewing, active listening, consultation with others, library or other research, and the observation of clients and systems

Critical Thinking Question: Organizations will often need to be open to pursuing grants, which requires them to collaborate with other entities. In what ways can organizations divide up the workload when collaborating on a grant proposal?

> Preparing for the unexpected, and planning for anything and everything to go wrong, can alleviate a number of unforeseen problems.

the opportunity to pool their efforts, allowing for the probability of better proposals and higher grant amounts. When agencies bring in new partners, new funding possibilities may become available. Agencies that have traditionally relied on grant opportunities that match the agency's areas of expertise may find that collaborating with other organizations can increase funding opportunities dramatically. Many funders seek proposals from agencies, or teams of agencies that can offer "one stop shopping" solutions to the challenges described in the request for proposals (RFP). According to Johns Hopkins University (2004), more often than not, successfully addressing problems requires a creative, broad-based, highly collaborative, horizontally and vertically integrated response. Partnerships among community agencies, schools, citizens, government, and other entities may be better able to address the complexity of an issue by working in tandem, than one agency may be able to address the issue by working independently. One suggestion for collaborative grant writing among organizations is to divide up the sections of the grant that need to be researched and written into manageable workloads for each participating organization.

The grant writing project should be prepared well in advance. It is best to begin by planning backward by first identifying the deadline date, then the shipping deadline, followed by the time it will take to ship the proposal, and then the time it will take for the proposal to arrive to the funder, and so forth. Preparing for the unexpected, and planning for anything and everything to go wrong, can alleviate a number of unforeseen problems.

Timing Is Everything

Grant proposal timelines can differ from proposal to proposal. Typically, timelines include three phases: the planning phase, the writing phase, and the submission phase. Following are common timelines and tasks that occur within each phase. This is only a representation of a timeline, as some timelines may be shorter and other timelines may be longer.

The Timeline

The planning phase typically begins 6 to 12 months before the proposal submission deadline. During this phase, agencies

- identify and discuss needs and resources.
- brainstorm and research projects and ideas.
- assess funding goals and resources.
- identify prior work and work accomplished by other agencies.

- establish a case for how the agency's programs and services differ from those of other agencies or complements the work of other agencies.
- identify potential funding sources, including funding priorities and applicant eligibility.
- contact the funding source and send letters of inquiry, if needed.
- inform the board of the intention to submit a grant and gain endorsements from the board, if necessary.
- develop a preliminary summary of the project.
- create a budget.
- choose a funding source that is compatible with scope and budget of the project.
- thoroughly read and review the proposal instructions, guidelines, timeline, and submission deadline.
- identify individuals who should be involved in the grant proposal.

The writing phase typically begins 2 to 6 months before the proposal submission deadline. During this phase, agencies

- outline the structure of the application.
- complete any required forms such as sponsor forms.
- plan and develop the first draft of the grant proposal.
- proof the draft and obtain feedback on the draft from qualified professionals.
- write all sections of the proposal.

The submission phase typically takes place 1 to 2 months before the proposal submission deadline. During this phase, agencies

- thoroughly proofread the completed proposal and make all necessary revisions to the proposal, including budget revisions.
- submit the final proposal to a proposal review office, if required or necessary, and make all revisions, if applicable.
- submit final grant proposal to the funding source at least 2 days before the deadline.

After the grant proposal has been submitted, the sponsor performs an initial screening of the proposal. Following the initial screening, most proposals are sent to peer reviewers for a more thorough screening. After the final review, an approval or rejection notice, along with comments, is sent to the agency. Refer to Chapter 10 for additional information on the review process.

Quality Trumps Deadlines

Although meeting deadlines is certainly a key goal of successful grant writing, producing a top-notch grant proposal is far more important than meeting a deadline. In other words, deadlines should not be put ahead of generating a quality proposal. Rushing the writing process can diminish the quality of the grant. Agencies that pull together last-minute proposals are better off slowing down in order to produce a noteworthy grant application. Henson (2003) recommends holding the proposal until the next year or submitting it to a similar funder once the proposal is ready.

Although meeting deadlines is certainly a key goal of successful grant writing, producing a top-notch grant proposal is far more important than meeting a deadline.

Contracting With a Professional Grant Writer

Researching and writing grants requires a lot of time, along with specialized research and writing skills. Some agencies may not have the time or available staff to dedicate to grant writing. If discretionary funds are available, contracting a professional grant writer, for a limited time, may be a viable option. In determining whether it is more advantageous for an agency to contract with a professional grant writer, Hired Gun Writing, LCC (2011a), recommends that organizations consider the cost of contracting with the grant writer. Other considerations include the grant writing talent of the agency's staff, the amount of time the staff has to devote to grant writing, and the agency's level of need for funding from a variety of sources. Another determinant is to weigh the pros and cons associated with hiring a professional grant writer. There are a number of pros, including the following:

- Agencies have more control over contracted grant writers. If the grant writer does not work out, the agency can contract with another grant writer for the next job. Letting a permanent employee go is much more difficult.
- Professional grant writers will be able to devote time exclusively to researching and writing the grant. Staff are often involved in other projects and meetings and do not have a block of time to dedicate solely to grant writing.
- Professional grant writers are more likely to have skills in choosing and searching grant maker databases and directories. These skills can come in handy in locating the best grantors for the agency's funding needs. However, it is important for organizations to develop these skills internally.
- Professional grant writers tend to have statistical expertise, which makes it easier for them to generate effective graphs and charts to visually illustrate the mission of the organization and to write results-oriented, data-driven grants. Staff may not possess the statistical expertise needed to inspire confidence in the agency's ability to meet its goals and objectives.
- Professional grant writers have exposure to trends and knowledge of the ins and outs of the application process and systems. They may also bring a fresh perspective to each project and take the perspective of the individuals who will be reading the grant. Inexperienced grant writers are less likely to have such exposure and knowledge.
- Professional grant writers are more likely to complete the grant proposal on time. Proposal deadlines are of paramount importance, and experienced grant writers know how to submit technically correct and complete proposals. Inexperienced grant writers are more likely to submit incomplete proposals and may not be as conscious of application deadlines.
- For agencies without grant writing expertise, a professional grant writer can teach the basics of grant writing to the agency staff. By having agency administrators shadow the grant writer, the administrators can learn about the grant writing process so that they will be able to write grant proposals in the future.

Along with pros, there are cons to contracting with a professional grant writer. For example,

- grants written by a contracted grant writer may lack the passion and personal voice that many funders prefer. Some funders would rather read a passionate plea from a novice grant writer than a well-developed proposal from a veteran writer who is isolated from the organization.
- contracted grant writers do not know the organization's grant history like someone within the organization does.
- choosing a professional grant writer who would be a suitable fit for the agency can be tricky. Because some professional grant writers are hired for one project at a time, a grant writer who was previously hired may not be available for the next project.
- contracting a professional grant writer can be quite costly, $200 an hour or more, although some rates may be as low as $25 to $50 an hour. Out-of-house grant writers work on a contractual basis. The best grant writers are often sought out by countless nonprofits and have a backlog of agencies waiting for their services. Although hiring the best and most experienced can be costly, the payoff to the agency may well be worth it. Agencies pay for these services only for a limited time based on the terms agreed upon. Therefore, organizations avoid paying the salary and benefits associated with permanent employees. In addition, professional grant writers tend to improve the odds that the agency's grant will be funded.

When an agency makes the decision to hire a professional grant writer, there are a number of guidelines that can assist in the selection process. Following are some helpful tips:

- Begin the process early. Many grant applications deadlines, or RFP (request for proposal) deadlines, are made public with only a 30-day notice. The search process for contracting with a professional grant writer can take several weeks.
- Ask for referrals from other nonprofits. Verify that the referring agency's needs matches the needs of the agency that is seeking a grant writer. Referring agencies with needs that do not align should be eliminated.
- Contact grant writer associations directly for referrals for grant writers.
- Decide if the grant writer will be contracted for a specific project, a longer period, or hired for a permanent position.
- Define the project and the skills and education needed in the grant writer. Detail fundraising objectives and grant targets. Determine the qualifications the agency is looking for in its grant writer. Use these criteria as a starting point for developing a job description.
- Advertise the grant writing position on websites where grant writers may visit, such as nonprofit websites, grant writer association websites, and freelance writing websites.
- Request resumes from candidates. Grant writing experience is essential. Grant writers, with many years of experience in grant writing, are likely to have a more successful and diversified background.

Information Management

Understanding and Mastery of . . . Obtain information through interviewing, active listening, consultation with others, library or other research, and the observation of clients and systems

Critical Thinking Question: Some agencies may not have the time or staff to dedicate to grant writing. When contracting for a professional grant writer, what background research should go into the selection of a professional grant writer?

- Request lists of submitted grant proposals with funded grants highlighted. These lists can help determine funding success rates. Candidates with diverse grant writing experience (i.e., grants from different sources) may be stronger candidates. Make sure the funding sources are in the same or similar categories as those the agency is seeking.
- Request copies of a few funded proposals the candidates authored. In addition, request copies of the award letters. Proposals can be used to examine writing skills, proposal appearance, attention to detail, and creativity. Grant writers must have verifiable relevant skills and experience to produce winning proposals. In addition, the grant writer should be able to write for the audience who will be reviewing the proposal.
- Request, from candidates, a list of three to five references. The references submitted should be of responsible individuals (i.e., board members, executive directors) and relate to recently funded proposals. All references should be checked.
- Provide candidates with a description of the work the organization does and the types of grants for which the organization plans to apply.
- If contracting a grant writer, inquire about the fees for the services.
- Meet with the grant writer to discuss the project and to assess whether the grant writer would be an excellent fit for the agency.
- Ask candidates how they would approach writing the grant proposal. Answers to this question can provide insight into the candidate's ability to meet the RFP requirements and focus on the organization's needs.
- Request a written synopsis of the candidates' grant writing model. This can provide information on their approach to grant writing and the procedures they follow.
- Ask if the grant writer has sufficient time to write the grant proposal.
- Once the grant writer has been selected, agencies should create a contract for the grant writer that includes the scope of the work; length of service; compensation; number of proposals; a non-compete agreement; a confidentiality statement; a non-disclosure agreement; a detailed list of the tasks the grant writer is expected to perform; pertinent grant targets; a cancellation clause that either the grant writer or the agency can use with appropriate notice; and a statement stipulating that the agency owns the completed proposal.
- Provide grant writers accurate information, including necessary background documents and financial statements. Supplying these documents to the grant writer can reduce time and expense. Preparedness affects the grant writer's fee.
- Design a plan to monitor progress, targets, and deadlines. Determine how often administrators will meet with the grant writer to monitor progress. Schedule time to meet with the grant writer.
- Provide feedback to the grant writer throughout the process.

Administration

Understanding and Mastery of ... Grant and contract negotiation

Critical Thinking Question: When contracting with a professional grant writer for a specific project, how might an agency go about negotiating for a reduced rate for contracting with the same grant writer for future projects?

There are a number of resources available to assist organizations in identifying potential grant writers. Following are several associations and organizations that provide resources, services, and directories to assist nonprofits in connecting with grant writers:

- *American Grant Writers' Association (AGWA) (2011).* AGWA is a nonprofit association of grant consultants, employees of state and local government agencies, institutions of higher education, and nonprofit organizations throughout the United States. AGWA consultants provide a number of services, including researching grant opportunities; writing proposals; reviewing proposals that have already been written; developing business plans; writing annual budgets; and training agency staff to research grant opportunities and write proposals.
- *Association of Fundraising Professionals (AFP) (2011).* The AFP represents over 30,000 members throughout the world and provides access to an online consultant and resource directory. The association provides fundraising professionals with a means to search for jobs, and agencies with a means to search for fundraising professionals.
- *Association of Proposal Management Professionals (APMP) (2010).* APMP provides members with access to tools, methods, and specialized expertise that can improve growth and competitiveness in the marketplace through proposal excellence. ARMP members are engaged in proposal management, strategic planning, proposal consulting, and proposal production, just to name a few. The professionals come from a number of industries, including the nonprofit sector.
- *CharityChannel (2011).* CharityChannel is comprised of thousands of professionals from around the world, who work in the nonprofit sector. The professionals volunteer information, advice, tips, articles, and their time, for the betterment of the community. CharityChannel.com provides teleclasses and on-demand classes on a variety of topics, including fund development. In addition, the organization provides access to a consultant registry.
- *Grant Professionals Association (GPA) (2011).* GPA is a nonprofit association with over 1,600 members and more than 3,000 grant professionals. It provides agencies with a means to connect with grant writers. The website offers members free resume access and resume search agents. Through the resume search agent, agencies receive automatic email notifications whenever job seekers match the agency's search criteria.

One final note regarding contracting the services of a professional grant writer is in regard to registration requirements. Although it is not necessary in every state, many states require non-employee grant writers to register with the state. If an organization operates in a state with a registration requirement and the outside contracted grant writer is not registered, the nonprofit may be subject to fines and penalties. Therefore, agencies should insist that contracted grant writers register in accordance with state law requirements (National Council of Nonprofits, 2010b).

> **Although it is not necessary in every state, many states require non-employee grant writers to register with the state.**

Summary

In order for a grant writing initiative to flourish, there are a number of crucial areas that should be considered. First, agencies should consider the advantages and disadvantages of collaborating with colleagues in developing grant proposals. Successful collaboration requires careful consideration to picking and choosing self-motivated and compatible team members and assigning tasks based on each member's skills and interests. Collaboration also extends beyond the walls of the agency. Collaborating with outside organizations can open the door to grant opportunities that may not be available without pooling the efforts and resources of other agencies. A successful grant writing initiative also relies on the development and adherence to a well thought-out timeline. A well-developed timeline serves as an essential guide through the grant writing process, from the initial planning to the submission of the proposal. Although meeting submission deadlines is critical, when proposals are not up to par, it is better to postpone submitting the proposal until another time or explore similar funders once the proposal is ready to submit. Finally, some agencies may not have the time or staff to devote to grant writing. In such cases, contracting with a professional grant writer may be a reasonable option. Contracting with a professional grant writer requires careful planning and screening, which can be a bit daunting. However, when agencies do not have the in-house expertise or the time to dedicate to grant writing, devoting time to planning and screening candidates can pay off in the form of potential grant awards.

The following questions will test your application and analysis of the content found within this chapter. For additional assessment, applying, analyzing, synthesizing, and evaluating chapter content with practice, visit **MySearchLab.com**

1. Typically, grant proposal timelines include a number of phases. Which phase involves proofing the draft of the proposal and obtaining feedback on the draft from qualified professionals?
    a. Preplanning phase
    b. Planning phase
    c. Writing phase
    d. Submission phase

2. You are working at an agency that provides services to immigrant workers. Your executive director came across a grant that he feels may be a good match for the mission of the agency. The grant proposal is due in 2 weeks. You work feverously on the proposal and feel it is not up to par; however, it is due tomorrow. You decide that the best course of action is to
    a. submit the proposal by the deadline.
    b. tell your executive director that you feel it's better to hold the proposal until the next year or submit it to a similar funder once the proposal is ready.
    c. contact the funding source and let someone there know that you will be submitting the proposal in another week.
    d. hire a professional grant writer to get the proposal up to par before you submit it tomorrow.

3. The American Grant Writers' Association, the Association of Fundraising Professionals, and CharityChannel are associations and organizations that can assist agencies in
    a. locating available grants.
    b. writing grant proposals.
    c. identifying professional grant writers.
    d. collaborating with other agencies in writing grants.

4. You have been asked to recruit a professional grant writer for your agency. Which of the following tips would be most helpful in securing a competent grant writer?
    a. Contact grant writer associations directly for referrals for grant writers.
    b. Post an announcement on the agency's bulletin board.
    c. Wait until a grant application, or RFP, is made public before searching for a grant writer.
    d. Use the same grant writer that a local agency is using.

5. Due to budget cuts and the fiscal environment in general, many nonprofits will need to be open to pursuing grants, which requires them to team up with other agencies. What are the benefits of collaborating with other nonprofits in seeking funding?

6. When planning to write and submit a grant proposal, it is important to develop and follow a timeline to ensure that the grant proposal is complete and ready to submit by the deadline. What are five tasks that are typically completed during the planning phase?

7. There are a number of pros associated with contracting with a professional grant writer. Explain three of the pros.

8. When an organization decides to contract with a professional grant writer, there are a number of guidelines that can assist the organization with the selection process. What are three tips that can assist a nonprofit in selecting a grant writer?

CHAPTER 9

Exploring Grant Possibilities and Searching Funding Databases and Resources

· ·

Learning Objectives
- Differentiate among the various types of federal grants.
- Distinguish among the various types of grant-making foundations.
- Describe funding databases along with their components.
- Identify funding resources and the information and services they provide.
- Share the benefits of affinity groups as funding resources.

Each day millions of dollars are awarded to nonprofit agencies to fund programs and services that impact the well-being of millions of people. The secret to acquiring funds is the knowledge of the various types of funding sources, the types of grants available, and where to locate the grants. This chapter is bursting with funding sources, database information, and additional resources to equip agencies with information beneficial to their fund-seeking initiatives. The first section highlights different types of grant-making sources, beginning with government-funded grants.

Government-Funded Grants

The federal government is the largest grant maker, with much of the federal grant budget moved to the states through block and formula grants. Once it is moved to the states, it is up to the states to decide how the money will be used. Some of the money is used to operate each state's programs, but some of the funds are redistributed through grants and contracts. Each government or agency has its own systems and procedures for redistributing funds through grants or contracts.

There tends to be some confusion regarding the differences between a grant and a contract. According to Coley and Scheinberg (1990), a grant is money given to an organization or an individual to address a need or problem in the community. On the other hand, a contract is a legal document that stipulates the services to be provided and the expected results in exchange for resources.

A federal grant is an award of financial assistance from a federal agency to an agency or other recipient to carry out a public purpose of support or stimulation as authorized by a law of the United States. Federal grants are not loans or federal assistance to individuals. In addition, they may not be used to acquire services or property for the federal government's direct benefit (Grants.gov, 2011b).

According to FederalGrants.com (2011a), there are several types of federal grants, including the following:

- *Project grants.* Project grants are awarded for medical or other kinds of research.
- *Categorical grants.* Categorical grants are awarded for narrowly focused purposes, where the beneficiary typically has to come up with funds to match the amount of federal funds given.
- *Block grants.* Block grants provide a little more leeway in how the agency uses the money.
- *Earmark grants.* Earmark grants are congressional appropriated grants. Earmark grants have come under public scrutiny because of instances where members of Congress have pushed through monetary awards in their own districts that support personal interests or specific agencies.

Information Management

Understanding and Mastery of . . . Compiling, synthesizing, and categorizing information

Critical Thinking Question: How might an agency go about determining the type of federal grant that is the best match for its funding needs?

When searching for a government grant, agencies must first identify principal federal agencies that fund their type of work and then track the distribution of the funds from Washington, DC, down to their locality. This sets the groundwork for prospecting for federal funds (The Grantsmanship Center, 2010).

Not only does the government fund the work of nonprofits, there are a number of grant-making foundations that are established with a mission of making grants to organizations that are unrelated to the grant-making foundations. The next section focuses on the various types of grant-making foundations.

When searching for a government grant, agencies must first identify principal federal agencies that fund their type of work and then track the distribution of the funds from Washington, DC, down to their locality.

Grant-Making Foundations

Grant-making foundations are nongovernmental entities that are recognized as nonprofit, corporate, or charitable trusts. The purpose of these entities is to make grants to organizations, agencies, institutions, and individuals for charitable purposes. There are a number of different grant-making foundations, including independent/private, family, community, corporate, corporate giving, and operational foundations.

Independent/Private Foundations

Independent foundations are grant-making organizations that are generally classified by the Internal Revenue Service (IRS) as private foundations. They are nongovernmental, nonprofit, self-governed organizations with funds. They are tax exempt under Code section 501(c)(3). The funds are usually derived from a single source, such as a family, an individual, or a corporation. The foundations are usually large, complex entities that are professionally managed by their own trustees or directors. According to Fundraising Dictionary (2007), they are established to aid or maintain social, educational, cultural, religious, or other charitable activities that serve the common welfare of society. Independent foundations must pay out roughly 5% of the market value of its assets each year. In addition, they must pay an annual 1 to 2% excise tax on their net investment income. Independent/private foundations are also known as general-purpose foundations, private non-operating foundations, and special-purpose foundations.

Family Foundations

Family foundations are independent, private foundations whose funds are derived from members of a family. According to Gersick, Stone, Grady, Desjardins, and Muson (2006), the term *family foundation* does not have a legal definition; this makes such foundations distinct from other private foundations. They are informally defined as being self-identified by including the word *family* in their name and having a living donor whose surname matches the foundation's name, and involving a minimum of two trustees whose surname matches a living or deceased donor's name. Therefore, the family plays a significant role in the grant-making decisions. Family foundations comprise 40 to 50% of all private and community foundations, and most are small and informal organizations. The largest family foundation is the Bill and Melinda Gates Foundation. From 1994 to 2010 the foundation has funded $23,910,000,000 in grants to help people around the world lead healthy and productive lives (Bill and Melinda Gates Foundation, 2011).

Community Foundations

Community foundations are 501(c)(3) organizations that make grants for charitable purposes within a specific geographic locality or region and usually focus primarily on community needs. A significant portion of the funds are usually raised from the public; therefore, it is not a "private foundation." Although the funds are usually derived from many donors, the funds are held in an independently administered endowment. The income earned by the endowment is used to make grants. Most community foundations are classified as public charities and are eligible for maximum income tax-deductible contributions from the general public (Fundraising Dictionary, 2007).

Corporate Foundations

Corporate foundations, also known as company-sponsored foundations, are the philanthropic arms created by corporations to manage requests for contributions (Fundraising Dictionary, 2007). Assets of corporate foundations are derived mainly from the contributions of for-profit businesses. Although corporate foundations may maintain ties to their parent companies, they are independent entities and abide by the same regulations that govern private foundations.

Corporate Giving Programs

Corporate giving programs, also referred to as direct giving programs, are established within a for-profit corporation and are usually administered by the public relations or marketing unit of the organization. The grant making is closely tied to the company's profits; a separate endowment does not exist. Grants and gifts from the corporation go directly to charitable organizations. The focus of the funding is typically on communities within which the company operates. Some corporations make charitable contributions through both corporate giving programs and company-sponsored foundations (Fundraising Dictionary, 2007). Corporate/direct giving programs are not subject to the same reporting requirements as are corporate foundations.

Operating Foundations

Operating foundations are 501(c)(3) organizations that are classified by the IRS as private foundations. The primary purpose of operating foundations is to conduct research, social welfare, or other programs that are determined by their establishment charters or governing bodies. Rarely are operating foundations also company sponsored. Operating foundations may make grants; however, the amount of funds is usually small compared to the funds used for the foundation's own programs (Fundraising Dictionary, 2007). Operating foundations generally operate libraries, research institutions, and museums.

Most grants awarded by foundations and corporate giving programs can be classified as either general-purpose/operating support grants or program development/project support grants (Minnesota Council on Foundations, 2010). General-purpose or operating support grants are grants that can be used to support the general operating expenses of the organization such as a particular service or program to utility bills. Program development or project support grants are funds connected to a specific activity with a specific start and end date. For the most part, this type of grant is restricted and must be used for the particular purpose for which it was intended. Examples of program development/project support grants include the following:

- *Planning grants.* Planning grants support initial project development work such as conducting planning activities.
- *Seed money.* Seed money or start-up grants assist a new organization or program during its first few years.
- *Management or technical assistance grants.* Management or technical assistance grants support an agency's administration or management.
- *Facilities and equipment grants.* Facilities and equipment grants provide funds to purchase a long-lasting physical asset such as a building.
- *Endowment grants.* Endowment grants funds invested in an endowment earn interest. The original sum remains in the endowment, and nonprofits spend only the interest earned.
- *Program-related investments (PRIs).* Program-related investments (PRIs) are loans made by foundations to nonprofits for projects that qualify for grant support. PRIs are typically made at low-interest or no-interest rates. PRIs must be paid back to the grant maker and are often used in building projects.

Information Management

Understanding and Mastery of . . . Using technology for word processing, sending email, and locating and evaluating information

Critical Thinking Question: How can technology be used to assist organizations in evaluating funding sources?

Knowing the funding sources is only one step in the grant-seeking process. Agencies must also be familiar with funding databases. Next, funding databases will be explored.

Funding Databases

Funding databases are searchable databases of funding sources available to support a variety of agency programs, services, and projects. The databases provide agencies with the ability to search for competitive grants representing thousands of funding opportunities. The following databases are listed in alphabetical order.

Catalog of Federal Domestic Assistance

The Catalog of Federal Domestic Assistance (CFDA) (2011) provides detailed descriptions for over 2,000 federal programs, services, projects, and activities that provide assistance or benefits to the American public. CFDA is the basic reference source of federal programs and assists users in identifying programs that meet the objectives of the applicant and assists applicants in obtaining general information on federal assistance programs. The resources are available to state and local governments and federally recognized Indian tribal governments; territories of the United States; domestic public, quasi-public, and private profit and nonprofit organizations and institutions; specialized groups; and individuals.

The CFDA contains a number of databases, including a database of programs that includes an advanced search option and a historical index of programs. The historical index dates back to 1965 and includes information on the subsequent action taken related to the programs.

There is also a database of agencies where users can click on the name of the agency to view the agency's programs. Users can use a keyword search to filter by agency, name, abbreviation, or description. Once the program has been identified, contact information is provided to enable agencies to contact the office that administers the program/s to obtain application instructions.

The CFDA website also includes information on regional agency offices. This database contains contact information for over 3,000 regional agency offices, including the contact name, address, and phone number.

FederalGrants.com

FederalGrants.com (2011a) provides free information on U.S. Federal Grants as well as information on qualifying and applying for government grants and what to do once one is approved for a grant. It is not endorsed by or affiliated with any government agency. The website is divided into three categories: tools, articles, and resources.

The tools section provides a search engine where one can search for grants via a keyword search, CFDA number, or a funding opportunity number (FON) search. Individuals can also browse grants by category or federal agency.

The site also provides links to a variety of grant-related articles. Topics range from "What is a Grant" to "Grants for Minorities." The resource section includes grant forums and links to miscellaneous sites such as quick loan, degree search, and credit score site.

Agencies will find FederalGrants.com a helpful resource for both locating federal grants and grant writing assistance. The website provides tips and guidelines from qualifying for a grant to what to do once approved for a grant.

The Foundation Center

The Foundation Center (2011a) is supported by almost 550 foundations and is touted as the top source of information about philanthropy worldwide. Through data, analysis, and training, it links people, wanting to transform the world, to resources they need to succeed. The Foundation Center maintains one of the most complete databases of information on nearly 100,000 U.S. and global grant makers and 2.1 million of its recent grants. In addition, it operates education, research, and training programs designed to advance knowledge of philanthropy at every level. Its website is visited by thousands of people daily who receive free access to information resources and educational programs. The access and information is made available through five regional library/learning centers (i.e., New York City, Atlanta, Cleveland, Washington, DC, and San Francisco) and a network of 450 funding information centers located in educational institutions, public libraries, community foundations, and educational institutions both nationally and globally. For nonprofits searching for funders, the Foundation Center offers a fact finder, funding source identifier, related tools, statistics, and local resources.

> **The Foundation Center maintains one of the most complete databases of information on nearly 100,000 U.S. and global grant makers and 2.1 million of its recent grants.**

- *Fact finder.* The fact finder provides basic information on grant makers in the United States, including private and community foundations, grant-making public charities, and corporate giving programs. Agencies can search for foundations by grant maker name, by geography, and/or by Employer ID Number (EIN). The 990 finder provides a means to search for organizations' IRS return. Trend tracker provides a means to review and compare grant maker data and create charts, graphs, and tables that display historical assets, expenditures, gifts received, and giving information.
- *Funding source identifier.* The funding source identifier provides an online foundation directory, which provides updated and comprehensive information on U.S. grant makers and their funding activities. It also includes an online database of corporate donors who support nonprofit organizations and programs through grants and in-kind donations of products, equipment, professional services, and volunteers. Another component of the funding source identifier is an online database of over 8,500 foundation and public charity programs that fund students, artists, researchers, and other individual grant seekers. The funding source identifier also provides print funding directories, lists of requests for proposals (RFPs), access to staff members, and an interactive map of direct grants by U.S. grant makers to non-U.S. recipients.
- *Related tools.* The related tools section provides a number of common grant application formats. Groups of grant makers have adopted these application formats to allow grant applicants to save time by producing a single proposal for a particular community of funders. Additional tools include prospect worksheets and the Foundation Center's Grants Classification System (GCS). The GCS uses indexing terms related to specific types of information, such as type of support, subject area or field of activity, beneficiary populations, and recipient auspice. The system uses the National Taxonomy of Exempt Entities (NTEE) for its subject, or field of activity, term list.

- *Statistics.* The statistics section provides statistics on the top 100 U.S. grant-making foundations, based on the market value of their assets. It also provides grant maker stats on national growth trends and grant stats on funding by subject area, by subject area and funder's region, and by subject area and foundation size.
- *Local resources.* The local resource section provides links to the five regional library/learning centers, New York City, Atlanta, Cleveland, Washington, DC, and San Francisco, as well as a link to the Foundations Center's cooperating collection. Each of the regional library/learning centers' websites provides training calendars, online libraries, podcasts, videos, blogs, and community resources. The cooperating collection is a fundamental collection of Foundation Center publications and a selection of supplementary materials and services in a variety of areas useful to grant seekers.

Agencies will find the Foundation Center's grant-seeking tools extremely beneficial. From online training and tutorials to foundation directories and resource libraries, the Foundation Center's extensive website provides a valuable network of grant-seeking resources.

GrantDomain.com

GrantDomain.com (2011), a product of The Grantmanship Center, is a membership-only service that provides members access to three different funding databases: Federal/State Funding, Foundation Grants, and Corporate Giving.

- *Federal/State Funding.* The Federal/State Funding database can be searched by keyword, announcement date, funding agency, program area, program title, and CFDA number. This database has a feature, so members can receive daily updates on new program announcements, news of any changes in the grant-making process, breaking news about state-level grant opportunities, and other relevant information that may impact grantees.
- *Foundation Grants.* The Foundation Grant database can be searched by keyword, foundation name, geographic giving preference, program area, and types of support. The foundations are pre-screened to ensure that the foundations have staff, that the foundations issue RFPs, or that the foundations otherwise indicate interest in receiving proposals. Members receive news updates and new foundation RFPs.
- *Corporate Giving.* The Corporate Giving database covers more than 1,200 corporations and 1,000 corporate foundations. Members can search by corporate location and can screen corporations by direct corporate giving, matching gifts, and donations of goods and services. Companies can be searched by keyword; company name; and city, zip code, or county. Members have access to daily corporate giving news updates.

GrantDomain.com also provides a guide to grant writing. In addition, through The Grantmanship Center, members can purchase a CD of winning grant proposals.

A CD set of multiple proposals cost $99 or a custom-made CD costs $29 for the first proposal and $20 for additional proposals. Subscriptions to GrantDomain.com run $495 for 1 year, $695 for 2 years, and $795 for 3 years.

Grants.gov

Grants.gov (2011a) was established as a result of the E-Grants Initiative, a part of the president's 2002 Fiscal Year Management Agenda. The objective of Grants.gov is to improve government services to the public. Grants.gov is a central clearinghouse of information on over a 1,000 grant programs. It provides access to approximately $500 billion in annual awards. All discretionary grants offered by the 26 federal grant-making agencies can be found on Grants.gov. There are a number of ways in which grant opportunities can be located on the site. Funding opportunities can be searched by keyword, CFDA number, or FON. Grant opportunities can also be searched by a variety of funding activity categories, lists of agencies offering grant opportunities, Recovery Act Opportunities, and more specific criteria such as eligibility, funding instrument type, or sub-agency. Each grant announcement includes a synopsis of the grant, a full announcement, and a link for an application. Individuals and agencies can also subscribe to receive email notifications of changes/modifications to grant opportunities of interest.

Individuals and agencies do not have to register to locate grants; however, they do need to register once they are ready to apply for a grant. The registration process can take anywhere from 3 to 5 business days or up to 4 weeks if all application steps are not completed in a timely manner. Grants.gov also provides applicants with System-to-System, a service that streamlines the application process. Through System-to-System, applicants with a high volume of application submissions can save time and resources by eliminating the need to reenter repetitious information into numerous individual application forms.

One of System-to-System's newest features is a self-help portal (iPortal). It provides entry points to live, 24-hour assistance. Key features of iPortal include

- searchable knowledge base with 400 answers to common issues.
- self-service help-ticket generator.
- live, web chat for one-on-one help.
- alerts and updates.

The U.S. Department of Health and Human Services is the administrative cohort of Grants.gov. Grants.gov is a comprehensive source for agencies seeking federal grants. Its database allows nonprofits to easily locate and apply for grants.

GrantStation

GrantStation.com, Inc. (2011), provides nonprofit organizations, governmental agencies, and educational institutions with opportunities to identify prospective funding sources and mentoring resources to assist with the grant-seeking process. GrantStation provides four searchable databases of grant makers and provides automated tours of each database. Proposals and inquiries are accepted from a range of organizations. The four databases include the following:

- *U.S. Charitable Giving.* U.S. Charitable Giving is a database of thousands of funder profiles from a variety of sources including independent, family, community, and corporate foundations, along with corporate giving programs, faith-based grant makers, and associations with grant-making programs. The database section is searchable by geographic focus, interest areas, and nature of support.
- *International Charitable Giving.* International Charitable Giving is a database of several thousand international funder profiles searchable by geographic location and interest areas.
- *Federal Grants & Loans.* Federal Grants & Loans database provides detailed program, contact, and application information on an abundance of U.S. federal grant and loan opportunities. The database is updated Monday through Friday; archived announcements are also available. The database is word searchable, and information is categorized by deadline dates.
- *State Grants & Loans.* State Grants & Loans database provides individual profiles for each state. It consists of links to state departments and agencies that oversee and administer grant and loan programs. The database also provides links to quasi-state agencies, such as the state arts council, children's trusts, and humanities forums.

In addition to the extensive databases, GrantStation publishes *GrantStation Insider* and *GrantStation International Insider*. *GrantStation Insider* is an e-newsletter that focuses on upcoming grant opportunities for U.S. nonprofit organizations, whereas *GrantStation International Insider* is an e-newsletter that focuses on forthcoming international grant opportunities.

Mentoring opportunities are available through the following GrantStation partner programs:

- *Co-Branded e-Newsletter.* The Co-Branded e-Newsletter program provides organizations with a means to strengthen their outreach efforts, build loyalty among their constituents, and add value to existing membership packages. Through this program, the *GrantStation Insider* is co-branded the organization's logo and mission statement and delivered weekly, free of charge, to the agency's email list.
- *Membership Value Program (MVP).* The Membership Value Program (MVP) provides organizations with a means to purchase GrantStation memberships at a considerable discount for the agency's constituent organizations.
- *GrantStation Technical Assistance Program (GS-TAP).* The GrantStation Technical Assistance Program (GS-TAP) provides organizations with an opportunity to purchase a volume of GrantStation memberships for their constituent organizations, members, or field offices. Along with access to the various databases, GS-TAP members are given access to customized online tour/webinars that provide guidance on using the GrantStation tools for research and grant writing, with refresher webinars offered half-way through the membership period. At the conclusion of the GS-TAP contract, GrantStation surveys the constituent organizations and develops a final report that identifies the partner organization's return on their investment.

Organizations can subscribe to the GrantStation's e-newsletters, become a member and receive membership benefits including subscriptions to the e-newsletters, or join as a partner. Partners receive all the benefits of members, but in addition, they receive discounted membership fees and customized website tours and online tours of each database. Membership dues range from quarterly dues of $189 to annual dues of $599.

U.S. Department of Education

The U.S. Department of Education (ED.gov) (2011) offers several kinds of grants. In addition to grants to help individuals attend college, the department provides formula grants to agencies using formulas determined by Congress, and discretionary grants to organizations, agencies, and individuals. Discretionary grants are awarded using a competitive process. Anyone meeting the eligibility requirements may apply.

ED.gov provides information on discretionary grants, including eligibility requirements, grant competitions, application openings, application procedures, supplemental priorities, and types of forms needed. Following is a list of information contained in each of these six sections.

The eligibility section provides a link to the

- Guide to Education Programs, where agencies can identify programs for which they are eligible to apply.

The grant competitions section provides links to

- discretionary grant application packages, which lists the majority of education competitions currently open along with links to applications for each competition.
- Federal Register notices that provide information on rules, deadlines, and applications.
- IES funding opportunities that provide information on research funding opportunities run by the Institute for Education Sciences, including funding for unsolicited grants.
- Grants.gov that provides a list of discretionary grant competitions from across the federal government. The lists also include many ED competitions.

The application openings section provides a link to

- grants forecasts, which can assist agencies in identifying competitions that may be opening soon.

The application procedures for discretionary grants section provides links to

- competition application packages or application instructions.
- ED's online application system that provides application packages for competitions that it hosts.
- downloadable application packages for various ED grant competitions.
- additional information on the grant application process.

The supplemental priorities section includes links to

- a general list of supplemental priorities that ED may choose to apply to discretionary grant competitions. The priorities are topics that ED is interested in focusing on; the list makes it easier for ED to assign priorities to individual competitions.

- the official Federal Register notice that provides detailed information of priorities and associated issues.

The forms section provides a link to

- grant applications and other forms that provide a list of grant-related forms. This link is in place just in case an application package, in the online application system, is missing forms. It is also useful should the applicant need to view other forms.

In addition to the aforementioned, agencies will find the "Forecast of Funding Opportunities" section helpful. This document lists nearly all programs and competitions the U.S. Department of Education has invited, or anticipates inviting, applications for new awards. Actual or estimated deadline dates for transmittal of applications are also provided.

U.S. Department of Health and Human Services

The U.S. Department of Health and Human Services (HHS) (2011) is the government's chief agency for protecting the health of Americans and providing vital human services, particularly for those who are the least able to help themselves. The HHS administers more grant dollars than all federal agencies combined. HHS.gov provides a variety of federal grant-making and funding information. The website is divided into four sections: U.S. Government Grants and Funding Resources, HHS Grant Information, HHS Education and Training Funding, and Contract Information.

The U.S. Government Grants and Funding Resources section provides links to

- finding and applying for grants.
- checking eligibility for government benefits.
- checking availability of government loans.
- finding business contracting opportunities.
- Finding descriptions of all federal assistance programs.

The HHS Grant Information section is divided into three parts: Find Grant Opportunities, Learn to Manage HHS Grants, and See Grants Awarded by HHS and Other Agencies. The Find Grant Opportunities section provides links to

- finding grant opportunities.
- searching and browsing forecasted HHS grant opportunities.
- funding opportunities for faith-based and community organizations.

The Learn to Manage HHS Grants section provides links to

- tips for preparing grant proposals.
- finding HHS grant management information.
- learning about the HHS grants management process.

The See Grants Awarded by HHS and Other Agencies section provides links to

- locating grant and award information by major activity type, HHS operating division, and by recipient class.
- learning how the federal government spends its funds.
- finding federal, state, and local government financial assistance award information.

The HHS Education and Training Funding section provides links to

- finding financial aid for health professions: students and practitioners.
- finding health care research training and education opportunities.
- locating public health training resources and opportunities.
- learning about the student training and extern program at the Public Health Service Commissioned Corps (PHS).
- finding information from the National Institutes of Health (NIH) on research training and research development news, extramural training funds, and NIH National Library of Medicine Associate Fellowship Program.
- finding information from Indian Health Service (IHS) on jobs and scholarships and student aid resources.

The Contract Information section provides links to

- finding HHS contracting opportunities at Federal Business Opportunities.
- HHS inventory of service contracts.
- HHS acquisition information on regulation, policies and guidance, and workforce training and certification.
- finding information for small businesses (Office of Small and Disadvantaged Business Utilization, OSDBU) on forecasting HHS contracting opportunities, small business at HHS, active HHS contracts, HHS Mentor-Protégé Program (MPP), and the *Pulse Newsletter*.

HHS.gov is a clearinghouse of grant information from all federal agencies. For many agencies, it can serve as a one-stop source for searching for and applying for federal grants.

Funding databases allow agencies to electronically locate and apply for grants. Most grants can be searched by conducting a keyword search or by searching via FON. Many databases provide means to browse by category or agency. Additional information can be found by accessing the database's search tips.

Although funding databases provide organizations with a means to search for, locate, and apply for grants, agencies can also benefit from funding resources. Funding resources offer information that agencies can use in tandem with, or separate from, funding databases.

Funding Resources

Funding resources provide an abundance of information and services ranging from legal information, charity reviews, public policy information, e-newsletters, audioconferences, access to membership directories, conference information, and webinars, just to name a few. The next section highlights, in alphabetical order, a variety of resources agencies may find helpful when exploring grant opportunities.

Administration

Understanding and Mastery of . . . Grant and contract negotiation

Critical Thinking Question: What information obtained through funding databases and funding resources might assist organizations in grant negotiations?

Funding resources provide an abundance of information and services ranging from legal information, charity reviews, public policy information, e-newsletters, audioconferences, access to membership directories, conference information, and webinars, just to name a few.

The Chronicle of Philanthropy

The Chronicle of Philanthropy (2011) provides print and online resources for leaders of nonprofit organizations, fundraisers, grant makers, and other individuals involved in philanthropy. Specifically, news and information is geared toward executives of tax-exempt organizations in education, health, religions, social services, the arts, and other areas. In addition to these fields, information is provided for fundraisers, professional employees of foundations, corporate grant makers, institutional investors, and charity donors. It offers resources, including lists of grants, fundraising techniques and ideas, reports on tax and court rulings, statistics, summaries of books, and a calendar of events. The print version of *the Chronicle* is published 18 times a year; however, an environmental-friendly digital version is also available, free of charge.

The fundraising section of the *Chronicle* covers a wide variety of topics, including

- annual giving
- big gifts
- capital campaigns
- direct marketing
- donor and prospect research
- events fundraising
- grant seeking
- marketing and communications
- online fundraising
- planned giving

The Chronicle of Philanthropy is one of the top news sources for nonprofits involved in philanthropy. It is read by over 110,000 people. Paid annual subscriptions include 18 issues and complete access to *the Chronicle*'s website. An annual print subscription costs $72; the digital version costs $52.50. Subscribers are able to create and manage custom job-search agents, participate in forums, forward *Chronicle* content to colleagues via email, and comment on news articles and blogs.

Council on Foundations

The Council on Foundations (2011) is a national nonprofit association consisting of roughly 2,000 grant-making foundations and corporations. It serves community foundations, corporate grant makers, family philanthropy, global philanthropy, and independent members. Among its many programs and services, the council provides legal information, public policy promotion, professional development, job information, and numerous publications.

The council's legal information services include access to council attorneys. In addition, it provides information and resources on foundation management; grant making; contributions and donors; and legislative, regulatory, judicial, and state legal resources; and information on the Pension Protection Act of 2006 that includes information on charitable reforms and incentives.

As the national policy voice for philanthropy, the council has an extensive public policy section. The section provides legislative updates regarding numerous public policy resources; a legislative action center; information on elected officials; legislative issues, alerts, and updates; an election guide; and a media guide for searching for local and national media contacts.

The professional development section offers online webinars and seminars, each geared toward specific populations, including community, corporate, family, private/ independent, international, and legal/memberships. Information on upcoming conferences is also provided. There are resources for CEOs and trustees, including a variety of professional development publications.

The council's job information section provides a means to post job announcements and search for jobs nationwide. Members of the council and collegial organizations can post job openings free of charge. Postings are displayed for 3 months or until the closing of the job search. In addition to jobs posted by council members and collegial organizations, job opportunities at the council are also posted.

The final section, the publication section, houses an online store where individuals and organizations can purchase books and digitally delivered publications on philanthropy-related topics. Some of the topics include grant writing, corporate giving, and foundation management.

Membership dues vary and are based on member category, total assets, and total grants. Member categories include private, community, public, tribal, and operating foundations; corporate grant makers; and non-U.S. foundations. Membership dues range from $500 to $55,000 depending on total assets and total grants. Benefits of membership include

- access to the member directory and council staff.
- early alerts regarding council conferences and programs.
- guidance on legal questions.
- access to research and benchmarking studies.
- awards programs.
- peer and education networking.
- governance documents.
- participation in council committees and/or board eligibility.
- discounts on online board portals, conferences, seminars, and webinars.
- complimentary electronic member listings.
- council e-newsletter, *Policy Update* e-newsletter, and various other publications.

The council welcomes private, community, operating, public, and corporate foundations; giving programs and emerging giving programs; grant-making organizations; and any conduit that brings people together in a philanthropic effort as its members. Although the council does not provide services to those seeking grants, it does provide support to grant makers in various aspects of foundation management.

Grantmakers in Health

Grantmakers in Health (GIH) (2011) is a nonprofit, educational organization devoted to assisting corporate giving programs and enhancing the health of all individuals. Through the fostering of communication and collaboration, GIH's mission is to bolster the grant-making community's knowledge, skills, and effectiveness. GIH was introduced in 1982 and is known as the professional home for health grant makers. It is a resource for grant makers and others seeking information and expertise in health philanthropy.

GIH generates and disseminates information about health concerns and grant-making strategies through issue-focused forums, workshops, annual meetings, continuing education and training, publications, consultation, technical assistance, and research of health philanthropy. GIH connects health grant makers with each other and with grant makers in other fields whose work has significant implications for health. In addition, GIH develops programs, services, and activities specifically targeted to its audience.

Some of the features of the GIH website include GIH press releases and events calendars as well as a funding partner network database, featured audioconferences, publications, job boards, links to other organizations serving philanthropy, and to issue topics. The funding partner network database is a searchable database of priorities, grants, and initiatives of health grant makers. It categorizes the work of health philanthropy based on foundation characteristics, health programming area, targeted populations, and funding strategy. It includes over 15,000 grants and initiatives from almost 400 foundations. Organizations can search the database to learn who funds issues of interest to the organization, as well as the types of strategies used by various funders.

The audioconferences series serves as a means to keep grant makers well-informed of issues of mutual interest. GIH currently offers the following 10 audioconference topics:

- Access
- Disparities
- Healthy eating/active living (health promotion)
- Maternal and child health
- Mental/behavioral health
- Oral health
- Public health
- Public policy
- Quality of care
- Social determinants of health

The publications section offers a wide selection of online publications, including the *GIH Bulletin*, a biweekly newsletter that provides updated news and information on the field including new grants, people, surveys, and studies. In addition, a monthly feature of the *Bulletin* is an issue focus that takes a comprehensive look at a health topic or philanthropic strategy. The *Bulletin* occasionally features *Views From the Field*, which are written by grant makers who share their insights on the practice of health philanthropy. Another online publication is a series titled *Inside Stories*, which uses narratives to create dialogue around challenging issues facing health philanthropy. In addition to the aforementioned publications, GIH offers survey results of a number of foundations, which provide publications and insight into serious challenges facing the field; in-depth reports focused on contemporary health topics; a look into their grant making; meeting reports on select proceedings, speeches, and presentations; and annual reports documenting GIH's activities and operations.

The job board posts current positions offered by GIH Funding Partners. The types of positions posted range from director of grant programs, to senior grant writer, to program officer.

Lastly, GIH provides direct links to a number of organizations serving philanthropy as well as links to issues highlighted on their website, including

- access
- aging
- children/youth
- disparities
- health promotion
- health reform
- mental health
- oral health
- public health
- public policy strategies
- quality
- social determinants of health
- foundation operations

In addition to these features, agencies will find the sample documents offered on the GIH website particularly helpful for their grant writing needs. Some of the sample documents include an example of a common grant application form, grant evaluation interim report, request of proposals, terms of award, and a conditions of grant document. Overall, GIH provides an array of resources and information helpful to nonprofit agencies seeking funding.

GIH is primarily supported by funding partners: foundations and corporate giving programs whose main function and activity is charitable grant making to multiple organizations or individuals. Recommended levels of support are based on giving patterns and foundation assets. Additional support is funded through fees for meetings, publications, and noteworthy projects.

GuideStar

GuideStar (2010) gathers and publicizes information on over 1.8 million IRS-recognized nonprofit organizations. Its database includes information on agencies' missions, programs, leaders, goals, accomplishments, and needs. The information is shared with donors, funders, governing agencies, professional service providers, researchers, educators, and media to assist them in making informed funding decisions.

There are a number of benefits to membership in GuideStar, including

- free marketing, fundraising, and management tools that help nonprofits to become more effective.
- access for donors and grant makers to Charity Check and TakeAction@GuideStar. Charity Check provides grant makers with a means to verify a nonprofit's charitable status, as well as the status of supporting organizations. TakeAction@GuideStar is a resource for donors that provides information on nonprofits that are making

differences in causes that are the most important to the donors. The database is categorized by subject, such as global health, child care, and homelessness. Donors are able to consult expert analyses, read and write charity reviews, and donate online directly from GuideStar.
- resources to assist nonprofits in gathering information on potential sources of financial support for their programs.
- access to data provided by GuideStar that can encourage individuals to become involved in the nonprofit sector.

GuideStar is funded through subscriptions and licensing fees for its services and from its foundation members, programs, contributions, and program-related grants. Suggested membership contribution ranges from $5,000 to $100,000 and is based on total foundation assets or grants/giving volume.

Nonprofit Works, Inc.

Nonprofit Works, Inc. (2007), provides courses, training, grant seeking, board training, and planning resources for nonprofit organizations. In regard to grant seeking, Nonprofit Works, Inc.,

- provides coaching and training to agency staff.
- researches and selects grants that best match agencies' needs.
- assists agencies in developing grant-seeking strategies and calendars.
- writes and prepares all types of grant applications and budgets.
- reviews grant applications written by agencies to ensure the applications are correct.

Agencies must contact Nonprofit Works, Inc., directly to discuss services and fees and to schedule an appointment.

The Philanthropy Journal

The *Philanthropy Journal* (2011) is a program of the Institute for Nonprofits at North Carolina State University in Raleigh, North Carolina. The website offers expanded news coverage of nonprofits and charitable giving, as well as "how-to" articles on fundraising and giving, nonprofit leadership and management, and nonprofit communication and marketing. Additionally, the website highlights announcements regarding charitable gifts and grants; features about people and organizations in the nonprofit sphere; and calendars of fundraising events, professional conferences, workshops, and networking opportunities. Through a daily website and free weekly email bulletins, the *Philanthropy Journal* delivers nonprofit news, resources, announcements, and job postings, free of charge. Readers are also able to subscribe to free email newsletters and email alerts offering information on online webinars and Lunch 'n' Learn workshops.

Although access to the information published on the *Philanthropy Journal* website is free, paid membership opportunities are also available. Costs of memberships range from $50 for an individual member, $100 for a nonprofit member with 10 or fewer employees, $250 for a nonprofit member with 11 or more employees, $500 for a corporate or foundation member, and $3,000 for a sustaining member. Membership benefits range depending on the membership category. Examples of some of the benefits are listing in a Resource Directory; invitation to submit organization profiles, discounts on PJ Webinars and lunch workshops; access to the editor's and publisher's quarterly report on nonprofit sector news and trends; free upgrade to a premium listing for any regular job posting purchased; and invitations to join other nonprofit leaders in informal advisory-group sessions with the *Philanthropy Journal*.

Miscellaneous Affinity Groups

Not only can agencies benefit from the broad-based, nonspecific resources mentioned earlier, agencies can also profit from more topic-focused resources. There are a number of affinity groups, each organized around a common ideology and concern for a given issue. Following are brief overviews of some of the more recognized affinity groups. The groups are arranged in alphabetical order. The synopsis does not do them justice. Therefore, readers are encouraged to visit the organizations' websites to learn more about their missions, programs, and services.

> **Not only can agencies benefit from the broad-based, nonspecific resources mentioned earlier, agencies can also profit from more topic-focused resources. There are a number of affinity groups, each organized around a common ideology and concern for a given issue.**

- The Communications Network (2011) provides resources, guidance, and leadership to improve philanthropic communication.
- Disability Funders Network (2011) offers resources to enhance the amount and effectiveness of grant making that benefits individuals with disabilities.
- Environmental Grantmakers Association (2011) promotes effective environmental philanthropy through collaborative knowledge, debate, leadership, and action.
- Funders Concerned about AIDS (2011) motivates and mobilizes funders to support relevant and effective initiatives related to key issues in the HIV/AIDS sector.
- Funders' Network for Smart Growth and Livable Communities (2011) shares knowledge, fosters networks, and encourages funder leadership in an effort to assist grant makers in creating prosperous, equitable, and sustainable regions and communities.
- Funders Together (2011) supports strategic and effective grant making to end homelessness.
- Grantmakers for Children, Youth, and Families (2011) serves as a point of contact for grant makers seeking collaborative and collegial relationships with other funders concerned with children, youth, and families.
- Grantmakers for Effective Organizations (2011) promotes strategies and practices that add to grantee success.
- Grantmakers in Aging (2011) promotes and strengthens grant making for an aging society by providing connections to key people, quality resources, and up-to-date ideas about aging and issues related to aging.
- Grantmakers Income Security Taskforce (2011) assists funders and philanthropic advisors in strengthening the self-sufficiency and economic well-being of low-income families in the United States.
- Neighborhood Funders Group (2011) works with grant makers who support social justice and social change to bolster the economic and social fabric of urban and rural low- and moderate-income communities.

Information Management

Understanding and Mastery of . . . Compiling, synthesizing, and categorizing information

Critical Thinking Question: Affinity groups are organized around a common philosophy and shared concern. In what ways can organizations seeking funding benefit from affinity groups?

Summary

Critical steps in the grant-seeking process include researching grant sources, searching databases, and exploring funding resources. Grants are funded by the government and by grant-making foundations such as family, community, and corporate foundations. Funding sources can be located on a number of funding databases, such as the Foundation Center, Grants.Gov, and the U.S. Department of Health and Human Services. Once grants are identified, agencies must monitor them, on a daily basis, so they are aware of when the funds become available. Successful grant quests are often the result of the readiness of the agency to seize upon the grant opportunity when it is presented. Funding resources, such as *The Chronicle of Philanthropy* and Guide-Star, provide funding information and directories helpful to nonprofit organizations. Becoming familiar with and comfortable with grant-seeking resources will give agencies a head start on their grant-seeking campaigns.

The following questions will test your application and analysis of the content found within this chapter. For additional assessment, applying, analyzing, synthesizing, and evaluating chapter content with practice, visit **MySearchLab.com**

1. Your agency just submitted a federal grant proposal that requires the agency to match the amount of federal funds given. Which of the following grants did your agency apply for?
   a. Earmark grant
   b. Categorical grant
   c. Block grant
   d. Project grant

2. A group of concerned citizens is interested in building a temporary shelter for community members who lost their homes in a recent hurricane. They are in need of seed money to build the shelter. The best type of grant-making foundation to approach for start-up money would be a/an
   a. independent/private foundation.
   b. community foundation.
   c. operating foundation.
   d. corporate foundation.

3. Your agency is in need of grant-seeking coaching and training for your board and staff. Another agency referred you to this organization, as it provides grant-seeking courses, training, and a number of related resources for nonprofit agencies.
   a. Nonprofit Works, Inc.
   b. GuideStar
   c. Council on Foundations
   d. GrantStation

4. For many nonprofits, this database can serve as a one-stop source for searching for and applying for federal grants. It contains a clearinghouse of grant information from all federal agencies.
   a. GrantStation
   b. Grants.gov
   c. FederalGrants.com
   d. U.S. Department of Health and Human Services

5. Family foundations are independent, private foundations whose funds are derived from members of a family. In what ways do family foundations differ from independent/private foundations?

6. One of the unique features of the Grants.gov database is its iPortal. Describe two key features of this self-help portal?

7. A number of funding resource sites charge fees. What are some services that fee-based resources offer to nonprofits that free resources may not?

8. Affinity groups are topic-focused funding resources organized around a common ideology and concern. In what ways can Affinity groups assist agencies with grant seeking?

CHAPTER 10

Writing, Submitting, and Revising Grant Proposals

. . . .

Learning Objectives

- Explain the initial steps of the grant writing process.
- Describe the various elements of a grant proposal.
- Apply suggestions for writing an offline and online grant proposal.
- Describe and apply ways to avoid common grant writing mistakes.
- Describe the grant proposal review criteria and the review process.

Although grant proposals vary in terms of funding source, amount of funds requested, and structure, one thing holds true: The competition for grant money has never been greater.

Grant writing is a craft. Just like any other craft, being a successful grant writer requires developing and refining the skills needed to be competent at grant writing. Some smaller agencies may believe that funders support only larger, well-known organizations. Although this may be the case in some situations, it is not the case in the majority of situations. Grant givers fund proposals that will provide the best return for their money. For the most part, funders look for organizations with reputations for effectively managing their budgets and delivering first-rate programs and services. Grant writing does not have to be a mysterious, complicated, anxiety-producing activity. Once basic grant writing skills are honed, the skills can be transferred to a variety of grant applications.

Although grant proposals vary in terms of funding source, amount of funds requested, and structure, one thing holds true: The competition for grant money has never been greater. Therefore, it is imperative that agencies put forth the time and energy necessary to create a well thought-out and well-developed grant proposal. A successful grant proposal makes a compelling case for funding and helps the grantor to envision the impact of its support. The complexity of grant writing can be overwhelming, especially for first-time grant writers; however, by breaking the process down into manageable steps, even the most novice grant writer can be successful.

Initial Steps of the Grant Writing Process

Throughout the grant writing process, it may be helpful for the agency to keep a journal or notebook to jot down ideas. It may also be beneficial for the agency to gather documents before the writing begins. Documents that may be helpful include tax exemption certificates and the organization's bylaws. Another useful tip is to develop a grant-tracking form to keep track of grant applications, funding cycles, funding received, and other valuable information. See Appendix D for a sample grant-tracking template.

The first step to writing grant proposals is to make a plan, beginning with identifying the agency's needs and focus. Once the needs and focus are identified, potential funders can be located. As discussed in Chapter 9, there are a variety of grant-making foundations and sources that can be explored in order to find a perfect match for the agency's project.

Once a funding source is located, a draft of the grant proposal can be prepared. The grant writer must know his or her audience before penning the first sentence of the grant proposal draft. Who will be reviewing the grant application? Do the reviewers work in the agency's field? Who do they report to? Ultimately, grant-making organizations report to someone, either their board or the public. Knowing who will be reviewing the proposal is the critical step to writing the draft of the grant proposal. At times, it may be necessary to contact the prospective funder by submitting a letter of inquiry/intent; however, this is not always needed. If a letter of inquiry is submitted, the agency would await a "request for proposal," also known as an RFP. An RFP is a document that describes a project's needs in a particular area and invites proposed solutions to the needs. RFPs are an increasingly popular vehicle for funders to publicize new projects and program initiatives.

Once the agency receives an RFP from the funder, if applicable, the agency structures the final version of the grant proposal based on the funder's precise instructions on how the proposal should be prepared. Applications should be thoroughly read, with questions in each section, of the application, identified. This can be a bit tricky, as some questions may appear to be asked several times. Grant proposals must speak to each aspect of the application. Grants are extremely competitive, and reviewers often look for minute mechanical reasons to eliminate competitors. See Appendix E for a sample RFP.

Knowing the reviewers and the structure of the grant application provides the necessary groundwork to writing a winning grant proposal. The next section provides tangible information on the common elements of a grant proposal.

Elements of a Grant Proposal

There are a number of elements to a grant proposal. Depending on each grant, the sections will likely vary. Therefore, it should be noted that the proposal sections described here are representative of common sections of a grant proposal, beginning with the letter of inquiry/intent.

Letter of Inquiry/Intent

Some funding sources prefer a letter of inquiry, or letter of intent, to determine whether the agency's project falls within the funder's criteria. When a letter of inquiry is requested, it is submitted in lieu of a cover letter. Although the format and segments may vary, a letter of inquiry typically

Information Management

Understanding and Mastery of . . . Compiling, synthesizing, and categorizing information

Critical Thinking Question: Grant writing requires agencies to organize information and assess its relevancy, accuracy, and validity. What steps can agencies take to ensure that grant proposals contain relevant, accurate, and valid information?

- includes the full name and position of the agency's contact person, along with the agency's name, address, and phone number.
- includes the grant provider's full name, title, organization, and address.
- is aimed at the individual overseeing the funding program.
- presents an overview of the agency and its mission.
- explains the reason for the letter, indicates the grant category for which the agency is applying, and provides the basis for the funding request.
- provides information on what the agency does, the need/problem that will be addressed, and how the grant would be beneficial to the agency's efforts.
- presents an overview of the project.
- provides the total amount requested (if required).
- lists other prospective funders for the project.
- includes a sincere statement of gratitude to the funder.
- outlines next steps to be taken.
- is signed by the person who can speak with authority on behalf of the agency.

If the funder determines the agency, and its project fits within the scope of the grant, the agency will be invited to submit a full proposal. If the funder determines that the agency and its project are not a suitable match for the grant, a decline letter will be issued. See Appendix F for a sample letter of inquiry/intent.

For grants that do not require a letter of inquiry/intent, an agency submits a cover letter with the application. The cover letter is the agency's introduction to the grantor.

Cover Letter

Just as a job search cover letter introduces an applicant to a prospective employer, a grant proposal's cover letter introduces an agency to the funder. Both types of cover letters highlight the attributes of the applicant and how the applicant is a perfect match for what the organization is looking for (i.e., an employee or a project to fund). The only way to show how a nonprofit is a perfect match for a potential funder is for the agency to do the research. Agencies must research potential funders in advance so that the cover letter is tailored to the reader. Cover letters should be upbeat, friendly, and have personality. The grantor should be introduced to the agency and assured that the project, for which the agency is seeking funds, has the support of the agency's board. In addition, the letter should specifically state what the agency is asking for (Carlson & O'Neal-McElrath, 2008).

Cover letters are typically used when writing proposals to foundations but normally not used when applying for federal or state grants. Federal and state funders rarely request a cover letter and only want items that they specifically request. According to Browning (2001), cover letters should be written after an agency completes the entire proposal; this allows the person writing the proposal to connect the agency's accomplishments, highlighted in the proposal, to the person who will be making the decision to make the agency's vision come true.

Quality cover letters

- are concise (no more than one page with three to four paragraphs maximum), clear, and accurate.
- do not simply duplicate information found in the proposal; they add new information of interest to the reader.
- should stand out, in a positive way, among competing organizations.
- demonstrate the agency's knowledge of the funder.
- charm the reader and display enthusiasm.
- communicate positively about how the agency's qualifications fulfill the funder's requirements.

Proposal cover letters are business letters, which can be written in a number of formats. The two most recognized formats are the full-block and modified block formats. The full-block letter format places all elements of the letter flush with the left margin. A blank line is placed between paragraphs, thereby eliminating the need for indenting. A modified block format is a bit less formal than a full-block format. The return address, date, complimentary closing, and signature block are placed right of center. The remaining elements of the letter are flush with the left margin. As with the full-block format, paragraphs are not indented, and a blank line separates paragraphs.

The elements of a proposal cover letter include the following (in this order):

- *Agency letterhead.* The letterhead should provide the agency's name, address, and phone number.
- *Date line.* The date line should be placed two to three lines under the letterhead. It should reflect the date the proposal application will be sent to the funder.
- *Inside address.* The inside address is placed two to three lines under the date line. The first line includes the grantor's corporate contact person's courtesy title (e.g., Mr., Mrs., Dr.) followed by his or her full name and title. Line 2 is the addressee's business title. Line 3 includes the grantor's name. Line 4 is the street address and/or post office box. Line 5 contains the grantor's city, state, and zip code. All information in the section should be confirmed with a phone call or an email, as this information tends to change frequently.
- *Salutation.* The salutation is placed two lines under the inside address. It normally begins with the conventional greeting, "Dear," followed by the personal title (e.g., Mr., Mrs., Dr.), last name of the addressee, and a colon. It is particularly important that the letter be directed to a specific person. If the name and title of the person is unknown, the foundation should be called to verify the name of the addressee and his or her title.
- *Text or body.* The text or body of the cover letter begins two lines following the salutation. It is single spaced, with one blank line left between paragraphs. This section is usually divided into three or four paragraphs. The opening paragraph is short and concise. It introduces the organization to the reader and states what the organization does, why the organization is writing the funder (i.e., tells the funder how much money the agency is requesting and why), and how the organization learned of the grant. The next two or three paragraphs are the main body of the

cover letter. The main body should be succinct. The agency should describe its purpose and how it matches with the grantor's mission of funding priorities. It should also state that the agency's board is in full support of the project for which funding is sought. Relevant information that may not be included in the proposal itself should be included. In the closing paragraph, agencies should include a statement about what the funding opportunity can mean to the agency's target audience. It should also mention any action the agency will take (e.g., contact the grantor in 10 days to ensure receipt of the proposal), along with an invitation for the grantor to contact the agency. The name and phone number of the agency's contact person should be included. This name may differ from the name of the person who signs the letter.

- *Signature block.* The signature block appears four or five lines below the complimentary closing. It contains the signature of the executive director or the chair of the board of directors, or both. Below the signature, the signer's name should be typed, including the signer's first name, middle initial, last name, and position title.
- *Enclosure notation.* The enclosure notation is placed two lines below the signature block. It reminds the reader of any enclosure that is included with the cover letter (i.e., grant proposal). Examples of enclosure notations are Enclosure, Enc., Enclosures (2), 2 Enclosures, and Enclosures. Agencies can also include the types of enclosures (i.e., grant proposal), although this is not necessary.

Letter writing is a skill. A well-written cover letter can captivate the reader and put the agency one step closer to its funding goals. See Appendix G for a sample cover letter.

The first page of the actual grant proposal is the title page. The format of the title page must follow the funder's formatting instructions. Errors in the title page can leave the grantor with an unfavorable first impression.

Title Page/Cover Sheet

The standard title page/cover sheet typically includes the project's title; the names of the principle investigator/s; the agency's name, address, phone, and fax number; the name and address of the funder; the project dates; the type of grant; the amount of funding requested; the grant period; and the signatures of the agency's authorizing personnel. The format, number of items, and order of items on the title page/cover sheet vary. Thought should be given to the title of the project. Titles should be as descriptive as possible though concise; titles over 60 letters or characters are discouraged. Projects should be identified with key words and clear adjective-noun combinations that accurately reflect the content of the project. Fillers should be avoided (e.g., An Intervention to Determine . . .). It is beneficial to examine titles of related projects that have been funded. Because funded grants are permanent records and are accessible to the public, jargon should be avoided, as limited and dated language can hamper readers' understanding of the project. See Appendix H for a sample template of a title page/cover sheet.

The next part of a grant proposal is the abstract/executive summary/introduction. This section serves as the synopsis of the proposal. This is among the first page or pages of a grant proposal; however, it is one of the last sections of a proposal that is prepared.

Abstract/Executive Summary/Introduction

The abstract/executive summary/introduction section is one of the shortest sections of the proposal; however, it is one of the most important and most read sections. It often forms the first impression, and for readers who are not the primarily proposal reviewers, it may be the only section they use to become acquainted with the proposal. This is where an agency convinces a grantor that its proposed program, project, or service is important. Remember, funders are investors shopping for outcomes, and therefore, the abstract/executive summary/introduction section must convince the grantor that the project is a good investment. According to Carlson and O'Neal-McElrath (2008), due to the gravity of its significance, this section may be the most difficult to write. Because of its brevity, it requires the writer to capture the most crucial elements of each part of the proposal in a concise style.

> Remember, funders are investors shopping for outcomes, and therefore, the abstract/executive summary/introduction section must convince the grantor that the project is a good investment.

A strong abstract/executive summary/introduction

- is concise (typically limited to one page) and does not exceed the specified word limit.
- is limited to key points included in the proposal.
- highlights key points that are important to the funder and fit with the grantor's priorities.

According to Yuen and Terao (2003), the funder's comprehension of the organization's proposal from the abstract/executive summary/introduction may be the basis used for determining the ranking of the proposal. Therefore, it is vital to make sure that the abstract/executive summary/introduction is well written and that it succinctly and accurately represents the proposal.

Typically, the abstract/executive summary/introduction includes the following information:

- Legal name of the agency, address, and name of the executive director; name and contact information of the person completing the proposal or application;
- Type of organization, including information about IRS 501(c)(3) nonprofit status;
- Organization's mission statement;
- Proposed program title and specific needs that will be addressed;
- The project's purpose, goals, and objectives;
- The agency's philosophy;
- The agency's track record with other funders;
- Success stories;
- Demographics of target population (i.e., age, ethnicity, gender, socio-economic status, special needs);
- Reason the project is important; a description of the community or regional needs and challenges that the project will address;
- Specific interventions planned;
- What the project will accomplish by the end of the specified time period;
- Location/s, and setting/s of the project;

- List of the board of directors of the organization and a brief biography of the board members;
- Total number of volunteers, especially those working on the project, total number of full-time and part-time staff;
- Link between the proposed project and the funder (i.e., relevance of the project to the funder);
- Proposed cost of the project and the amount requested from the funder, the granting period, and acknowledgment of any previous support from the funder in the last 5 years;
- A sincere statement of gratitude to the prospective funder.

The abstract/executive summary/introduction may also be used for the agency's project summary and for a number of other reports such as a report to the board of directors and to the community. It may also be used internally by the agency for its own reporting as well as for orientations to various constituencies (Yuen & Terao, 2003). See Appendix I for a sample abstract/executive summary/introduction.

For some grant proposals, the abstract/executive summary/introduction is followed by a literature review. The literature review lets grantors know that the agency has done background research necessary to undertake the project.

Literature Review

Some grant proposals require a literature review. Literature reviews highlight published writings on subjects related to the project for which the agency is seeking funding. They provide crucial background information for understanding the need for the proposed project. Literature reviews are not new contributions to the body of knowledge but are cohesive accounts of relevant bodies of both ideas and arguments of others. A basic literature review is comprised of three sections, the introduction, body, and conclusion.

- *Introduction.* The introduction identifies the topic, area of concern, or issue, and points out what has been published regarding overall trends, conflicts, conclusions, and gaps in research. The introduction also establishes the writer's reason for the literature review, the criteria used for analyzing the literature, and the sequence of the literature review.
- *Body.* The body of the literature review groups studies, reviews, and other types of literature according to common themes. Articles are summarized with more significant studies garnering more space.
- *Conclusion.* The conclusion summarizes the most significant articles and studies, points out significant flaws or gaps in research, and summarizes issues and areas related to the project. This section concludes with a link between the literature review and the subject of the grant proposal (i.e., the project for which the agency is seeking funds).

A substantial literature review achieves the right amount of breadth and depth. It is not exhaustive, but is comprehensive; it includes all relevant works. In addition, it is neither too broad nor too narrow. It provides an analysis of a portion of published works in order to provide a broader understanding of what has been comprehensively investigated in the past and in what areas valuable work is still needed. See Appendix J for a sample of a literature review embedded in a needs/problem statement.

Following the literature review is the needs/problem statement. The needs/problem statement answers the question, "What is the need that our organization will address?"

Needs/Problem Statement

The needs/problem statement provides the impetus behind a grantor's conclusion that the proposed project meets a vital societal need. It is a key element of the grant proposal and makes a clear, well-supported statement of the problem that will be addressed. It addresses the need and how the agency's clients are affected. A needs/problem statement is both quantitative and qualitative in nature. According to Coley and Scheinberg (1990), a needs/problem statement examines what is happening that requires attention, makes an effort to explain why it is happening, and describes what is currently being done to address the need. There are a number of resources that organizations can use to collect data and information about the need/problem. Information can be collected through both formal and informal means. Various types of data can be helpful in supporting the needs/problem statement. Some of these include historical, geographical, statistical, qualitative, and quantitative data. Local, regional, and state government planning offices are a wonderful resource and can likely provide background information. Highlighting these findings in the needs/problem statement can be valuable.

A quality needs/problem statement

- provides the working hypothesis that guides the development of the proposal.
- presents the purpose for developing the proposal.
- clearly relates the addressed need with the agency's mission.
- matches the funder's mandate/mission.
- focuses on the people the agency serves as opposed to the agency's needs.
- describes how the agency came to realize the problem exists.
- describes what is currently being done to address the problem.
- uses narratives anchored in hard data.
- is well supported with comparative statistics, expert opinions, and trends.
- substantiates the agency's ability to respond to the need (i.e., discusses the agency's history or expertise in dealing with the problem).
- describes the specific manner through which the need might be resolved.
- discusses the consequences of not dealing with the problem; presents a sense of urgency but not a sense of defeat.
- provides information on sustainability plans.
- explains what will happen to the project, program, or service once funds have been exhausted.

A well-written needs/problem statement avoids circular reasoning or tautology. According to Yuen and Terao (2003), circular reasoning is like a dog chasing its own tail; it will go round and round in a circle. In other words, circular reasoning pertains to the presentation of the absence of the agency's solution as the actual problem;

Planning and Evaluating

Understanding and Mastery of . . . Analysis and assessment of the needs of clients or client groups

Critical Thinking Question: What precautions can an organization take to ensure that its needs/problem statement avoids circular reasoning?

it supports the premise with the premise rather than a conclusion. For example, an agency seeking funds to support a drug rehab intervention may state that the intervention is needed because the intervention does not exist. Some may argue, however, that the drug rehab intervention does not exist because it is not needed. The statement has no end and no beginning. To eliminate circular reasoning in a needs statement, agencies should state exactly why the community needs the proposed project. For example, what would happen if the drug rehab intervention were not funded? In other words, needs/problem statements should focus on why the intervention is needed and what would happen if the intervention were not funded.

Needs assessments identify gaps in programs and services and describe discrepancies between what is and what should be. Well-written needs assessments can convince the grantor that what the agency proposes to do is crucial and that the agency is the best choice to do it. See Appendix J for a sample needs/problem statement.

Once the needs are explained, the organization must describe what it intends to do about the problem. This is achieved through carefully written goals and objectives.

Goals and Objectives

The needs/problem statement is the driving force to the development of goals and objectives. Goals and objectives provide a map to the project, influence the design of the program, determine the methods and strategies needed to achieve the goals and objectives, and guide the evaluation process.

The terms *goals* and *objectives* are sometimes confusing and often used interchangeably; doing so, however, is inaccurate. Goals are derived from an agency's mission statement, and in the case of grant proposals are linked back to the needs/problem statement. They are overarching and long-term in nature and are not necessarily measurable or achievable in the short run. Goals help agencies to operationalize their mission statement. According to Netting, Kettner, and McMurtry (1993), goals are broad statements of expected outcomes. Goals are statements of hopes or expectations. On the other hand, objectives are narrow, precise, relatively short term, tangible, concrete, and measurable. Objectives clarify the details for each goal in measurable terms, including the process to achieve the goals and the expected outcomes. If the proposal is funded, the stated objectives will likely be used to evaluate the progress of the funded project, program, or service. Browning (2001) suggests using the acronym S.M.A.R.T. When writing objectives, one should make them *S*pecific, *M*easurable, *A*ttainable, *R*ealistic, and *T*ime-bound.

Here are some guidelines for writing quality goals and objectives:

- Link goals and objectives to the agency's needs/problem statement.
- Use concrete terms to form the basis of objectives (e.g., to identify, to reduce, to increase, to assess).
- Avoid general terms to form the basis of objectives (e.g., to understand, to fully appreciate, to know, to have an awareness of).

- Include all relevant groups and individuals in the target population. Who is involved?
- Provide details and realistic numbers. Each objective must be measurable.
- Develop a feasible timeline to accomplish the objectives. When will the objectives be met? What is the finish date for the goal?
- Develop means to measure each objective. What tools or instruments (e.g., surveys, focus groups, tests) will be used to measure each objective?
- Budget money for the measurement (evaluation) of the objectives.

It is an excellent idea to start thinking about program evaluation when developing goals and objectives. Agencies should select outcomes that can be measured and tracked. In addition, organizations should reflect on the types of data that will be needed, where the data will come from, and how the data can be regularly collected.

Some grant applications will ask for a project goal and a list of objectives and rarely will the funder explain what it means by a project goal and a list of objectives. At other times, the funder's guidelines may provide different definitions of what it defines as goals and objectives. If the funder provides such guidelines, agencies should go with what is on the funder's application. See Appendix K for a sample of a goal and its objectives.

Once the goals and objectives are written, the design/methods/strategies of the project are described. This portion of the grant proposal provides methods for achieving the goals and objectives.

Program Design/Methods/Strategies

Following the development of the project's goals and objectives, methods for achieving those goals and objectives are specified. The program design/methods/strategies must include sound models based upon the nonprofit's or others' success. It must be closely tied to the program's objectives and needs/problem statement. This section of the grant proposal is typically long; therefore, use of subheadings can help keep the reader from getting confused. The subject of the subheadings will depend on the project and the grant proposal. Examples of subheadings include setting, participants, and interventions. The program design/methods/strategies must be suitable and adequate for answering the question and/or solving the problems expressed in the goals and objectives section.

Here are some guidelines for writing the program design/methods/strategies section:

Interventions and Direct Services

Understanding and Mastery of . . . Skills to facilitate appropriate direct services and interventions related to specific client or client group goals

Critical Thinking Question: The program design/methods/strategies section of a grant proposal must include sound models. How can an agency make certain that its proposed program design, methods, and/or strategies are reliable and valid?

- Although this section does not require an introductory paragraph, it is useful to begin with a few sentences that provide an overview of the time frame for the project.
- Write this section as though the reader knows nothing about your agency. Assuming the reader is familiar with the agency can be a colossal mistake, as the proposal will likely be vague and confusing.
- Justify the rationale for choosing the project's methods or activities by including support statements, such as citing research, expert opinions, personal communications, and past experience. Explain why these methods or activities were chosen.

- State who will be served and how they will be chosen.
- Connect the program design/methods/strategies to the requested resources in the proposal budget. Ensure that the activities are feasible for the proposed budget.
- Clearly state how the data will be collected and how the data will address each of the project's objectives. Plan for measurable results.
- Accurately present the activities the agency will be undertaking. State who will perform each activity and include any related resources that will be needed.
- Justify the course of action that will be taken. For example, the most economical method should be used as long as the method does not sacrifice or compromise the quality of the project, program, or service.
- If possible, agencies should include tables or figures to support the narrative of this section. A flow chart of the features of the project can also be created. The chart can illustrate how the segments of the chart interrelate, where staff may be needed, and what staff will be expected to do. The chart can also be used to identify the types of facilities and support services that will be needed. The tables, figures, or charts can be embedded in the narrative or placed at the end.
- Highlight the innovative characteristics of the proposal that set the proposal apart from other proposals that may be under consideration.
- End the section with a paragraph that discusses expected outcomes, including expected results and practical implications of the results.
- Supplementary data, references, work schedules, timetables, and other details should be included in appendices and not embedded in the body of the narrative. These documents, although supportive of the proposal, may distract the reader if embedded in the narrative. When placed as addendums, readers have instantaneous access to the information.

The program design/methods/strategies section can be written in a number of ways. Regardless of the way it is written, it should contain a hook. The hook tailors the description of the project to the interest of the funding source. It aligns the project with the purpose and goals of the funder. This is a vital component of the program design/methods/strategies section because it determines how compelling the proposal will be to the reviewers. See Appendix L for an example of a program design/methods/strategies section.

Once the proposal has a comprehensive program design/methods/strategies section, the proposal writer can turn to the evaluation plan. The evaluation plan is perhaps one of the most valuable sections of the proposal for the grant reviewers.

Evaluation Plan

The evaluation plan has become increasingly essential in the development of proposals. Funders want to ensure that agencies will be using objective measures to evaluate their projects, and they want hard evidence that their support was beneficial. Therefore, it is essential that agencies clearly and carefully define how success will be determined.

So what is an evaluation plan? An evaluation plan involves carefully collecting information about a project or program in order to make necessary decisions regarding the project or program. Specifically, an evaluation plan

- clarifies the purpose of the project.
- chronicles the progress of the project and assesses the effectiveness of the project in meeting its goals and objectives.
- assists in making strategic decisions.
- aids in re-examining the course of the program.
- obtains feedback from the individuals served as well as from community members.
- assists in determining whether the project's outcomes can be ascribed to the project itself or to other factors.
- helps to determine if an impact were made on the identified need.
- facilitates project improvement midstream, if needed, to insure the project's success.
- improves delivery methods to be more cost-effective.
- provides information that can assist funders.
- examines and describes successful projects for duplication somewhere else.

The type of evaluation an agency undertakes depends on what the agency wants to learn about the project, and what the agency and funder need to know in order to make critical program decisions. There are a variety of different types of evaluations; some are highly structured and some are less structured. The type or types of evaluations chosen should reflect the planned frequency of data collection for evaluation purposes. Funders are interested not only in the type of evaluation but also in the planned frequency of data collection. According to Duggan and Jurgens (2007), the three most common types of evaluations are process evaluations, outcome evaluations, and impact evaluations.

- *Process evaluations.* Process evaluations, also known as formative evaluations, are descriptive and ongoing. They evaluate how well a project or program was designed, implemented, and completed. They measure actions that were taken, decisions made, and procedures followed in developing the project or program. They describe the services delivered, how the program operates, and functions that the program carries out. Process evaluations are useful for monitoring program implementation, for identifying changes that need to be made, and for improving the project or program.
- *Outcome evaluations.* Outcome evaluations, also referred to as summative evaluations, help in identifying whether a project's outcomes have been achieved. They provide information for decision-making regarding future programming needs. Many agencies are proactive in documenting results of their programs in order to have something to show potential funders in their grant proposals.
- *Impact evaluations.* Impact evaluations assess the changes that can be attributed to a particular project, intervention, program, or service. Impact evaluations are structured to answer the question, How would the outcomes have changed if the project, intervention, program, or service had not been undertaken? Duggan and Jurgens (2007) state that impact evaluations are not as common in the human services field as are process and outcome evaluations. One of the main reasons is that impact evaluations require measurement over long periods of time, and change is sometimes slow or difficult to maintain.

There are numerous tools that can be used to collect evaluative information. The choice of evaluation tools should be based on the project's goals and objectives and the funder's requirements, if applicable. Some common tools include questionnaires, surveys, checklists, interviews, observations, focus groups, case studies, and documentation review. Agencies should choose the tools that have the greatest potential of providing the necessary information.

Here are some tips for writing the evaluation plan of a grant proposal:

- Determine whether quantitative and/or qualitative methods will be used for data collection.
- Describe the evaluation methods that will be used and the rationale for the methods.
- Ensure that the evaluation section is consistent with the program design/methods/strategies section.
- Explain how the evaluation plan will measure whether the project met its objectives.
- Describe who will conduct the evaluation.
- Specify how the agency will use the findings.
- Provide a clear plan on how the evaluation results will be disseminated.
- State whether the agency will be conducting an internal evaluation or hire outside expertise.

Evaluation plans guide agency efforts from start to finish and end when all necessary information has been collected. They require the collection of appropriate data before, during, and after the project. If the evaluation design cannot be developed before the project begins, then a thorough review of the project design may be necessary. Needs/problems and project designs that are not well defined and carefully examined may be difficult to evaluate. Quality evaluation plans can lead to winning proposals. See Appendix M for a sample evaluation plan.

The next piece will describe what to include in the organizational information section of the grant proposal. This section establishes the nonprofit's credibility in delivering the proposed project.

Organizational Information

The organizational information section of the grant proposal provides a concise and convincing argument of the agency's credibility to accomplish the goals and objectives of the project. It offers general background information about the agency and is typically no more than two pages in length. Information included in the organizational information section should be limited only to those items that position the nonprofit as the best agency to implement the proposed project. Common elements of this section include

- the full, legal name of the agency, including its legal status (i.e., 501(c)(3)).
- the location of the agency headquarters as well as other operating sites.
- the history of the organization, including when it was founded, who founded it, and for what purpose.

- the agency's mission statement.
- an overview of the nonprofit's programs (or those most relevant to the project).
- a description of the people and/or constituents served, as well as the reason for serving the identified people and/or constituents.
- the agency's most significant achievements, including any awards or noteworthy recognitions received.
- financial information, including the organization's budget, annual donations, and how money is raised.
- a concise statement about the agency's board, staff, and volunteers, and their qualifications.
- the position of the nonprofit in the community, including its role and collaborations with other organizations.
- a statement of what sets the agency apart from other agencies, and what makes the agency uniquely positioned to be successful with the project.

Again, the purpose of this section is to establish the organization's credibility, and to convince the grantor that the organization can accomplish the goals and objectives of the project. Information included elsewhere in the proposal should not be included in this section unless it is in an abridged form. See Appendix N for an example of an organizational information section of a grant proposal.

The next section of the grant proposal is the budget section. The budget section describes the program's administrative and project costs and delineates costs to be met by the funding source and funds that will be provided by other parties.

Program's Budget and Budget Narrative

A budget is a plan that estimates the cost for implementing a project and the allocation of these costs. With increased accountability and the need to monitor how nonprofits spend public money and donations, well-developed budgets are vital (Yuen & Terao, 2003).

The budget spells out both administrative and project costs. It usually consists of a spreadsheet or table with detailed line items and a budget narrative, or budget justification. The budget narrative is attached to the budget and explains how the budget will be spent, why each item is needed, and why the budget is cost-effective. The narrative must not only tell the grantor why the funds are needed, but must provide a clear picture of the significant impact that can be made with the requested funds. It must be professionally written in order to assure the funder that the agency is financially competent. The program's budget and budget narrative section convey how much the project will cost, provide an explanation of each expense, and list expected income that will be earned or contributed.

There are three common budget categories: direct costs, indirect costs, and in-kind contributions. Perhaps the most crucial part of the grant proposal's budget is the direct cost section. Direct costs are expenses for activities or services that can be identified specifically to benefit the project. Direct costs can be directly assigned to a project fairly easily and with a high degree of accuracy. These are expenses grantors will fund such as:

Personnel-related expenses:

- Salaries or wages for full-time, part-time, temporary, and/or seasonal project personnel (excluding general operating/administration costs for the organization)
- Benefits that the agency pays for each employee, such as payroll taxes, FICA, state unemployment insurance, medical benefits, life insurance, paid sick leave, retirement 401(k), childcare allowances, and Worker's Compensation insurance
- Cost-of-living increases
- Bonuses
- Increases in legal minimum wage
- Uniforms, clothing, footwear
- Hiring costs such as employment ads, drug screenings, background checks, license verification, education verification, and employment verification
- Fees for consultants and contractors
- Volunteer costs

Facility-related expenses (prorated as needed):

- Facility expenses such as rent/mortgage payments
- Utilities, including electricity, gas, and water
- Telecommunications, including phones, cell phones, Internet, pagers, fax, along with the costs of equipment, installation, long-distance and monthly charges
- Maintenance, repairs, and inspections for equipment and major electrical, gas, and plumbing systems
- Maintenance contracts, equipment lease fees, and depreciation.
- Furnishings

Other expenses:

- Expendable or consumable supplies, including letterhead, envelopes, pens, books, publications, copy paper, binders, and ink cartridges
- Postage, shipping, and courier services
- Special-purpose office equipment, computers, and software
- Travel expenses (e.g., mileage, parking, and airfare) of project personnel by purpose of travel. (e.g., training seminars, professional development, technical assistance, meetings, and conferences)
- Marketing and advertising, including ad design, production, displays, brochures, flyers, printing, public relation campaigns, and press releases

Indirect costs are those costs that are incurred for common or joint objectives and, therefore, cannot be easily identified with a particular project. They are sometimes referred to as overhead costs. Most grants do not fund indirect costs unless the grant specifies an approved indirect cost rate. The following costs are normally indirect, but may be approved directly under exceptional circumstances (i.e., the costs can be specifically identified to work performed under the project or the grantor accepts the cost as part of the project's direct-cost budget):

General operating/administration:

- Salaries and fringe benefits of administrative and clerical personnel unless under unusual circumstances (e.g., the project requires extensive data accumulation, analysis, and entry)
- General office supplies (paper, pencils, pens, markers, file folders, binders)
- Accounting and financial audit expenses
- General-purpose equipment maintenance and repairs
- General-purpose computer software
- Fundraising expenses
- Membership dues

Rather than a donation of cash, an in-kind contribution is a donation of goods or services. Examples of in-kind contributions include the following:

- Pro-bono professional services
- Donated space, such as the use of a building and its utilities in order to hold a meeting
- Advertising, such as public service announcements
- Training for staff and volunteers
- Volunteers
- Project staffing and oversight
- Transportation

According to Kramer (2011), the value of in-kind contributions is estimated based on their "fair market value." For example, what would the nonprofit pay if the good or service were not donated? For instance, the value of volunteers for an unskilled position might be assessed based on the minimum wage. Documentation of in-kind contributions is just as vital as the documentation of other expenditures. For in-kind contributions, both the donation and the value of the donation must be recorded along with the basis for determining their value.

In-kind contributions often impress grantors because they show evidence of community support for the agency and its programs. They are also a terrific means of showing funding sources how the agency will get the most out of each of the grantor's dollars.

Here are some tips for writing the program's budget and budget narrative section:

- Include all items requested by the funding source.
- Include all items paid for by other sources.
- Include costs that will be incurred at the time the project is implemented.
- Include direct costs, indirect costs (if applicable), and in-kind contributions (if applicable).
- Verify that all budget amounts are justified.
- Double-check all figures for accuracy.
- Organize the budget so it is reader friendly.
- Ensure that the proposed budget is sufficient to perform the tasks described in the program's design/methods/strategies section.

It is beneficial for organizations to anticipate that the funds from the grant will not be the only support for the project. This consideration should be given to the overall budget requirements, especially those items most likely to be subject to inflation. Agencies should refrain from inflating cost predictions but strive to account for possible inflation.

A well-prepared budget justifies all expenses and is consistent with the abstract/executive summary/introduction section of the grant proposal. When developing the budget, special consideration should be given to the following:

- *Equipment purchases.* Equipment should be the type of equipment permitted by the funder.
- *Additional space and equipment.* If additional personnel will be hired to assist with the project, additional space and equipment may be needed.
- *Increases in the cost of insurance.* If the project requires additional office space, the cost of insurance for the additional space should be considered.
- *Salaries.* Salaries in the proposal should reflect the salaries of the staff working at the agency.
- *Indirect costs.* If indirect cost rates apply, the indirect and direct costs should reflect the funder's approved formula.
- *Matching funds.* When matching funds are required, the contributions to the matching funds should be removed from the budget, unless otherwise the application specifies differently.

See Appendix O for a sample proposal line-item budget.

Most grantors want assurance that their funds are an investment in the future of the agency. Therefore, potential funding sources want to know the agency's plans for future project sustainability. This portion of the grant proposal is known as the other funding/sustainability section.

Other Funding/Sustainability

> Funders want to ensure that their contributions will produce positive results and that the project can persevere in the future, whether it is with or without additional assistance from the grantor.

Funders want to ensure that their contributions will produce positive results and that the project can persevere in the future, whether it is with or without additional assistance from the grantor. If sustainability is a required component of the grant and the project cannot be sustained with relative assurance after the grant period ends, it likely is not a smart idea to apply for the grant. In the other funding/sustainability section of the grant proposal, nonprofits describe their long-term continuation play or vision for the project after the grant period has ended. Specifically, agencies must explain how they will raise funds to carry on the project, including future grant requests and/or any reserve money that may be available at the conclusion of the grant period. This future funding plan can contain a combination of different sources and strategies. There are a number of recommendations for creating a sustainability plan. Clarke (2009) recommends charging fees for services; developing entrepreneurial business ventures, such as selling merchandise at consignment shops; creating membership programs that charge dues; developing major-gift programs; using the Internet for online donations; securing corporate sponsorships for funding charity events; establishing employer-based fundraising through federated campaigns such as United Way; and connecting with local, state, or federal agencies that fund related projects.

Here are some guidelines for writing the other funding/sustainability section:

- Detail specific future fundraising strategies.
- Illustrate minimal reliance of future grant support.
- Present a solid blueprint of how the agency will raise money to continue the project or program in the future.
- Assure that the fundraising plans are practical, given the agency's resources.
- Refrain from indicating that the organization will approach the grantor for additional funding.
- Include a list of other funders approached on behalf of the project.
- If needed, include information on hiring additional staff or independent contract workers.

See Appendix P for a sample of a funding/sustainability statement.

In addition to all of the aforementioned sections of grant proposals, sometimes additional items are requested. These items are referred to as supplemental materials.

Supplemental Materials

The majority of the previously mentioned sections are almost always required when submitting a grant proposal; however, additional supplemental items may also be required. Some of the more commonly requested supplements include

- IRS tax-exempt verification letter
- list of board of directors and their affiliations
- list of staff experience
- financial statement for the previous year
- current fiscal year's budget
- next fiscal year's budget
- letters of commitment or endorsements from individuals who will be affected by the project (e.g., a collaborating organization)
- lists of clients served
- annual report

Although less common, the following supplements may be requested:

- Organizational literature (e.g., an agency brochure, an article, a newsletter)
- List of current funding sources
- List of programs, projects, and services
- Program statistics
- Resumes of project staff
- Agency's by-laws
- Diagrams for building request or equipment request
- Documentation that the request was approved by the board of directors

It is crucial to carefully review the RFP to determine which supplemental materials are required, if any, so that all necessary documents are submitted. On another note, nonprofits should not submit supplemental materials that are not requested.

Once the proposal is finished, it should be reviewed and proofed by a neutral third party. The proposal should be reviewed

- for continuity, reasoning, and clarity.
- to ensure that it does not contain any unsupported assumptions, unnecessary language, or jargon.
- for neatness. Proposals should be carefully inspected to ensure consistency from the first page to the last page.

Constructive criticism can provide the agency with an opportunity to iron out glitches and strengthen the proposal before it is reviewed by the funder.

Once the proposal is ready, it is crucial to copy the entire application before mailing it to the grantor. The copy should be kept with the agency. This can be used to track the results of the agency's grant applications. The original should be clipped together with a paperclip or bound with clamps or hard covers. Agencies should check with the grantor to determine the grantor's preference. A well-organized and appealing proposal package can impress the funding organization.

The proposal should be placed in an envelope and mailed or submitted per the grantor's instructions—before the deadline. Enough time must be allotted for the proposal to reach its destination. Missing a deadline can result in missing a funding opportunity.

Should the agency not hear back from the funding source 1 week after mailing the proposal, a follow-up call should be placed. The follow-up call is a means for the agency to verify that the proposal was received and to ask when the results can be expected. The date when the follow-up call should be made, and the date the call is placed, should be marked on a calendar.

More and more grantors now request online grant applications. The process may require some modifications.

Online Grant Applications

Agencies must adapt their grant proposals to a paperless format with limited space. Not only does this require some transition, online applications limit the amount of space for each section of the proposal. Although this may take some getting used to, it can actually lead to easier and faster proposal development. Online grant applications can substantially improve the efficiency and accuracy of the grant proposal submission process. Applications can easily be reviewed online from remote locations. Organizations can receive email notifications of the status of their applications. In addition, some programs can automatically verify the agency's IRS tax-exempt status.

As with technology in general, there are instances when problems can arise, such as servers going down preventing the agency from accessing the site and meeting the funder's deadline. If the application is submitted online, agencies should not wait until the application due date. The day the grant is due, many people are trying to submit their applications and servers often crash. If the application does not go through by the deadline, it is rare that the funding agency will approve an extension. With possible setbacks aside, more and more grantors are choosing to streamline their application process and go paperless.

Whether submitting grant applications online or offline, grant writing mistakes can have a serious impact on the success of the proposal in securing funds. Even the most minor mistakes can have an adverse effect on the credibility of an agency's grant proposal.

Grant Writing Mistakes

There are some common grant writing mistakes that more often than not stem from inexperience with grant writing, unfamiliarity with the grantor, or insufficient resources, such as time. According to Hired Gun Writing, LLC (2011b), some common mistakes include writing proposals that are generic; lack detail or are excessively detailed; lack measurable objectives or specific action plans; contain grammatical and typographical errors, circular reasoning, unrealistic or inadequate cost analysis; and lack quantitative data. Other mistakes include writing proposals that

- are hastily assembled.
- are too lengthy.
- are written in first person.
- use too many complex words, jargon, acronyms, buzzwords, and/or clichés.
- state objectives that are far different from the funder's objectives.
- include false, inaccurate, or embellished cost estimates.
- include impossible promises or inflated rhetoric.
- overkill a point.
- include discrepancies between the program design/methods/ strategies section and the budget section.
- have sections that do not logically follow previous sections.
- do not follow the grantor's formatting instructions.

Administration

Understanding and Mastery of . . . Developing budgets and monitoring expenditures

Critical Thinking Question: One common grant writing mistake is when there are discrepancies between the program design/methods/ strategies section and the budget section. How can these discrepancies be eliminated?

It can be quite easy to make some of these common mistakes. However, avoiding these pitfalls can be just as easy. To increase the likelihood of getting the proposal accepted, the grant should be carefully proofed by a neutral party who is knowledgeable and experienced in grant writing. A proposal should be sound, before it is submitted.

Once the grant proposal is ready for submission, it is forwarded to the funding source, by the funder's deadline. The next step is the review process.

The Review Process

Proposals are reviewed with varying degrees of rigor and competition. Typically, proposals are scored using grading rubrics or a similar means to ensure consistency of evaluations across review criterion.

Proposal Reviews

According to Yuen and Terao (2003), for the majority of federal human service grants, proposal review committees are formed from experts in the fields of practice, as well as representatives from various constituencies. These committees are responsible for the review and recommendations of all submitted proposals.

The review criteria are the guidelines that the reviewers follow when determining which proposals to fund. Each funding agency or organization will have its own specific criteria on how to format and prepare the proposal. Applying agencies should keep these criteria in mind when developing proposals, as reviewers will likely assign scores to these criteria or may evaluate the proposal's responsiveness to the criterion. In some cases, proposals that do not address the merit criteria are returned without review. Examples of criteria include the following:

- *Significance.* Is the project significant? Does it address an important need/problem? What will be the effect of the project on the field?
- *Approach.* Is the design, methods, and evaluation reasonable and appropriate to the goals and objectives of the project? Does the applying agency acknowledge potential areas of concern and consider alternative approaches?
- *Innovation.* Is the project original (e.g., will the project be launched as opposed to maintained)? Does the project employ innovative approaches and concepts?
- *Competence.* Are the project facilitators/implementers qualified and competent to carry out the project? Do they have the necessary level of experience and skills needed to complete the project? Does the team bring integrated and complementary expertise to the project?
- *Match/fit.* Is the project a good match for the mission of the funding source? Will it help the grantor meet its overall funding goals? Is it an appropriate project for funding based on the grantor's funding objectives?
- *Quality.* Is the quality of the proposed project substantial?
- *Environment.* Will the environment in which the project will take place contribute to the overall probability of success? Is the support of the agency and available resources adequate for the success of the project?
- *Overall impact.* What will be the overall impact of the project on the clients, customers, and community? What will be the potential benefits to society?
- *Timely.* Was the proposal submission deadline date met?
- *Preparation.* Does the proposal meet the grantor's preparation requirements, such as formatting and page limitations?

Although the grant review process can vary depending on the type of grant (i.e., project grants, categorical grants, block grants, and earmark grants), the federal grant review process typically consists of the following steps:

1. Review committee members are invited to review a set of grant proposals before a committee review meeting. Each committee member is assigned as primary readers for several proposals, and as secondary and tertiary readers for the remaining few. Proposals are reviewed, evaluated, and scored.

2. A review committee meeting is held, which may last 4 to 5 days. During the meeting, each primary reader is responsible for presenting a summary of the proposals for which he or she was assigned. The primary reviewers also provide their critiques and comments of the proposals.
3. Following the primary readers' presentations, the secondary reviewers present their comments and underscore disagreements and agreements they have with views of the primary readers.
4. The tertiary readers then state their observations.
5. Following the presentations and commentaries of all the readers, proposals are given priority ratings and the proposal committee votes and makes its recommendations to the funding decision makers. The funding decision makers have the final say on which grant/s will be funded.

The review process for foundation grants may differ from the review process for federal grants. The following steps are typical of the foundation review process:

1. Foundation staff verifies the applicants' eligibility and conducts a review of the application materials in relation to the grant proposal guidelines.
2. Representatives of the foundation conduct an internal review of the proposals. Occasionally, they may schedule a site visit to gain a better understanding of the project. If needed, additional documents may be requested. The internal reviewers create analysis reports and present them to members of a grant review panel.
3. The grant review panel, comprised of community members and members of the board of directors, review the grant applications independently and then meet to discuss the merits of each request. Applications are given a priority rating, and recommendations for funding are presented to the full board of directors.
4. The board of directors reviews the recommendations, and the approved applicants are notified, usually in writing.

The aforementioned illustrations are only examples of review processes. Each funder's review process, whether a governmental agency or a foundation, will likely differ in some way. For example, with some review processes, the grant reviewer's ratings remain confidential. In such cases, the median or average scores for each proposal are calculated, and these scores are used to determine recommendations for funding. It is helpful for agencies to seek information on the review process, before writing and submitting grants. This will help ensure the likelihood of a positive outcome.

Once the review process is complete, letters are issued to the grant applicants. Agencies whose proposals have been chosen for funding will receive a terms of award letter, or a letter of agreement. The terms of award letter serves as the official notice of the award. It is the grantor's obligating document.

Terms of Award Letter

Congratulations! The grant was funded! Now what? First and foremost, the terms of award letter must be carefully read. The terms of award letter specifies the obligations of both the grantor and the grantee. It states the terms and conditions of the award. Award letters vary considerably from the explicit to the brief. Some, and at times all, of the following elements are included in terms of award letters:

- Terms of the award including, but not limited to, payment, conditions on activities, and expenditures of funds.
- Reporting requirements including, but not limited to, financial reports and progress reports.
- Public policy requirements including, but not limited to, ongoing reporting, financial conflicts of interest, and protection of human subjects.

Once the terms of award letter is received, agencies should immediately verify their address with the award committee to ensure that the grant funds arrive properly. Every award letter should be followed up with an acknowledgment letter on the agency's letterhead within a week of receipt of the award letter. According to Queenin (2011), the acknowledgment letter should include a thank you, a declaration that the awarded funds will be used as stated in the grant proposal, a statement of how the funds will benefit the work of the nonprofit, and a statement that the funder is not benefitting by making the grant. This statement will fulfill IRS regulations.

The agency should update its website and list the grantor as one of its funding sources. For larger grants, a press release should be issued (with the grant maker's permission). Agencies should keep funders informed through newsletters, news coverage, emails, and miscellaneous publications. Funders should be invited to events that are related to the funded project (Queenin, 2011). Copies of all articles appearing in print media should be saved and included in future grant requests. This shows future grant administrators that the agency is a gracious recipient of the funds, gives credit where credit is due, and confirms that the project is worthy of funding.

Terms of award letters are, of course, the goal of a grant proposal. So what if the grant proposal results in a rejection letter? Receiving a rejection letter from a funding source can be an enormous letdown; however, the best way to handle a rejection letter is by remaining optimistic and creating a plan for getting funding elsewhere.

Rejection Is a Step to Future Success

> When a grant proposal is rejected, it does not mean that the proposal was rubbish; it may just mean that there was another proposal that better matched the grantor's criteria.

The acceptance rate for funding of projects varies depending on the funding source. On average, the success rate for most federal grants is less than 25%. Even the most experienced grant writers receive a rejection letter at one time or another. When a proposal is rejected by a funder, it is essential not to take the rejection personally. Be optimistic. When a grant proposal is rejected, it does not mean that the proposal was rubbish; it may just mean that there was another proposal that better matched the grantor's criteria. If possible, organizations should request the reviewers' evaluations and comments. When asking, it is imperative to be gracious, courteous, and polite. Information regarding possible flaws, weaknesses, and recommendations can be valuable resources in preparing future proposals. If the grantor funds projects on a regular basis, agencies should inquire when the next round will take place and whether the organization is eligible to reapply. If the grantor permits the agency to reapply, the proposal should be revised to fit the funder's needs. If it is necessary to start over again and locate another funder, agencies should search for grantors that are more likely to fund the project. Nonprofits should apply to as many grantors as possible. Agencies should not assume that all proposals are funded and will be fully funded. Sometimes projects are funded for less than the amount requested. By applying for a number of grants, agencies increase the probability of receiving the financial backing they need in order to fund their projects. Lastly, nonprofits should be persistent. Information obtained from rejected proposals can provide critical insight into the proposal's weak points. This is a tremendous opportunity to learn ways to improve the proposal and work out any quirks in order to increase its likelihood of future funding success.

Summary

A successful grant proposal takes more than the agency's inspiration and a funding source; it takes knowledge and skill to leave a positive first impression on the funder and the reviewer. Winning grants effectively reveal the what, why, when, how, where, and who of the project. They clearly illustrate how the agency's clients and the community will benefit from the project. They are related to the grantor's mission and help the grantor meet its goals and objectives. Planning ahead is an important step to successful grant writing. Keeping a journal, collecting necessary documents, and writing a first draft can help an agency get an early start on its grant writing. Becoming familiar with and skilled in writing the various sections of a grant proposal is crucial to writing successful proposals. More and more funding sources are requesting online applications to improve the efficiency and accuracy of the submission process. Agencies must modify their grant proposals to this paperless format that limits the amount of space for each section of the grant proposal. Regardless of whether the grant application utilizes a paper or paperless format, following application guidelines is just as important as avoiding common grant writing mistakes. Becoming familiar with both will enhance the probability of receiving a terms of award letter. If the grant is not funded, agencies can gain helpful insight from the review process. This information can strengthen future proposals and future funding success.

The following questions will test your application and analysis of the content found within this chapter. For additional assessment, applying, analyzing, synthesizing, and evaluating chapter content with practice, visit **MySearchLab.com**

1. You have just completed a grant proposal and are in the process of writing a cover letter. Which of the following guidelines should be followed when writing the cover letter?
   a. The cover letter should be at least 3 pages long.
   b. The salutation should contain the addressee's first name.
   c. The signature block should appear four or five lines above the complimentary closing.
   d. The text or body of the cover letter should be divided into three or four paragraphs.

2. When writing goals and objectives it is important to
   a. use general terms.
   b. avoid restricting the goals and objectives to a specific group.
   c. link the goals and objectives to the funder's criteria.
   d. include a timeline.

3. You are developing an evaluation plan to include in a grant proposal. You will be evaluating the program's design, implementation, and completion. The best type of evaluation to meet these needs would be a/an
   a. formative evaluation.
   b. outcome evaluation.
   c. impact evaluation.
   d. summative evaluation.

4. At times, a grantor will request supplemental materials to include with a grant application. Which of the following is an example of a supplemental item?
   a. Other funding/sustainability
   b. Agency's by-laws
   c. Budget narrative
   d. Executive summary

5. Some funders may request that agencies submit a letter of inquiry/intent. What is the purpose of a letter of inquiry/intent?

6. One of your colleagues has just finished writing a goal for a grant proposal. The goal reads, "To assist clients in adjusting to their disabilities." Rewrite the goal by following the guidelines for writing quality goals and objectives.

7. Many grantors request online grant applications. The process for submitting an online application may require the agency to make some modifications. Describe two modifications that must be made when submitting online applications.

8. The review process for foundation grants differs from that of federal grants. Describe one major difference between these two review processes.

CHAPTER 11

Implementing, Managing, and Closing a Funded Project

Once the grant proposal has been accepted, and funding for the project is approved, the agency begins the process of carrying out the grant proposal. In the majority of cases, there is a window of time between receipt of the award letter and the beginning of the funding period. These precious days can be put to good use by taking advantage of the time.

Taking Advantage of Time

Most grants are awarded for a specified period, the funding period. The grant award letter will include a date on which the funding period will begin. The funding period is the total time for which support of the project has been approved, along with any extensions, if applicable. Typically, the funding period begins 30 days or more from the date of the letter. During the period between the receipt of the letter and the start of the funding period, agencies should get organized.

Organizing 101

Agencies should use this time to get organized. FederalGrants.com (2011b) offers a few basic suggestions for getting organized; these include creating a binder or a folder, meeting with the team, and putting a record-keeping system in place.

A binder or folder should be created and set aside specifically to house all the paperwork related to the grant. Examples of paperwork to include in the binder or folder are a copy of the grant application, the grant award letter, the signed grant contract, and all correspondence to and from the funder. Placing the binder or folder aside will help ensure that it does not get mixed up with the agency's other paperwork. This is essential so that the information is easily accessible should the funder call. The funder will be impressed when the documents can be easily retrieved on short notice.

Learning Objectives
- Apply tips on getting organized before the funding period.
- Select and develop data collection instruments; organize and analyze data.
- Apply suggestions for monitoring grant expenditures.
- Keep everyone apprised of funded project; share information with constituents.
- Describe the process for submitting reports and closing out grants.

Another task that can be completed while waiting for the start of the funding period is to hold a meeting with the team to review the grant and the tasks that must be completed as outlined in the grant. Keeping the staff involved and aware of progress during the waiting period is paramount. If personnel will be hired and/or volunteers will be recruited, the recruitment process can get under way. Responsibilities can be assigned, and preliminary tasks can be completed.

Lastly, a record-keeping system can be put in place. The record-keeping system can track the progress of the project, including the number of people served, the results of the evaluations, and other matters of importance directly related to the money awarded to the nonprofit.

Selecting and Developing Data Collection Instruments

There is a wide variety of data collection instruments available to assist nonprofits in gathering information needed to evaluate the project, program, or service. When agencies use existing tools, they should assess the instrument's prior use as well as the instrument's validity and reliability (Duggan & Jurgens, 2007). When agencies develop their own data collection instruments, the tools must be well developed and well thought out. Examples of data collection tools are

- anecdotal record form: used to record critical events that transpire during the development and implementation of the project. Anecdotal record forms provide "human stories" of significant incidents that take place during various stages of the development and implementation of the project.
- in-person surveys: used to gain answers to basic questions.
- direct or participatory observations: used when the person who is collecting the data is a participant in the project.
- expert review checklist: used for both process and outcome evaluations. It is given to experts in the field and used to critique all aspects of the project that the nonprofit would like reviewed. The expert review checklist can be in the form of a Likert-type survey, where experts are asked to rate various components of the project.
- focus group protocol: used to collect data about focus group members' opinions or reactions to the project, program, or service. The focus group protocol is the evaluation tool used to assess the actual focus group. It consists of a number of questions regarding the project, program, or service that are asked to sample groups of constituents.
- formative review log: is used to review the project during its formative phase. It is divided into three columns. The first column records the part of the project that is being evaluated. The second column records the evaluator's reactions, comments, questions, and/or recommendations. The third column records the actions taken as a result of the reviewer's feedback (Center for Education Integrating Science, Mathematics and Computing (CEISMC), n.d.; Duggan & Jurgens, 2007).
- implementation log: used to gather information about the actual implementation of the project. It consists of four columns. The first column describes what was

planned to happen. The second column describes what happened. The third column is used to comment on the differences between what was planned to happen and what actually happened. The fourth column is reserved for any additional questions, regarding the implementation of the project (Center for Education Integrating Science, Mathematics and Computing (CEISMC), n.d.; Duggan & Jurgens, 2007).

- interview protocol: used to collect consumers' and constituents' reactions to the project, program, or service. The interview protocol is typically in the form of a survey.
- questionnaires: used to systematically obtain data about the project from large numbers of respondents. Questionnaires are perhaps the most used data collection tool. When developing a questionnaire, these tips are worth considering:
  1. Use language appropriate to the average reading level of the group completing the questionnaire.
  2. Use vocabulary familiar to the respondents. Avoid ambiguous words. Bear in mind the respondents' frame of reference. Do not ask for opinions on subjects that are unfamiliar to the respondents. Consider whether the respondents have enough information to answer the questions.
  3. Ensure that the words used in the questionnaire have the same meaning for each respondent. Make sure to give culturally appropriate options in choices of answers.
  4. Avoid absolute language such as "all," "always," and "never" in the stem of questions (e.g., On a scale ranging from "strongly agree" to "strongly disagree," all participants benefited from this program).
  5. Avoid general terms such as "often," many," and "usually."
  6. Include only a single idea in each question. Avoid merging two or more ideas into a single question.
  7. Be specific when asking questions about quantity or frequency.
  8. State all questions neutrally; do not include biased items.
  9. Pay attention to how the questionnaire is formatted. For example, when using a Likert-type scale, ensure that all items match the scale and that all interval alternatives are equal.

Information Management

Understanding and Mastery of . . . Using technology for word processing, sending email, and locating and evaluating information

Critical Thinking Question: In what ways can technology be used to develop data collection instruments and organize and analyze collected data?

The selection of data collection tools should be based on the agency's data collection goals and objectives. The advantages and disadvantages of each tool should be weighed and considered so that agencies select the best instruments that have the greatest probability for providing the information needed.

After data has been collected, agencies must organize and analyze the data. The type of data that has been collected will determine how the data should be organized and analyzed.

Organizing and Analyzing Collected Information

The type of data an agency collects will ultimately determine the type of analysis that is performed. When there are lots of numbers to crunch, spreadsheets or data analysis tools are beneficial. On the other hand, if the data is non-numeric, such as the case of qualitative data that consist of a lot of text, identification of patterns and themes is

When there are lots of numbers to crunch, spreadsheets or data analysis tools are beneficial. On the other hand, if the data is non-numeric, such as the case of qualitative data that consist of a lot of text, identification of patterns and themes is necessary.

necessary. Analyzing qualitative data can be a fascinating but complex task. Qualitative data must be categorized in terms of emerging themes or key topics of interest. Glasser and Strauss (1967) and Lincoln and Guba (1985) recommend the following steps for organizing and reorganizing focus group data: Review data and resolve any record-keeping discrepancies; code the responses based on similarities; complete another round of sorting to form smaller, more meaningful key categories; and compare suggested findings with existing literature. Hall (2011) suggests the following steps for organizing and analyzing qualitative data in general: Read and review the data; write notes while reviewing the data, code the data, interpret the data, and draft a report detailing the findings.

Agencies should not wait until the end of their project to organize and analyze collected information. Interim analyses of data can help ensure whether the data is logical, valid, and was properly entered. The analyses can also measure trends, and if problems are revealed during the course of the grant, solutions can be developed.

Monitoring Finances

Agencies are responsible for monitoring grant expenditures for accuracy and timeliness. Money must be spent according to the funding source's guidelines as well as according to agency policies. Maintaining up-to-date accounting information throughout the life of the grant is crucial. Agencies must keep excellent records, which verify that expenditures are within the allocated budget.

Selby-Harrington, Donat, and Hubbard (1993) recommend setting up meetings between budget personnel and staff to review accounting policies and forms. They also recommend organizing budget information by designing a chart that lists each accounting form, its purposes, completion instructions, required signatures, and routing directions. The chart is a helpful tool, especially at the start of the grant period.

Up-to-date accounting information is necessary to ensure that expenses are within the allotted budget. Selby-Harrington et al. (1993) suggest that agencies compare expenditures with anticipated expenses at predetermined times (e.g., quarterly) during the budget year. This information can help organizations determine whether unexpected needs can be met and can help with the planning of future budgets. Monitoring grant expenditures is only one instance where timelines are essential. Effective grant management requires agencies to adhere to timelines as specified by the funding source.

Administration

Understanding and Mastery of . . . Developing budgets and monitoring expenditures

Critical Thinking Question: Accurately monitoring grant expenditures is crucial. How can agencies ensure that their grant expenditures are accurately monitored when they are collaborating with other agencies on one grant?

Adhering to Timelines

Looking toward the future, anticipating potential problems, and making sure that tasks are completed properly are ways in which an agency can ensure adherence to timelines. One of the first steps to adhering to a timeline is to break the timeline down into manageable steps and share the timeline with agency staff. Some of the larger steps can be broken down into smaller steps. The duties and their subsequent deadlines can be assigned to various project staff. Developing sequential checklists to guide staff members in completing the tasks can help the process by verifying when tasks are completed. In addition, it can alert the agency when a task may need to be assigned to another staff member (Selby-Harrington et al., 1993).

> **One of the first steps to adhering to a timeline is to break the timeline down into manageable steps and share the timeline with agency staff.**

Even with the most careful planning and the most detailed timeline, problems will occur. If handled properly, obstacles can become valuable learning experiences that can guide future projects.

Keeping the Communication Channels Open

Regardless of the type of grant, the scope of the project, or the size of the agency, communication between the agency, its staff, agency constituents, and funding sources is key. Keeping everyone apprised of progress and obstacles can provide stakeholders with a sense of partnership in the funded project. Communication among project partners can be enhanced by holding regular meetings to update parties on grant activities and to seek their feedback. Other means of communicating with project partners include creating and disseminating newsletters and bulletins, mailing letters, sending faxes, posting information on agency websites, writing articles for local newspapers, and sending emails. Not only are these means of communication helpful in keeping everyone involved with the grant in the loop, so to speak, the information shared can be helpful when developing and writing future reports, continuation applications, manuscripts, and other such documents.

Disseminating Information

The impact and results of a funded project often rest in the success of an organization's dissemination activities. The goal of dissemination, according to the National Center for the Dissemination of Disability Research (NCDDR) (2009), is utilization. In other words, dissemination can lead to decision-making, making revisions, and/or taking other actions to improve the outcomes of the project. Effective dissemination is the process of matching the information shared with the correct format, language, content, and media that is the best match for the targeted audience. Well-implemented dissemination activities can lead to agency recognition and awareness. Publishing reports and journal articles should not be the only method of disseminating information. Dissemination methods must be oriented toward recipients, and methods to disseminate the information should be varied. Some additional ways to publicize funded projects are through workshops, conferences, meetings, CDs, newsletters, websites, letters, person-to-person contact, newspaper articles, list serves, and radio and television interviews.

The timing of the dissemination is critical. The initial planning of the dissemination strategy should take place early on in the grant implementation process. This will provide the organization with sufficient time to connect with other organizations, develop opportunities to share information with stakeholders, involve experts in the field, and budget for dissemination strategies that will effectively reach targeted groups (NCDDR, 2009).

An effective dissemination plan is not designed to reach all targeted parties in one vast sweep through a single event of publication. According to NCDDR (2009), the most successful plans choose from a wide array of tools and tailor strategies to meet the nonprofit's dissemination goals.

Submitting Continuation Applications

In cases where an extension or continuation is needed, the grantee must submit a written request to the funding agency. Some funders require that requests for extensions or continuations be submitted at least 90 days before the termination date. Such applications typically entail that the agency provide information on the agency's progress in meeting the grant's goals and objectives, as well as information on the allocation of resources and management of project activities. According to Selby-Harrington et al. (1993), the application usually includes a budget and plan for the next year and an overview of staff responsibilities. In addition, any changes made to the original project or budget must be justified. According to Selby-Harrington et al. (1993), depending on the funding source, some continuation applications are reviewed by agency staff, by outside reviewers, or by both. Whatever the case, the agency must be available to justify its decisions, provide additional information about its proposed plans, and answer questions that may arise during the review process.

Submitting Required Reports

The schedule for submitting required reports is typically set by the funding source. The grant contract will include guidelines on the reporting requirements, including what to report and when the reports are due. The types of reports requested will vary depending on the type of grant and the funding source; however, most granters will want detailed financial statements, information on the project's outcomes or expected results, and whether the agency delivered on the promises as stated in the grant proposal (Satterfield, 2007). Even if the funder does not require a report, it is best to submit one. A well-written grant report can have a positive effect on how grantors view the agency and can impact the probability of the agency securing future grants. Although the types and number of reports will likely vary, common information requested in reports include

- a summary of the original request and any modifications made to the original request, if applicable. If modifications are made, the effects of the adjustments should be stated.
- an overview of data collection strategies and methods along with a report of interim findings.

- a summary of the results and overall impact of the project. A synopsis of measurable outcomes as detailed in the original request and progress made toward achieving these outcomes. An explanation of any outcome changes, including why the outcomes changed and the effect the changes had on the project.
- an overview of the strengths and weaknesses of the project. If unexpected challenges were faced, the report should include how the challenges were resolved. If the findings can benefit other organizations, the report should provide information on how the information will be shared with others.
- information regarding any additional resources that were acquired since the launch of the project, including other funding sources, along with the amounts received, and other resources such as services, supplies, publicity, and people. A summary of a sustainability plan on how the agency will secure additional funding for the future should also be included.

> **Planning and Evaluation**
>
> Understanding and Mastery of . . . Skills to evaluate the outcomes of the plan and the impact on the client or client group
>
> **Critical Thinking Question:** What evaluative information should an organization include in its grant report? Explain.

Reports should be well-written and well-organized. Satterfield (2007) recommends organizing the report using subheadings and bullet points; including charts and graphs to illustrate findings and results; incorporating stories about people who were helped; keeping reports brief; adhering to deadlines; and saying thank you. When grant reports are well-written and well-organized, agencies can bolster their relationships with grantors and set the stage for future funding.

Closing Out the Grant

A grant is considered closed when all the work, as stipulated in the grant contract, has been performed to the satisfaction of the funder, or upon the termination date as specified in the award. In some cases, the grantor will send a notice to the grantee indicating the anticipated termination date. Typically, the closing-out process requires the nonprofit to complete and submit various forms and reports. The following illustrates the typical steps involved in closing out a grant:

> **A grant is considered closed when all the work, as stipulated in the grant contract, has been performed to the satisfaction of the funder, or upon the termination date as specified in the award.**

1. The nonprofit receives a notice from the funder that the grant will be expiring. This is usually sent 30 to 60 days before the termination date.
2. Upon receipt of the letter, or before the termination of the grant, the agency reviews its expenditures to ensure that
   - all services performed, and goods received within the grant period are processed and accounted for in the financial documents. Services and goods not received before the termination date of the grant are typically not covered by the grant, unless authorized by the sponsor.
   - all open requisitions are followed up on to ensure timely receipt of goods and services, as well as timely receipt of invoices from vendors.
   - all expenditures are allowable.

- credits and charges, which were not permitted under the grant contract, are transferred to an appropriate budget.
- there are no unposted charges or credits.
- indirect costs are accurate.
- cost share pledges are met, when applicable.
- negative balances are resolved.
- termination paperwork is completed for all staff funded by the grant, and if required, payroll changes are made for staff members assigned elsewhere in the agency or to other grant projects.

3. A final project/program progress report is developed. The final project/program report is usually required for any grant that is terminated. The report may also be required for any award that will not be extended through a new segment of the project. In preparation for developing the final project/program progress report, any programmatic reports that were previously submitted should be reviewed. The final project/program progress report typically includes

- a summary of progress toward meeting the originally stated goals and objectives. If the grant proposal contained quantifiable goals, the report should address whether the project produced the desired results. Numbers can be helpful in reporting the overall impact of the project. If the project did not meet the agency's initial goals and objectives, the agency should provide an honest assessment about what may have gone wrong.
- a list of significant results and outcomes, whether positive or negative. The report should speak to the project's overall impact. Positive and measurable outcomes should be highlighted. This allows the funders to see the positive impact their funds have made on the lives of people and on their community.
- a list of publications funded by the grantor, which credit the funding source.
- information on the lessons learned. The final project/program progress report should include information on the project's major takeaways, including challenges and problems the agency encountered and ways the agency would resolve the challenges in the future. Describing ways in which problems can be overcome shows the grantors that the organization is unlikely to make the same errors in the future.
- the agency's sustainability plan. The sustainability plan should outline a plan for continuing the project. The plan helps to persuade grantors to renew the grant or even increase the amount of funding in the future.

Clark and Fox (2006) recommend a number of tips for preparing an effective grant report. These tips include emphasizing important information; using charts and graphs; including stories; keeping to the point; meeting deadlines; and saying thank you.

- *Use subheadings, bullet points, and bold text.* Emphasizing important information by using subheadings, bullet points, and bold text makes the information stand out in the report. Overemphasizing text in the report, however, can defeat the purpose.

- *Use charts and graphs.* Charts and graphs should be used to display key successes and findings. Charts and graphs can bring attention to important points.
- *Include anecdotes and testimonials.* Including stories, anecdotes, and testimonials from those who benefited from the project can make the report more appealing. To give the report more life, photographs can be included.
- *Make it succinct.* Funders have numerous reports to read, so reports should be limited to the maximum number of pages allotted by the funding source. If a page limit is not stipulated, agencies should limit the report to no more than 10 pages.
- *Meet the deadline.* Deadlines are not only important when submitting a grant application, they are also important when submitting final reports. If the deadline cannot be met, grantors should be contacted.
- *Exercise courtesy.* Thanking the funder is not only the right thing to do, it can increase the agency's likelihood of obtaining future funding.

Other individuals, who played a key role in implementing the grant, should have an opportunity to review the final progress report and provide input before submission of the report.

4. The agency assembles the closeout package. The contents of the closeout package are determined by the funding source. Agencies must review the final reporting requirements to ensure that all required documents are included. The closeout package typically includes the following:
   - *Final fiscal status report.* The final fiscal status report is a financial statement that includes all costs related to the project, including salaries, travel expenses, and equipment purchases. Each funding source will have its own guidelines for the final fiscal status report. Generally, funders will want to see how the actual budget matched the original budget. The final fiscal report should be as thorough as possible, as some funders may request an audit of the agency's financial records.
   - *Disposition of property and supplies report.* The disposition of property and supplies report describes the agency's plan for proper disposition and allocation of property, equipment, and supplies purchased with grantor's funds.
   - *Final project/program progress report.* The final project/program progress report is described in step 3.
5. The agency returns the closeout package to the funding agency by the due date, usually within 3 months after the grant ends. The agency ensures that all reports included in the closeout package contain the grant number or other identifying information.

All grant-related electronic records, files, and paperwork should be retained for 7 years. This includes all communication with the grantor; meeting agendas, minutes, and sign-in sheets; copies of all accounting documents; and any other documents related to the program, project, or service funded by the grant. These files and documents should be clearly inventoried. The inventory list should include the physical location of the boxes and containers. Each box and container should be marked with its contents. All documents, boxes, and containers must be retained in a safe and secure manner.

It is the agency's responsibility for reviewing the final reports and other items as part of the closeout process. It is critical to close out the grant in a timely and efficient manner. Doing so demonstrates the agency's ability to effectively manage grants. Turning in forms on time and accurately documenting how the funds were spent are vital to the nonprofit's continued grant success. This information becomes a component of the nonprofit's funding history. Depending on the grant, this information may be shared with the grantor's reviewers should the nonprofit submit a future proposal to the same funding source. It cannot be stressed enough the importance of maintaining integrity throughout the grant management process.

Arranging for the Disposition of Property and Supplies

Supplies purchased with grant funds are usually property of the granting agency. If the property is no longer needed to sustain the grant activities, the property must be offered for return. When the grant is completed, it is the agency's responsibility to submit all required reports and arrange for the proper disposition or final allocation of equipment, property, and supplies. When preparing a budget for a grant proposal, agencies must identify equipment and supplies needed for their projects. In addition to identifying needed equipment, federally funded agencies, as well as other grantors, often request that applicants state the disposition plan for the property and supplies once the project is completed. It is imperative that agencies thoroughly review the grantor's disposition options, as the options will vary. Some funders use an acquisition cost of $5,000 as a benchmark to determine whether the equipment must be returned to the funding source. For example, if the equipment has an acquisition cost under $5,000, the agency may be permitted to retain or sell the equipment without compensating the funder. On the other hand, tangible property with a value over $5,000 may need to be returned, or if retained or sold, the agency may need to reimburse the funder for its share of the fair market value of the equipment.

Looking Ahead: Preparing for Future Grants

The best time to prepare for a future grant is before the current grant expires.

The best time to prepare for a future grant is before the current grant expires. The knowledge and skills put forth in carrying out the current grant can improve the possibility of landing another grant. One of the many benefits of having a successful funding experience is that the transition between one funded project to the next can be a less complicated one. An agency's grant experience will likely enhance the organization's likelihood of being awarded future funding. The agency will have experienced staff, volunteers, and other individuals who were instrumental in the success of the project. This seasoned team can work together to determine the best and most suitable source of future funding. Through their efforts, the next successful grant proposal will be right around the corner.

Summary

Implementing, managing, and closing a grant are perhaps the most gratifying periods of a funded project. These phases are when the agency's preliminary work comes to fruition and the projects, services, and programs are carried out and lives are changed. Once an agency learns that its proposal will be funded, the agency should take advantage of any available time, before the start of the funding period, to get organized. Creating a binder or folder for documents related to the grant, getting together with the team, and creating a record-keeping system are some valuable tasks that can be accomplished while waiting for the funding period to begin. During the funding period, there are a number of activities that will occupy the agency's time; effectively managing these activities is critical in the successful implementation of the funded project. These activities include selecting and developing data collection instruments; organizing and analyzing collected information; monitoring finances; adhering to timelines; keeping the communication channels open; disseminating information; and submitting continuation applications and required reports. Once the funding period concludes, the agency must close out the grant and arrange for the disposition of property and supplies. The satisfaction of implementing, managing, and closing a grant can serve as a springboard of confidence that agencies can use when applying for future grants.

The following questions will test your application and analysis of the content found within this chapter. For additional assessment, applying, analyzing, synthesizing, and evaluating chapter content with practice, visit **MySearchLab.com**

. . . .

1. You need to develop a data collection instrument to gather information needed to evaluate the effectiveness of your agency's food pantry program. Specifically, you need to evaluate the project during its development and implementation. Which of the following tools is best suited for your evaluation?

   a. Formative review log

   b. Expert review checklist

   c. Implementation log

   d. Anecdotal record form

2. When developing a questionnaire it is important to

   a. ensure that the words used in the questionnaire have the same meaning for each respondent.

   b. use absolute language such as "always," "all," and "never."

   c. merge two or more ideas into a single question.

   d. be general when asking questions about frequency or quantity.

3. You are working on a funded project and realize that the project will not be completed by the deadline you originally provided to the funder. Therefore, you need to request an extension. Typically, the extension must be filed at least

   a. 30 days before the termination date.

   b. 60 days before the termination date.

   c. 90 days before the termination date.

   d. 120 days before the termination date.

4. You are new to an agency and have been asked by the executive director to go through boxes of grant-related paperwork and electronic records and dispose of the documents that are no longer needed. Based on your executive director's request, it should be safe to destroy records that are

   a. over 1 year old.

   b. over 3 years old.

   c. over 5 years old.

   d. over 7 years old.

5. You just received a grant award letter and the funding period will begin in 3 weeks. What can you do in regard to the grant to make the best use of your time before the funding period begins?

6. Nonprofits are responsible for monitoring grant expenditures for accuracy and timeliness. What are the two tips that can assist an agency in effectively managing grant expenditures?

7. Despite the type of grant or size of the agency, keeping everyone apprised of the project and possible obstacles can provide stakeholders with a sense of partnership in the funded project. Describe two ways in which communication between the agency and its constituents can be enhanced?

8. After closing out a grant, an agency must arrange for the disposition of equipment, property, and supplies. How does an agency determine what needs to be returned, if anything?

Appendix A

Organizational Chart of a Nonprofit's Fundraising Team

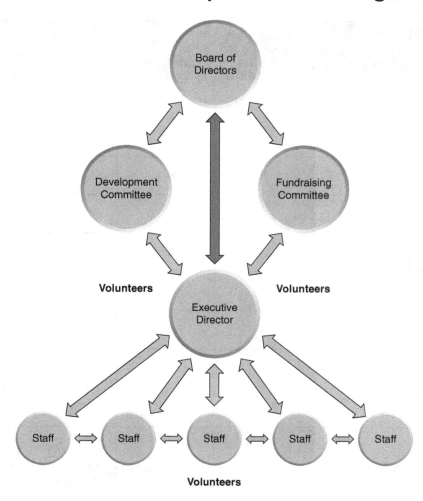

Generic Gift Chart for $2,000,000 Goal

Gift Amount ($)	Number of Gifts Required	Number of Prospects Required	Subtotal ($)	Cummulative Total ($)	Cummulative Percentage
200,000	1	4	200,000	200,000	10
150,000	1	4	150,000	350,000	18
100,000	2	8	200,000	550,000	28
75,000	3	12	225,000	775,000	39
50,000	5	20	250,000	1,025,000	51
38,000	8	32	304,000	1,329,000	66
25,000	10	40	250,000	1,579,000	79
13,000	12	48	156,000	1,735,000	87
5,000	12	48	60,000	1,795,000	90
Under 5,000	82	328	205,000	2,000,000	100
Totals	**136**	**544**		**2,000,000**	**100**

Generic Fundraising Campaign Timetable

Fundraising Campaign	Jan	Feb	March	April	May	June	July	Aug	Sept	Oct	Nov	Dec
Annual Donor Recognition Dinner			X									
Recruit Fundraising Committee Members				X	X							
Identify and Cultivate New Donors/Prospects				X	X	X						
Regular Fundraising Committee Meetings				X	X	X	X	X	X	X	X	X
Agency Branding and Marketing Campaign				X	X	X	X	X	X	X	X	X
Solicit Major Gifts						X	X	X	X	X	X	X
Direct Mail Campaign								X	X	X	X	X
Annual Fundraising Monte Carlo and Dinner									X			
Annual Haunted Forest Fundraiser										X		
Holiday Craft Show Fundraiser											X	

Appendix D

Grant-Tracking Template

Funder Name and Contact Information	Past Support (if Applicable); Purpose	Funding Cycle; Due Date to Submit Request	Suggestions from Funder	Actions Taken	Follow-up and Comments

Appendix E

Sample RFP from a City Targeted to Improve the Job Placement Rate of Individuals with Disabilities

Request for Proposal (RFP) for:
The City of XYZ's
Job Placement Improvement Project for Individuals with Disabilities
RFP #12260JD-TD

Summary

The City of XYZ is seeking proposals to reduce the city's unemployment rate of individuals with disabilities. The city's focus is to support the efforts of city-based nonprofit organizations to implement initiatives at the city level.

Under this Request for Proposals (RFP), the City of XYZ is inviting local nonprofit organizations to apply for funding initiatives to develop comprehensive approaches to assist individuals with disabilities with job placement.

Applicants may request up to $75,000 for the planned project. However, available funding is dependent on the amount of funding in the city's 20XX budget.

If your organization wishes to be considered, the City of XYZ is requesting a written proposal that speaks to the points detailed in this RFP. Applications will be accepted on April 20, 20XX.

Project Overview

The purpose of this RFP is to provide interested organizations with information needed to prepare and submit a proposal for a Job Placement Improvement Project for Individuals with Disabilities. The City of XYZ intends to use the results of this process to fund a number of city-wide initiatives and activities, the goal of which is to improve the low job placement rates of individuals with disabilities who reside in the City of XYZ. The funding available through this RFP will assist the city in reducing these unemployment rates through innovative programs created and implemented by nonprofit organizations.

Priority ranking will be given to projects which support the employment aspirations of individuals with disabilities, provide job skills training to individuals with disabilities, create linkages with area employers, and produce projects that can serve as city-wide, long-term models.

This RFP is for projects which range from 1 to a maximum of 3 years to complete.

Salaries and benefits for existing staff and routine administrative and operating expenses, with the exception of project-related professional and legal fees, are not eligible for funding.

Available Funds

A total of 300,000 will be made available in the first year of funding under this RFP. Funds awarded under this solicitation will be for the period of July 1, 20XX through June 30, 20XX. Based upon satisfactory performance and availability of funds, successful proposers receiving funds under this RFP may be eligible to apply for additional awards, on a year-by-year basis through June 30, 20XX.

Eligibility

Funding eligibility is limited to nonprofit organizations located within the City of XYZ and nonprofit organizations located outside the city but who provide programs and services to the residents of the City of XYZ. Organizations must provide documentation of their nonprofit 501(c)(3) status. Applying organizations must have a governing Board of Trustees and an Executive Director who is responsible for the daily operations of the agency. Applying organizations must be fiscally sound and must have the appropriate organizational competencies to receive and administer public grant funds.

Administrative Requirements

For the organizations selected, city funds will be granted through the City of XYZ.

Reports of both project and fiscal activity will be required to ensure that projects follow the purpose stated in the original proposal. Funded organizations will be required to submit one-page, written reports to the City of XYZ annually and upon completion of the project. Reporting requirements will be identified in the agreement between the successful proposers and the City of XYZ. Should an organization not use the funding for the approved purpose stated in its application, the organization will be required to reimburse the City of XYZ the full award amount and may be subjected to additional expenses.

Termination of Agreement

The City of XYZ may cease this agreement at any time at its sole discretion by providing 30 days written notice to the grant recipients. Should a grant recipient choose to terminate this agreement, the grant recipient must deliver a 30-day written notice to the grantor. In addition, the grant recipient must refund the City of XYZ all payments received for activities not completed. Such termination will require the grant recipient to submit its refund within 30 days of said termination.

Submittal of Application

Applications will be accepted on or after April 15, 20XX. The closing date for the receipt of applications will be June 15, 20XX. Applications will be accepted and considered received on time if the application is received at the address below, by 4:00 p.m. on June 15, 20XX.

Applications may be mailed or hand delivered. Faxed applications will not be accepted. Applications must be signed by the organization's Board Chairperson or Executive Director.

Submit one original, signed application to:

The City of XYZ
1 Main Street
XYZ, State, Zip
Attn: The Job Placement Improvement Project for Individuals With Disabilities

Application Content and Format

1. Cover sheet on the agency's letterhead. The cover sheet must contain relevant contact information, including the name of the contact person, his or her phone number, and a brief and concise overview of the proposed project.
2. Proposal not to exceed 10, one-sided, single-spaced pages that include:
   a. Project cost, not to exceed $150,000.
   b. Project goals and objectives and how the project will assist in resolving the problem.
   c. Target population that will be served by the proposed project including age, sex, ethnicity/race, education level, income, type of disability.
   d. Project activities including a detailed description of the proposed project and how it will improve the job placement rates for individuals with disabilities.
   e. Staff who will be responsible for the project.
   f. Data collection and evaluation plan based on the project goals and objectives.
3. Organization's qualifications, including the organization's background, history, mission, and experience in job placement and in working with individuals with disabilities.
4. Detailed budget for the project including a statement detailing the nonprofit's ability to implement the project within the maximum budget of $150,000.
5. The following Appendices:
   a. IRS tax-exempt status determination letter.
   b. Certificate of Incorporation.
   c. By-laws.
   d. List of staff and board of directors.
   e. Most recent annual audited financial statement and current general operating budget.
   f. Current annual report (if available).
   g. List of additional current funding sources and uses.
   h. Letters of commitment from any project consultants or subcontractors.
   i. Two to three letters of support.

Evaluation Criteria, Potential Points to Be awarded, and Procedures

All proposals received in accordance with the requirements specified in this RFP will be reviewed by an evaluation committee. The funding awards will be made on a highest-ranked basis. For consideration of an award, a proposal must score at least 150 points or 75% of the total points possible in the evaluation process unless the evaluation committee concludes it is in the best interest of the City of XYZ to award an applicant who scores less than 150 points. Proposals will be evaluated according to the following criteria:

a. Organization's qualifications
b. Applicant organization's staffing qualifications
c. Project's goals and objectives
d. Target population that will be served
e. Project activities
f. Data collection and evaluation plan

Appendix F

Sample Letter of Inquiry/Intent

The Open Hearts Center
2211 Belmont Park
City, State, Zip

May 6, 20XX

Mr. Joseph McCarthy
Trustee
McCarthy Family Foundation
P.O. Box 138
City, State, Zip

Re: Letter of Inquiry/Intent

Dear Mr. McCarthy:

It was a pleasure meeting you at the Foundations Conference last week. I was especially appreciative of the time you took to meet with representatives of our nonprofit organization, The Open Hearts Center, and learn about our mission and current projects. Your enthusiasm for our vision of assisting the newly immigrated population is a noteworthy acknowledgment of our 10-year dedication to serving this often underserved population.

We are aware that the McCarthy Family Foundation distributes a number of grants for new initiatives geared toward assisting the newly immigrated population. I am pleased to write to you about our new Open Hearts/ Open Arms initiative. It is our hope that your Foundation will invite a proposal from our organization. We are requesting an investment of $100,000 a year for the next 3 years to support our new program. This grant would provide funds needed for us to offer comprehensive adjustment services to at least 250 newly immigrated individuals each year.

Poverty, despair, and harsh living conditions lead numerous individuals to flee their homeland to come to the United States for an opportunity to live the "American dream." However, many immigrants experience frustration and anxiety when arriving to the United States. This can be due to acculturation issues and difficulties in finding suitable employment. Immigrants to the United States often face the challenge of successfully adjusting to a new social environment while simultaneously valuing and preserving their own ethnic identity. In addition, many immigrants find themselves working in some of the most dangerous environments, yet having the fewest resources to protect them. This acculturative stress can lead to both mental and physical health concerns thereby impeding their ability to function in their host country.

Within the past 10 years, The Open Hearts Center has assisted over 4,000 newly immigrated individuals and their families with housing and English-language education. This past year we piloted a new comprehensive program, to assist the newly immigrated with adjustment difficulties. Our new initiative, Open Hearts/Open Arms, provides adjustment counseling, medical care, childcare, and job placement services, along with housing and English-language education. This has proven to be extremely successful; out of the 15 individuals who participated in our pilot, 11 have secured full-time employment and 13 have shown significant decreases in symptoms associated with acculturative stress.

We critically need funds to expand our Open Hearts/Open Arms initiative. Despite our best fundraising efforts, cuts in government financing continue to take a toll on the services we are able to provide. It is our initial goal to provide comprehensive adjustment services to a minimum of 250 newly immigrated individuals a year for the next three years.

We are sincerely grateful to the McCarthy Family Foundation for its dedication to providing necessary resources to improve the lives of the newly immigrated population. We look forward to your consideration of our request and the opportunity for The Open Hearts Center to submit a formal proposal. Please do not hesitate to contact me at 555-555-XXXX should you have any questions or need additional information.

Respectfully,

Judith M. Greis

Judith M. Greis
Executive Director
Enclosures: IRS 501(c)(3) designation, 20XX annual report, audited financial statement

Appenix G

Sample Cover Letter

Hyun Li
Chair, Board of Trustees
Cottage Quarters
3605 6th Avenue
City, State, Zip

November 4, 20XX

Dr. Guadalupe Lopez
CEO
JKL Corporation
1421 City Center
City, State, Zip

Dear Dr. Lopez:

Cottage Quarters is excited to submit this grant proposal. We are requesting an investment of $250,000 to support our collaborative efforts to offer outreach services to seniors residing in the Baker Community. We learned of this opportunity through the Foundation Center website. This grant would provide a portion of the funds needed for us to launch our new Cottage Quarter's Senior Center.

For the past 7 years, Cottage Quarter's has provided transportation services, meal delivery, and senior companionship to over 300 seniors a day. The new Cottage Quarter's Senior Center will be an all-inclusive center providing comprehensive healthcare and social services to the seniors of Baker Community. Our diverse Board of Trustees, staff, and volunteers are well-versed in diversity issues and trained in culturally appropriate service delivery. A number of our staff are bilingual with fluencies in Spanish, Korean, Chinese, and Italian. These skills make our agency well prepared to serve our community's ethnically diverse senior population.

The senior population has grown significantly over the past few decades and is expected to continue to grow. Over the next 10 years, it is anticipated that the population of seniors will increase from 21 percent to almost 29 percent. Seniors often live alone. Some are reliant on family members to care for them.

Many of these family members work full or part-time, making it difficult for them to provide adequate care to their elderly relatives. As a result, our seniors often find themselves isolated and cut off from the community. These challenges have compelled many communities to find creative ways to serve their senior citizens. Through the new Cottage Quarter's Senior Center, seniors of Baker will have access to a community clinic and to numerous programs including arts and crafts, recreational activities, health and fitness, performing arts, workshops, lifelong learning classes, and a number of special events. These services fit well with your corporation's commitment to community outreach.

We have secured $100,000 to seed the program. Your investment in the Cottage Quarter's Senior Center will provide us with funds needed to purchase equipment and supplies and hire additional personnel to staff the center.

Thank you in advance for your consideration of our request. We envision building upon our success by opening our new Cottage Quarter's Senior Center to better serve the seniors of the Baker Community. I will follow up with you in the next 10 days to speak with you about the possibility of meeting with you to discuss the merits of our proposal. Should you have any questions in the interim, please do not hesitate to contact me at (555) 555-XXXX. I look forward to hearing from you.

Sincerely,

Hyun Li

Hyun Li
Chair, Board of Trustees

Enc: Grant proposal

Appendix H

Sample Template of a Title Page/Cover Sheet

20XX–20XX Grant Application Cover Sheet

Contact Person and Title	
Principle Investigator/s	
Name of Organization	
Address	
Phone	( ) -
Fax	( ) -
Title of Project	
Purpose of Grant	
Grant Period	
Total Organizational Budget	
Type of Application (check one only) ☐ Planning Grant ☐ Seed Money ☐ Facilities and Equipment Grant	
Signature/s of Authorizing Personnel	

Appendix I

· ·

Sample Abstract/Executive Summary/Introduction

Proposal Number: 7632-JCF

Organization: Second Chance
                   89 Pleasant Ridge
                   City, State, Zip

Executive Director: Tamara Brown
                   (555) 555-XXXX

Program Title: 13th Step

Our organization, Second Chance, is a nonprofit organization and is tax exempt under Section 501(c)(3) of the Internal Revenue Code. The organization serves individuals in the northern region of the state who are recovering from substance abuse and are at risk of relapse. The ethnic demographic of the population served mirrors the ethnic demographic of the northern region of the state (i.e., 33% Caucasian, 27% African American, 19% Latino/a, 12% Asian, and 9% other). Second Chance serves adult males and females aged 18 and older. The majority of those served are of lower and middle SES.

Some of the identified risk factors for relapse include physiological and psychological factors, social stressors, and environmental factors such as stress from a job, academic problems, and difficulty with family and friends.

The Mission of Second Chance is to help people recovering from substance abuse by providing an unmatched treatment experience allowing them to live as responsible and productive individuals. Our mission is directly related to the mission of your foundation, to improve the quality of life and thereby reduce the likelihood of relapse for individuals recovering from substance abuse. Our philosophy is that recovery from substance abuse is possible only when the complexity of the condition is recognized. This means taking into account psychological, physiological, social, and environmental factors.

Second Chance has an impressive track record of providing unmatched treatment experiences for our clients. Our programs are based on the latest research on substance abuse recovery and provide an unmatched treatment experience for our clients. We are proud of our reputation and boast the lowest relapse rate of all substance abuse treatment facilities in the state.

In an effort to build on our existing programs and bridge the gaps in the area of supportive services, Second Chance has identified a way to reduce the likelihood of relapse, through a comprehensive social-skills and coping-skills training program. We are seeking funds to implement our "13th Step" program. If funded, this grant will allow us to offer social-skills and coping-skills training to adults in recovery in a safe, supportive, nurturing, and drug-free environment.

Some of the anticipated outcomes for those completing all eight modules of the "13th Step" program include:

- Reduced risk of relapse
- Higher levels of responsibility
- Improved social and professional relationships
- Sustained employment

The total cost of our new 13th Step initiative is estimated at $35,000 a year. We have raised approximately $27,000 and have received donations of office supplies, workshop space, and refreshments. We are requesting $5,000 from your foundation. Your generous contribution would fund staff training and module software for 1 year. Your consideration of this request is greatly appreciated.

Appendix J

Sample Needs/Problem Statement

Self-injury is a phenomenon where emotional wounds are brought to the surface and manifest in the form of visible self-inflicted wounds and scars. Recent reports indicate that rates of self-injury appear to increase, with incidence ranging from 14 to 39% (Nock & Prinstein, 2005). However, statistics on the incidence of self-injury can be unreliable, underestimating the true incidence of self-injury. The reality is that many incidents will be dealt with by the individual, in private, and will never reach the attention of medical services or mental health professionals (McAllister, 2003). Research indicates that self-injury is three to four times more common in women than men (McAllister, 2003). However, these findings are not without controversy. Many argue that the statistics are much higher for men. However, men may be less likely to report self-injury and human service professional may not be as adept at examining self-injury among the male population.

Self-injury rarely exists in isolation. The behavior is highly correlated with bipolar disorder, depression, and anxiety. Additionally, research indicates individuals who self-injure may be at an increased risk for suicide. Findings suggest that approximately 55 to 85% of individuals who self-injure have made at least one suicide attempt. Additionally, the individual who self-injures is 18 times more likely than the rest of the population to commit suicide (Favazza & Conterio, 1989; Stanley, Gameroff, Michalsen, & Mann, 2001).

Dr. Laurie Craigen, the executive director of Compassion Retreat, first became aware of the issue of self-injury 10 years ago, after meeting a woman who was struggling socially, academically, and emotionally. The young woman revealed that she was cutting herself, using knives, razors, and broken glass. When the young woman lifted her sleeve, she displayed a patchwork of fresh cuts that spanned the length of her arm, and her embarrassment and shame were evident. This young woman shared a story of overwhelming pain, suffering for many years with the behavior on her own. Further, she talked about the negative experiences she encountered within the mental health arena. Unfortunately, her story was not unique; many who receive treatment for self-injury are dissatisfied with the services they receive (Craigen & Foster, 2009).

Within the mental health community, many providers feel uncomfortable working with this population and lack a clear understanding of self-injury, inappropriately leading them to pathologize the behavior. In fact, the majority of human service professionals have little or no pre-service training in their undergraduate or graduate training programs on the topic of self-injury (Craigen & Hays, in press). Consequently, helping professionals erroneously categorize self-injury as a criterion of Borderline Personality Disorder and refuse to work with individuals who self-injure, labeling them as manipulative and difficult. In emergency room settings, individuals who self-injure have reported unethical treatment (Stone & Sias, 2003). For example, women seeking treatment have been sutured without anesthesia, scrubbed with wool surgical sponges on open wounds, and refused medical treatment because their injuries are self-inflicted.

These approaches have long-lasting effects upon patients, resulting in both negative views of the self and helping professionals. This approach is likely to be harmful; when a client is rejected for treatment, he or she feels wounded and even untreatable (Kiselica & Zila, 2001).

There are few organizations that provide holistic interventions to those who self-injure. In fact, Compassion Retreat is the only nonprofit agency in the southern part of the state that provides holistic interventions to both females and males struggling with issues related to self-injury. Our mission is "to provide a safe and inclusive environment to foster spiritual renewal and transformation in those individuals affected by self-injury." Our mission matches your organization's mission of "transforming the lives of others."

For the past 6 years, Compassion Retreat has hosted over 50 retreats for both males and females who self-injure. Our month-long retreats encompass a number of holistic (i.e., mind/body/spirit) interventions including yoga, meditation, health and wellness, stress management, and personal growth. Our staff are well trained in the areas of self-injury and holistic service delivery. Each staff member has earned a minimum of a bachelor's degree in human services or other help-related fields. Compassion Retreat has received a number of honors including the Honor of Distinction for Outstanding Commitment to the Wellbeing of Others.

Parents and guardians of those who engage in self-injury are also unaware of how to work effectively with their child who is self-injuring. Many parents and guardians feel overwhelmed and helpless and don't know where to turn for help. The majority of parents and guardians lack understanding and education on the topic and many blame themselves for their child's behavior.

Compassion Retreat proposes to expand its services and offer retreats for parents and guardians of those who self-injure. We intend to offer one-week long, holistic retreats for parents and guardians with a goal of promoting their education, understanding, and awareness of self-injury. This will be accomplished through educational workshops and holistic interventions, including, but not limited to, relaxation techniques, stress management, guided visualizations, and relational communication skills.

A truly holistic approach to treating self-injurious behavior supports those most directly affected by the behavior; those who self-injure along with their parents and guardians. True healing is possible only when those closest to the situation are assisted.

This program has been designed with sustainability in mind. Compassion Retreat has received seed money of $25,000 for program development. It has also received a pledge from Healthful Meals, to donate meals to the retreat center for the next 3 years. With the support of your corporation, Compassion Retreat will be able to hire additional staff and provide training seminars for all new and existing staff in order to effectively meet the unique needs of parents and guardians of those who self-injure.

References

Craigen, L., & Foster, V. (2009). A Qualitative investigation of the counseling experiences of adolescent women with a history of self-injury. *Journal of Mental Health Counseling, 31*(1), 76–94.

Craigen, L., & Hays, S. (in press). Assessing the effectiveness of a pilot training program for self-injury treatment. *Journal of Human Services*.

Favazza, A. R., & Conterio, K. (1989). Female habitual self-mutilation. *Acta Psychiatra Scandinavica, 79*, 283–289.

Kiselica, M., & Zila, L. (2001). Understanding and counselling self-mutilation in female adolescents and young adults. *Journal of Counselling and Development, 79*, 46–52.

McAllister, M. (2003). Multiple meanings of self-harm: A critical review. *International Journal of Mental Health Nursing, 12*, 175–185.

Nock, M. K., & Prinstein, M. J. (2005). Contextual features and behavioral functions of self-mutilation among adolescents. *Journal of Abnormal Psychology, 114*, 140–146.

Stanley, B., Gameroff, M., Michalsen, V., & Mann, J. (2001). Are suicide attempters who self-mutilate a unique population? *American Journal of Psychiatry, 158*, 427–432.

Stone, J. A., & Sias, S. M. (2003). Self-injurious behavior; a bi-modal treatment approach to working with adolescent females. *Journal of Mental Health Counseling*, 112–114.

Appendix K

Sample Goal and Objectives
Schooling's In, Dropping's Out

Goal

- The goal of the "Schooling's In, Dropping's Out" program is to reduce the dropout rate of high-school students in the 10th District.

Objectives

During the 20XX–20XX academic year, "Schooling's In, Dropping's Out" will:

- Provide 2 hours per week of afterschool tutoring for each of 150 at-risk, high-school students in the 10th District.
- Facilitate one "Classroom Etiquette Seminar," during the first week of the academic year at each high school located in the 10th District.
- Mediate monthly planning conferences between the 150 participating students and their parents/guardians to celebrate successes, discuss challenges, and identify solutions.

Appendix L

· ·

Sample Program Design/Methods/Strategies

Carol's Place provides temporary shelter to survivors of intimate partner violence, regardless of sex, race, age, ethnicity, culture, and sexual orientation, who reside in Carol County. Carol's Place accommodates families including those with adolescent male and adult male head-of-households.

Carol's Place is seeking funds to build an addition onto one of its six existing shelters. One of its shelters is inadequate to serve the increasing needs of the community. The new addition will enable Carol's Place to provide housing for 20 additional residents. The planning process has taken into account all legitimate and sound expenses related to the construction of an addition to one of its shelters. The agency has experience in building additions; this will be the fourth addition made to one of its shelters. As such, Carol's Place has put to use this knowledge and experience in devising its budget, designing the project, and creating the project timeline.

This project is based on an 18-month timeline which takes into account possible delays due to weather, shortage of labor/volunteers, and/or delays in receiving pledged funds (see detailed timeline in Appendix Q). Through an innovative agreement with a local technical college, 90% of the construction (i.e., carpentry, plumbing, electrical, and masonry) will be completed, for material costs only, by students enrolled in the college's building construction program. Twenty students will be recruited for the project each semester and will receive academic credit for their labor and for attending class. No other compensation will be provided to students. The project will be supervised by four faculty in the building construction program through in-kind donations through the college. The remaining 10% of the construction costs will be paid to contractors, specialists, and security guards.

Building supplies and materials are estimated to cost $240,000 (i.e., 3,000 square feet × $80 per square foot). All costs for the project are realistic and reasonable and are itemized in the budget worksheet (see Appendix R). The costs are significantly less than purchasing an existing property to house 20 individuals.

Program Design

This project is based on a unique partnership between Carol's Place and a local technical college. Through this partnership, students enrolled in the college's building construction program will receive academic credit and hands-on experience. College faculty and a professional building contractor will supervise the students throughout the project.

Whenever possible, community resources will be utilized. For example, it will be necessary to work with the city in securing approval for the addition and in acquiring a building permit. Carol's Place has considerable experience in managing the construction of additions to its shelters and this experience will be put to good use. Careful planning at the early stages of the project will help to ensure that any potential problems are promptly eradicated.

Potential Problems and Solutions

The planning process will be focused on the recruitment and retention of students enrolled in the building construction program at an area technical college. Carol's Place will work with the admissions office at the technical college to determine the availability of resources for recruiting students. Carol's Place will assist with recruiting students through their agency's website, e-newsletters, and other agency marketing materials.

Prior to the implementation of the project, representatives from Carol's Place (e.g., board of trustees, administrative staff) will work closely with the building construction program's faculty and students. This will enable all project participants to understand the scope of the project and the roles, responsibilities, and expectations of each project member.

Because some students may not have transportation to the construction site, all students will be transported to and from the construction site via an agency van.

In order to protect the anonymity of Carol's Place residents, residents of the shelter for which the addition will be built will be temporarily relocated until construction is complete. In addition, all project participants will sign confidentiality agreements prohibiting them from disclosing the address or location of the shelter. Twenty-four-hour onsite security will be provided by trained security guards.

Training

Students recruited for the project will be trained through the technical college's building construction program. Each student will attend 2-hour weekly in-class seminars and will work onsite an additional 20-hours per week, per semester. Students will be supervised by faculty members and the project's general contractor. Safety will be emphasized throughout the project.

Students will be actively engaged in learning the relevant construction jobs, both onsite and in the classroom. Students will become familiar with construction terminology and work tasks in building construction, electrical, plumbing, and masonry trades. The ratio of students to supervisors will be no more than 6:1. See Appendix S for flow chart of training. Data will be collected each semester through student and faculty evaluations and test scores. The data will be used to evaluate the overall project in meeting the goals and objectives of the agency, building construction program, and the faculty.

Construction Plan

Construction will take place at Building "C" of Carol's Place. Ten bedrooms with attached bathrooms, a common living area, and kitchen will be added to the existing structure. See Appendix T for the project blueprint.

Project Staff

Four faculty from the local technical college will be required to train and supervise the students. Each faculty member will specialize in one of the four specialty trades (i.e., building construction, electrical, plumbing, and masonry). Phillip Gordon of Acme Construction will serve as the general contractor and oversee the project. Mr. Gordon served as the general contractor for three prior construction projects at Carol's Place. Twenty-four-hour security will be provided by AAA Security Services. See Appendix U for work schedule.

Implications

Since 2002, Carol's Place has provided temporary shelter to survivors of intimate partner violence regardless of sex, race, age, ethnicity, culture, or sexual orientation. Carol's Place is the only agency in Carol County that accommodates families including those with adolescent male and adult male head-of-households. The need for such shelters is far greater than the available resources. The new addition will provide additional shelter to accommodate and protect 20 additional survivors.

Appendix M

Sample Evaluation Plan

To evaluate the success of the "Community Outreach Project," an agency-developed outcome survey will be utilized. The survey consists of three sections. Sections 1 and 2 utilize a five-point Likert-type scale and section 3 employs a ranking method. Section 1 asks volunteers to indicate their level of satisfaction with the community service activities they participated in during the 4-week project. Section 2 asks volunteers to indicate the probability of their participation in next year's "Community Outreach Project." Section 3 asks volunteers to rank the top three community service activities they feel most accomplished the project's goal of "providing needed assistance to community agencies and to the people served by the agencies." The survey was piloted on 10 volunteers who participated in community service projects through their community college.

Sample Organizational Information

In 1978, Rufus Jones, a formerly homeless father, recognized that a number of families in the City of LMN were on the verge of homelessness or were homeless. In 1990, Rufus earned a bachelor's degree in human services. The bachelor's degree was a long time coming. Ten years prior, Rufus was a homeless father of two. His partner had died 2 years previously of breast cancer. The medical expenses and the time Rufus took off of work led his family to poverty. Eventually Rufus lost his home and he and his two children found themselves living out of his pickup truck. With no shelter in the area that took in families, Rufus vowed to do whatever he needed to do to ensure that families with similar needs would have a safe haven. Ten years later, Northern Homeless Services opened its doors.

The mission of Northern Homeless Services is to conquer homelessness by addressing a wide range of issues related to homelessness and by offering a continuum of services and programs to support families through their transition from homelessness to permanent housing.

Northern Homeless Services is the only agency in a 100-mile radius of the City of LMN that provides programs and services to families who are homeless. In 2005, Northern Homeless Services forged a partnership with the area's Community Services Board and Anthony University. The partnerships allowed Northern Homeless Services to provide comprehensive case management services to families year round. In 2009, Northern Homeless Services was the recipient of the city's Golden Hands award for superlative service to the citizens of the city.

Northern Homeless Services is a nonprofit organization and tax exempt under Section 501 (c)(3)of the Internal Revenue Code. It was established in 1988 as an independent agency by the City of LMN and supports homeless families by providing outreach services, meals, transportation, drop-in shelters, transitional housing, and assistance with securing permanent housing to families who are homeless. Northern Homeless Services serves a highly diverse population, with 55% of its consumers from racial and ethnic minority groups.

The following is an overview of the agency's board and staff:

Board of directors (resumes attached):

- Danette Mitchell, Chairperson; Administrator, LMN Community Hospital
- Joy Danielle, Vice-Chairperson; President/CEO, Century Autos
- Terence Rodriguez-Flores, Secretary; Member, LMN Community Services Board
- Rodney Grote, Treasurer; President, Grote Accounting Services
- Dustin Phillips, Member; Assistant Principal, LMN Middle School
- Loretta Palmer, Member; Professor, LMN Community College

Staff (resumes attached):

- Rufus Jones, Executive Director, B.S. in Human Services
- Yukio Ito, Assistant Director Development
- Santianna Russell, Assistant Director Operations
- Dahnay Robinson, Assistant Director Finance

Northern Homeless Services coordinates and manages over $1.3 million annually. It operates entirely on contributions raised through grants and fundraising efforts. The majority of its support comes from federal grants and foundations. The balance comes from individual donations, corporate sponsors, and local churches and synagogues. Sources of funding include:

- Federal government: 35%
- Other government: 12%
- Community contributions: 36%
- Donated services and donated property: 14%
- Other: 3%

Funds are used in the following ways:

- Programs and services: 87%
- Administrative and general expenses: 9%
- Fundraising: 6%

Appendix O

Sample Grant Proposal Line-Item Budget

LINE ITEM	REVENUE	PROJECT	GRANT REQUEST
1	Grants	38,500	15,000
2	Corporate contributions	12,100	
3	United Way	0	
4	Membership	0	
5	Foundations	7,000	
6	Fundraising events	9,300	
7	Individuals	10,900	
8	Miscellaneous	1,510	
9	**Total**	**$79,310**	**$15,000**
10	**In-kind**	**$10,400**	
11	**Total Revenue**	**$89,710**	**$15,000**
LINE ITEM	**EXPENSES**	**PROJECT**	**GRANT REQUEST**
12	Project staff salaries and wages	50,500	10,000
13	Fringe benefits and taxes	11,110	2,200
14	Room rental and utilities	1,900	
15	Supplies and materials	1,230	1,500
16	Printing	1,550	1,000
17	Travel to conferences	2,125	
18	Marketing and promotion	2,200	300
19	Workshop facilitator training	2,350	
20	**Subtotal**	**$72,965**	**$15,000**
21	General operating (indirect)—8%	6,345	
22	**Total**	**$79,310**	**$15,000**
23	**In-kind**		
24	Accounting services (260 hours × $40)	10,400	
25	**Total In-kind**	**$10,400**	
26	**Total Expenses**	**$89,710**	
27	**Revenue over Expenses**	**$0**	

Sample Funding/Sustainability Statement

Sustainability is built into this plan, partially through the pooling of resources. By pooling resources, Morgan County Foster Care will be able to provide more services for children, and there will be less duplication of services and programs countywide. The plan also ensures that other funding alternatives will continually be investigated to make certain that the sustainability of benefits, from this grant, will continue. Partnerships with area colleges will ensure that interns will be secured in order to manage some of the agency's programs and services. In addition to these partnerships, several foundations have been approached for support; Morgan County Foster Care is pleased to announce that $3,800 was received from Freemon Broadcasting, and $2,200 was received from Adreanne Electronics. Currently Morgan County Foster Care has three grant proposals pending, requesting a total of $75,000. Additionally, several fundraising events (i.e., Monte Carlo Night, Silent Auction, and Golf Tournament) have been planned.

References

Acceptiva. (2010). *Customized online payment and donation service.* Retrieved from http://www.acceptiva.com/.

Airey, D. (2008). *5 useful logo design tips.* Retrieved from http://www.davidairey.com/5-vital-logo-design-tips/.

Alise, C. (2010). Valentine fundraising ideas. *eHow: How to do just about everything.* Retrieved from http://www.ehow.com/way_5251556_valentine-fundraising-ideas.html.

AllBusiness.com, Inc. (2010). *Integrating online and offline marketing efforts for your small business.* Retrieved from http://www.allbusiness.com/marketing/strategic-marketing/3920-1.html.

American Grant Writers' Association. (2011). *American Grant Writers' Association.* Retrieved from http://www.agwa.us/.

Andreasen, A. R., & Kotler, P. (2003). *Strategic marketing for nonprofit organizations* (6th ed.). Upper Saddle River, NJ: Prentice Hall.

Association of Fundraising Professionals. (2008). *Code of ethical principles and standards.* Retrieved from http://www.afpnet.org/files/ContentDocuments/CodeofEthicsLong.pdf.

Association of Fundraising Professionals. (2009). *Guidelines, codes, standards.* Retrieved from http://www.afpnet.org/Ethics/content.cfm?ItemNumber=3093&navItemNumber=536.

Association of Fundraising Professionals. (2011). *Association of Fundraising Professionals.* Retrieved from http://www.afpnet.org/.

Association of Proposal Management Professionals. (2010). Welcome to APMP. *APMP: Association of Proposal Management Professionals.* Retrieved from http://www.apmp.org/default.aspx.

Association of Small Foundations. (2010). *Association of Small Foundations.* Retrieved from http://www.smallfoundations.org/.

Axiom Consulting Partners. (2010). *Employee engagement.* Retrieved from http://www.axiomcp.com/firm/our-capabilities/employee-engagement?gclid=CMeS762k7qICFQVGnQod1k9Aag.

Barker, L. (2010). How to create a nonprofit operating budget. *eHow.* Retrieved from http://www.ehow.com/how_4927144_create-nonprofit-operating-budget.html.

Bennett, M. (2009). *How to write a nonprofit case statement.* Retrieved from http://www.howtodothings.com/careers/how-to-write-a-nonprofit-case-statement.

Bill and Melinda Gates Foundation. (2011). *Foundation fact sheet.* Retrieved from http://www.gatesfoundation.org/about/Pages/foundation-fact-sheet.aspx.

Blackbaud, Inc. (2010). *Gift range calculator.* Retrieved from http://www.blackbaud.com/company/resources/giftrange/giftcalc.aspx.

Blue Fountain Media. (2010). *How to choose a tag line that delivers your company's message effectively.* Retrieved from http://www.bluefountainmedia.com/business/onlinemarketing/how-to-choose-a-tag-line-that-delivers-your-company%E2%80%99s-message-effectively/.

Bluejay, M. (2009). Website design tips. *Website Helpers.com.* Retrieved from http://websitehelpers.com/design/.

BoardSource. (2007). *Board members and personal contributions.* Retrieved from http://www.boardsource.org/Knowledge.asp?ID=1.109.

Boggon, P. (2009). Insight: Commitment is a 2-way street. *Tarnside.* Retrieved from http://www.tarnside.co.uk/Insight12.php.

Brockman, A. (2010). *Using Foursquare for fundraising.* Retrieved from http://www.achieveguidance.com/blog/?p=148.

Browning, B. (2001). *Grant writing for dummies.* New York: Wiley.

BusinessDictionary.com. (2010). Charitable gift annuity. *BusinessDictionary.com.* Retrieved from http://www.businessdictionary.com/definition/charitable-gift-annuity.html.

Capital Venture. (2010). *Development committee tips.* Retrieved from http://www.cvfundraising.com/resources/tip_sheets/development_committee.

Carlson, M., & O'Neal-McElrath, T. (2008). *Winning grants step by step* (3rd ed.). Hoboken, NJ: Jossey-Bass.

Carson, J. (2010). Why online fundraising auctions work. *About.com: Nonprofit Charitable Orgs.* Retrieved from http://nonprofit.about.com/od/fundraising/a/auctions.htm.

Catalog of Federal Domestic Assistance. (2011). *Catalog of Federal Domestic Assistance.* Retrieved from https://www.cfda.gov.

Center for Community Change. (2010). *Board versus staff roles in fundraising.* Retrieved from http://www.cccfiles.org/resources/orgdevtools/downloads/boarvst.pdf.

Center for Education Integrating Science, Mathematics and Computing (CEISMC). (n.d.). Evaluation tools. Retrieved from http://www.ceismc.gatech.edu/MM_Tools/evaluation.html.

CharityChannel. (2011). About CharityChannel. *CharityChannel.* Retrieved from http://www.charitychannel.com/.

CharityFacts. (2010). *Telephone fundraising: How it works.* Retrieved from http://www.charityfacts.org/fundraising/fundraising_factsheets/telephone_fundraising/how_it_works.html.

Charitymeter.com. (2009). *Charitymeter.com: Charity news, articles, products, and more!* Retrieved from http://www.charitymeter.com/.

Checco, L. (2005). *Branding for success.* Bloomington, IN: Trafford Publishing.

Chhabra, S. S. (2010). Nonprofits, here's what NOT to do on social media. *The Case Foundation.* Retrieved from http://www.casefoundation.org/blog/nonprofits-what-not-do-social-media?utm_source=feedburner&utm_medium=feed&utm_campaign=Feed%3A+casefoundation+%28Case+Foundation+-+Investing+in+People+and+Ideas+that+Can+Change+the+World%29.

ChipIn. (2010). *ChipIn: The easy way to collect money.* Retrieved from http://www.chipin.com/.

Chronicle of Philanthropy, The. (2011). About the Chronicle of Philanthropy. *The Chronicle of Philanthropy.* Retrieved from http://philanthropy.com/page/About-The-Chronicle-of/235/.

Ciconte, B. L. (2005). Developing an effective fundraising board: A senior development professional shares tips on how to motivate even the most reluctant board members to become successful fundraisers. *The Public Manager, 34.* Retrieved from

http://www.questia.com/googleScholar.qst;jsessionid
=M8GGqVmQcJW10F7nshFxfWGPN3VlyQMnRbyJThKDfB1
hSD5nQKGZ!1330981764!1896127874?docId=501084622.

Clark, C. A., & Fox, S. P. (2006). *Grant proposal makeover: Transforming your request from no to yes.* San Francisco, CA: Jossey-Bass.

Clark, R. (2008). *What motivates people to be charitable?* Retrieved from http://ezinearticles.com/?What-Motivates-People-To-Be-Charitable?&id=951444.

Clarke, C. A. (2009). *Storytelling for grantseekers: The guide to creative nonprofit fundraising* (2nd ed.). San Francisco, CA: Jossey-Bass.

Coley, S., & Scheinberg, C. (1990). *Proposal writing.* Newbury Park, CA: Sage.

Communications Network, The. (2011). *The Communications Network: Strengthening the voice of philanthropy.* Retrieved from http://www.comnetwork.org/.

Constant Contact, Inc. (2011). *Constant Contact home.* Retrieved from http://www.constantcontact.com/index.jsp.

Corporation for National and Community Service. (2010). *Accepting online donations.* Retrieved from http://nationalserviceresources.org/accepting-online-donations.

Council on Foundations. (2010). *Council on Foundations.* Retrieved from http://www.cof.org/.

Council on Foundations. (2011). About the council. *The Council on Foundations.* Retrieved from http://www.cof.org/about/index.cfm?navItemNumber=14828.

Cravens, J. (2010). *Nonprofit organizations and online social networking: Advice and commentary.* Retrieved from http://www.coyotecommunications.com/outreach/osn.html.

Darling, R. (2010). What are the duties of a Fundraising Committee? *eHow.* Retrieved from http://www.ehow.com/about_5372428_duties-fundraising-committee.html.

David, S. (2008). Different sources of non-profit fundraising. *Articlesbase.* Retrieved from http://www.articlesbase.com/fundraising-articles/different-sources-of-nonprofit-fundraising-352102.html.

DeMartinis, R. (2005). Internet fundraising. *Nonprofit and fundraising resources: Professional, practical and free!* Retrieved from http://nonprofit.pro/internet_fundraising.htm.

DiJulio, S., & Ruben, M. (2007). *People to people fundraising: Social networking and Web 2.0 for charities.* Hoboken, NJ: Wiley.

Disability Funders Network. (2011). *Disability Funders Network.* Retrieved from http://www.disabilityfunders.org/.

DoJiggy, LLC. (2010). *Fundraising tips.* Retrieved from http://www.dojiggy.com/s/Fundraising-Tips/.

Duggan, M. H., & Jurgens, J. C. (2007). *Career interventions and techniques: A complete guide for human service professionals.* Boston, MA: Pearson/Allyn & Bacon.

eBay. (2010). *Fees for selling on eBay.* Retrieved from http://pages.ebay.com/help/sell/fees.html.

eHow. (2010a). *How to set up a web site for a nonprofit organization.* Retrieved from http://www.ehow.com/how_17220_set-web-site.html.

eHow. (2010b). *How to write a nonprofit case statement.* Retrieved from http://www.ehow.com/how_2122727_write-nonprofit-case-statement.html.

Environmental Grantmakers Association. (2011). *Environmental Grantmakers Association.* Retrieved from http://www.ega.org/.

Extraordinaries, The. (2010). *The micro-volunteering network: An online collaboration platform for nonprofits and skilled professionals.* Retrieved from https://app.beextra.org/.

FastTrack Fundraising Tips and Articles. (2009). *Fundraising committee management—documentation.* Retrieved from http://www.fasttrackfundraising.com/fundraisers/category/fundraising-tips/teamwork/.

FederalGrants.com. (2011a). Welcome to Federal Grants. *Federal Grants.* Retrieved from http://www.federalgrants.com/.

FederalGrants.com. (2011b). You're awarded the federal grant, now what? *Federal Grants.* Retrieved from http://www.federalgrants.com/youre-awarded-the-grant.html.

Fisher, R. J., Vandenbosch, M., & Antia, K. D. (2007). *An empathy-helping perspective on consumers' responses to fundraising appeals.* Retrieved from http://www.bus.wisc.edu/nielsencenter/research/TVOManuscript%20final%20(October%2030,%202010).pdf.

Ford, J. (2010). Board members: How much money should boards expect their members to give? *Ezine Non-Profit Articles.* Retrieved from http://ezinearticles.com/?Board-Members---How-Much-Money-Should-Boards-Expect-Their-Members-Give-to-Their-Nonprofits?&id=3960541.

Forhan, C. (2008). Successful meetings: 14 tips. *PTO Today.* Retrieved from http://www.ptotoday.com/pto-today-articles/article/212-successful-meetings-14-tips.

Forum of Regional Associations of Grantmakers. (2007). *More giving together: The growth and impact of giving circles and shared giving.* Washington, DC: Forum of Regional Associations of Grantmakers.

Forum of Regional Associations of Grantmakers. (2008). *Hosting a giving circle: The benefits and challenges of giving together.* Washington, DC: Forum of Regional Associations of Grantmakers.

Foster, W. L., Kim, P., & Christiansen, B. (2009). Ten nonprofit funding models. *Stanford Social Innovation Review.* Retrieved from http://www.ssireview.org/articles/entry/ten_nonprofit_funding_models/.

Foundation Center. (2010). *Highlights of foundation giving trends.* Retrieved from http://foundationcenter.org/gainknowledge/research/pdf/fgt10highlights.pdf.

Foundation Center. (2011a). *About the Foundation Center.* Retrieved from http://foundationcenter.org/about/.

Foundation Center. (2011b). *Proposal writing short course: The statement of need.* Retrieved from http://foundationcenter.org/getstarted/tutorials/shortcourse/need.html.

Foursquare. (2011). *Foursquare.* Retrieved from http://foursquare.com/.

Frederiksen, L. W., & Taylor, A. E. (2010). *Spiraling up: How to create a high growth, high value professional services firm.* Reston, VA: Hinge Research Institute.

Fritz, J. (2010a). Capital campaign. *Nonprofit Charitable Orgs.* Retrieved from http://nonprofit.about.com/od/c/g/capitalcamp.htm.

Fritz, J. (2010b). Charitable giving through a private or family foundation. *About.com: Nonprofit Charitable Orgs.* Retrieved from http://nonprofit.about.com/od/fordonors/a/familyfound-give.htm.

Fritz, J. (2010c). *5 steps to defining your nonprofit's brand.* Retrieved from http://nonprofit.about.com/od/nonprofitpromotion/fr/branding.htm.

Fritz, J. (2010d). Fundraising fundamentals. *About.com: Nonprofit Charitable Orgs.* Retrieved from http://nonprofit.about.com/od/fundraising/a/fundraising101.htm.

Fritz, J. (2010e). How to start an endowment for your nonprofit. *About.com: Nonprofit Charitable Orgs.* Retrieved from http://nonprofit.about.com/od/fundraisingbasics/a/startendowment.htm.

Fritz, J. (2010f). New 990 makes nonprofit fundraising registration unavoidable. *About.com: Nonprofit Charitable Orgs.* Retrieved from http://nonprofit.about.com/od/fundraisingbasics/a/frregistration990.htm.

Fritz, J. (2010g). The art of recognizing and thanking your donors. *About.com: Nonprofit Charitable Orgs.* Retrieved from http://nonprofit.about.com/od/fundraising/a/donorrecog.htm.

Fritz, J. (2010h). *12 tips for nonprofits on getting started with social media.* Retrieved from http://nonprofit.about.com/od/socialmedia/tp/Tipsstartsocialnetworking.htm.

Fritz, J. (2010i). Writing a case statement: Answer these 5 questions for your case statement. *About.com: Nonprofit Charitable Orgs.* Retrieved from http://nonprofit.about.com/od/fundraisingbasics/a/casestatement.htm.

Funders Concerned about AIDS. (2011). Funders Concerned about AIDS. Retrieved from http://www.fcaaids.org/.

Funders' Network for Smart Growth and Livable Communities. (2011). Smart growth and the future of regions and communities. *About Funders' Network.* Retrieved from http://www.fundersnetwork.org/about.

Funders Together. (2011). Funders Together: Homelessness ends here. *Funders Together.* Retrieved from http://funderstogether.org/content/view/home-for-good.

Fundraiser Help: Fundraising Ideas and Resources. (2009). *Art fundraising.* Retrieved from http://www.fundraiserhelp.com/art-raffle-fundraiser.htm.

Fundraising Dictionary. (2007). *Fundraising dictionary of terms.* Retrieved from http://fundraising-dictionary.com/.

Fundsnet Online. (2010). *Fundsnet services online.* Retrieved from http://www.fundsnetservices.com/.

Gaebler Ventures. (2010). Effective capital campaigns. *For entrepreneurs: Nonprofit management.* Retrieved from http://www.gaebler.com/Effective-Capital-Campaigns.htm.

Garcia Abadia, M. (2009). Nonprofit cost analysis—Step 3: Allocate direct costs. *The Bridgespan Group.* Retrieved from http://www.bridgespan.org/nonprofit-cost-analysis-toolkit-allocate-direct-costs.aspx.

Garecht, J. (2010). *How to build your prospect list. The fundraising authority: Tools and information for schools, churches, and other non-profits.* Retrieved from http://www.thefundraisingauthority.com/fundraising-basics/prospect-list/.

General Mill's Box Tops for Education. (2010). *General Mill's box tops for education.* Retrieved from https://www.boxtops4education.com/common/Register.

aspx?sid=14348&WT.mc_id=topnavJoin&WT.mc_id=paid_search_100505_636117&WT.srch=1&esrc=15783.

Gersick, K. E., Stone, D., Grady, K., Desjardins, M., & Muson, H. (2006). *Generations of giving: Leadership and continuity in family foundation.* Lanham, MD: Lexington Books.

Giving USA Foundation. (2006). Charitable giving rises 6 percent to more than $260 billion in 2005. *Charity navigator: Your guide to intelligent giving.* Retrieved from http://www.charitynavigator.org/index.cfm/bay/content.view/cpid/445.htm.

Glasser, B. G., & Strauss, A. L. (1967). *The discovery of grounded theory.* Chicago: Aldine.

Gottlieb, H. (2008). *Board recruitment and orientation: A step-by-step common sense guide* (3rd ed.). ReSolve, Inc. d/b/a Renaissance Press.

Grant Professionals Association. (2011). *Grant Professionals Association.* Retrieved from http://grantprofessionals.org/.

GrantDomain.com. (2011). GrantDomain.com. *Welcome to Grant-Domain.com.* Retrieved from www.grantdomain.com.

Grantmakers in Aging. (2011). *Grantmakers in Aging.* Retrieved from http://www.giaging.org/imis15_prod/internet/default.aspx.

Grantmakers for Children, Youth, and Families. (2011). *Grantmakers for Children, Youth & Families.* Retrieved from http://www.gcyf.org/.

Grantmakers for Effective Organizations. (2009). *Grantmakers for Effective Organizations.* Retrieved from http://www.geofunders.org/home.aspx.

Grantmakers for Effective Organizations. (2011). About GEO. *Grantmakers for Effective Organizations.* Retrieved from http://www.geofunders.org/aboutgeo.aspx.

Grantmakers in Health. (2011). About GIH. *Grantmakers in Health.* Retrieved from http://www.gih.org/info-url_nocat2663/info-url_nocat.htm?requesttimeout=500.

Grantmakers Income Security Taskforce. (2011). *Grantmakers Income Security Taskforce.* Retrieved from http://www.gist-funders.org/.

Grants.gov. (2011a). About Grants.gov. *Grants.gov.* Retrieved from http://www.grants.gov/aboutgrants/about_grants_gov.jsp.

Grants.gov. (2011b). What is a grant? *Grants.gov.* Retrieved from http://www.grants.gov/aboutgrants/grants.jsp.

Grantsmanship Center, The. (2010). *The Grantsmanship Center's Federal funding sources.* Retrieved from http://www.tgci.com/funding.shtml.

GrantStation.com, Inc. (2011). About us. *GrantStation.* Retrieved from http://www.grantstation.com/public/Company_info_px/about_us.asp.

GreaterGood.org. (2010). *GreaterGood.org.* Retrieved from http://www.greatergood.org/.

GuideStar. (2010). *GuideStar.* Retrieved from http://www2.guidestar.org/Home.aspx.

Hall, S. (2011). How to analyze qualitative data. *eHow.* Retrieved from http://www.ehow.com/how_5188889_analyze-qualitative-data.html.

Harmon, J. (2010). 6 reasons your website sucks. *Marketing for nonprofits: New voices for a new world.* Retrieved from http://www.marketingfornonprofits.org/.

Hawkins, V. (2009). *How to find your nonprofit organization's target audience*. HowToDoThings.com. Retrieved from http://www.howtodothings.com/careers/how-to-find-your-nonprofit-organizations-target-audience.

Henson, K. T. (2003). Debunking some myths about grant writing. *The Chronicle of Higher Education*. Retrieved from http://chronicle.com/article/Debunking-Some-Myths-About/45256/.

HighBeam Research, Inc. (2009). *Cause marketing*. Retrieved from http://www.reference.com/browse/wiki/Cause_marketing.

Hired Gun Writing, LCC. (2011a). Hiring a professional grant writer. *Hired Gun Writing*. Retrieved from http://www.content-professionals.com/Hiring-a-Grant-Writer.php.

Hired Gun Writing, LLC. (2011b). *Nonprofit grant writing mistakes and grant writing tips*. Retrieved from http://www.content-professionals.com/Grant-Writing-Tips.php.

Hoffman, B. R. (1992). *ARCH factsheet number 6: Some general principles of charitable nonprofit fundraising*. Retrieved from http://www.archrespite.org/archfs6.htm.

Hoffman, B. R. (2002). *ARCH factsheet number 7: Marketing for charitable nonprofit organizations*. Retrieved from http://marketing.about.com/gi/o.htm?zi=1/XJ/Ya&zTi=1&sdn=marketing&cdn=money&tm=22&gps=231_16_1276_770&f=11&tt=14&bt=1&bts=1&zu=http%3A//www.archrespite.org/archfs7.htm.

IDonateToCharity.org. (2009). *A charitable auctions website*. Retrieved from http://www.idonatetocharity.org/.

Investment Dictionary. (2010). Investment Dictionary. *Answers.com*. Retrieved from http://www.answers.com/topic/charitable-remainder-trust.

InvestorWords.com. (2010). Charitable lead trust. *InvestorWords.com*. Retrieved from http://www.investorwords.com/829/charitable_lead_trust.html.

IRS.gov. (2009). *Tax information for charities and other non-profits*. Retrieved from http://www.irs.gov/charities/index.html.

Jacobs, K. (2009). Marketing materials. *Kathy Jacobs design and marketing*. Retrieved from http://www.kathyjacobs.com/marketing-materials.html.

Jenne, K. J., & Henderson, M. (2000). Hiring a director for a nonprofit agency: A step-by-step guide. *Popular Government*. Retrieved from http://www.sog.unc.edu/pubs/electronicversions/pg/pgsum00/article4.pdf.

Johns Hopkins University. (2004). The importance of collaboration and leadership. *Center for Technology in Education: A Partnership of the Maryland State Department of Education*. Retrieved from http://cte.jhu.edu/courses/ssn/grantwriting/ses1_act1_pag2.shtml.

Jones, T., & Kasat, R. (n.d.). *How to write a great case statement*. Retrieved from http://www.epa.gov/watertrain/sustainablefinance/files/case_howto.pdf.

Jordan, R. R., & Quynn, K. L. (2009). *Planned giving: A guide to fundraising and philanthropy*. Hoboken, NJ: Wiley.

Kapin, A. (2010). The keys to fundraising on Foursquare. *Frogloop.com*. Retrieved from http://www.frogloop.com/care2blog/2010/6/24/the-keys-to-fundraising-on-foursquare.html.

KnowHow NonProfit. (2009). *Legacy fundraising: Getting started with legacy fundraising and ways to expand your existing legacy base*. Retrieved from http://www.knowhownonprofit.org/funding/fundraising/individual-giving/legacy/legacy-fundraising.

Kotler, P., & Armstrong, G. (2010). *Principles of marketing* (13th ed.). Upper Saddle River, NJ: Prentice Hall.

Kramer, H. J. (2011). Getting your grant proposal budget right: Budgets for grant proposals are simple once you know the basics. *About.com: Nonprofit Charitable Orgs*. Retrieved from http://nonprofit.about.com/od/foundationfundinggrants/a/grantbudget.htm.

Kronberger, B. (2010). Take time to cultivate relationship with donor. *Portland Business Journal*. Retrieved from http://portland.bizjournals.com/portland/stories/2001/12/17/focus5.html.

Krupin, P. J. (2010). The essentials of a fundraising news release. *About.com: Nonprofit Charitable Orgs*. Retrieved from http://nonprofit.about.com/od/nonprofitpromotion/a/newsrelease.htm.

Lansdowne, D. (2006). *Fundraising realities every board member must face: A 1-hour crash course on raising major gifts for nonprofit organizations*. Medfield, MA: Emerson & Church.

Leduc, B. (2010). Five successful marketing techniques. *Business know-how*. Retrieved from http://www.businessknowhow.com/marketing/5marktech.htm.

Lincoln, Y. S., & Guba, E. G. (1985). *Naturalistic inquiry*. Newbury Park, CA: Sage.

Lysakowski, L. (2003). What's in it for me? *New Directions for Philanthropic Fundraising, 39*, 53–64.

Lysakowski, L. (2005). *Nonprofit essentials: Recruiting and training fundraising volunteers*. Hoboken, NJ: Wiley.

Mal Warwick Associates. (n.d.). Rating the writing: How to assess a telephone fundraising script. *Mal Warwick Associates*. Retrieved from http://www.bridgeconf.org/site/DocServer/Warwick__Mal__Master_Class__Assessing_a_telefundraising.pdf?docID=482.

Martinelli, F., & Biro, S. (2010). Developing a board recruitment plan. *Creative information systems*. Retrieved from http://www.createthefuture.com/developing.htm.

Marts & Lundy. (2008). M & L minute #2: Board giving. *Counsel online*. Retrieved from http://www.martsandlundyinc.com/counsel/archive/june08/minute_1.php.

Masaoka, J. (2009). Should board members be required to give? *Blue Avocado*. Retrieved from http://www.blueavocado.org/content/should-board-members-be-required-give.

Masters, J. (2003). *Profit making for nonprofits and social enterprise tool kit*. Retrieved from http://www.cencomfut.com/SocialEnterpriseManual.pdf.

Mercer, E. (2005). *How can we use the Internet for fundraising?* Retrieved from http://www.idealist.org/if/idealist/en/FAQ/QuestionViewer/default?section=0&item=1511.

Minnesota Council on Foundations. (2010). Common types of grants. *Minnesota Council on Foundations*. Retrieved from http://www.mcf.org/nonprofits/common-types-of-grants.

Multi-State Filer Project. (2010). *The Unified Registration Statement*. Retrieved from http://www.multistatefiling.org/index.html#yes_states.

Mutz, J., & Murray, K. (2010). *Fundraising for dummies* (3rd ed.). Hoboken, NJ: Wiley.

National Center for the Dissemination of Disability Research. (2009). *Developing an effective dissemination plan.* Retrieved from http://www.researchutilization.org/matrix/resources/dedp/.

National Center for Family Philanthropy. (2010). *National Center for Family Philanthropy.* Retrieved from http://www.ncfp.org/.

National Consumer Supporter Technical Assistance Center. (n.d.). *Fundraising basics.* Retrieved from http://www.ncstac.org/content/materials/FundraisingBasics.pdf.

National Council of Nonprofits. (2010a). *Accountability practices in fundraising.* Retrieved from http://www.council-ofnonprofits.org/resources/resources-topic/fundraising/accountability-practices-fundraising.

National Council of Nonprofits. (2010b). Professional fundraising consultants and grant writers. *National Council of Nonprofits.* Retrieved from http://www.councilofnonprofits.org/resources/resources-topic/fundraising/professional-fundraising-consultants-and-grant-writers.

Neighborhood Funders Group. (2011). About NFG. *Neighborhood Funders Group.* Retrieved from http://www.nfg.org/.

Netting, F. E., Kettner, P. M., & McMurtry, S. L. (1993). Social work macro practice. New York: Longman.

Network for Good. (2010). *Network for Good.* Retrieved from http://www1.networkforgood.org/.

Network for Good. (2009a). *Register for a badge.* Retrieved from https://www.networkforgood.org/pca/PcaLandingPage.aspx.

Network for Good. (2009b). *The keys to fundraising on foursquare.* Retrieved from http://www.fundraising123.org/article/keys-fundraising-foursquare.

NFP Consulting Resources, Inc. (2010). *Developing a strong fundraising board: A "how-to" guide.* Retrieved from http://www.nonprofitlocal.com/tips.tip.116/how-to-develop-a-strong-fundraising-board.html.

Nonprofit Hub.com. (n.d.). *Telephone fundraising.* Retrieved from http://www.nonprofithub.com/articles/telephone-fundraising-overview.htm.

Nonprofit Works, Inc. (2007). Nonprofit Works, Inc. *Nonprofit Works, Inc. about us.* Retrieved from http://www.nonprofitworks.com/about/default.asp.

Nonprofits Assistance Fund. (n.d.). *Managing restricted funds: A resources article by Nonprofits Assistance Funds.* Retrieved from http://www.nonprofitsassistancefund.org/files/MNAF/ArticlesPublications/Managing_Restricted_Funds.pdf.

NTEN, Common Knowledge, & thePort. (2010). *Nonprofit social network benchmark report.* Retrieved from www.nonprofitsocial-networksurvey.com.

Panas, J. (n.d.). *The no nonsense guide to help you prepare a statement of your case.* Retrieved from http://www.panaslinzy.com/assets/No%20Nonsense%20Guide.pdf.

PayPal. (2010). *Paypal.* Retrieved from https://www.paypal.com/.

Perlman, S., & Chang, K. I. (2007). Cause marketing: How far can the quid pro quo go? (REGULATION). *The Non-profit Times.*

Retrieved from http://www.entrepreneur.com/tradejournals/article/167254308_1.html.

Philanthropy Journal. (2011). About the Philanthropy Journal. *Philanthropy Journal.* Retrieved from http://www.philanthropyjournal.org/about.

Philanthropy Roundtable. (2006). *Philanthropy Roundtable.* Retrieved from http://www.philanthropyroundtable.org/.

PlannedGiving.com. (2010). *What is planned giving?* Retrieved from http://www.plannedgiving.com/whatisplannedgiving.php.

Poderis, T. (2009a). Addendum: Capital campaign construction expense budget. *Fund-Raising Forum.* Retrieved from http://www.raise-funds.com/1099aforum.html.

Poderis, T. (2009b). *A development director needs more than "A smile and a shoeshine," but it's a good start.* Retrieved from http://www.raise-funds.com/699forum.html.

Poderis, T. (2009c). *Building donor loyalty.* Retrieved from http://www.raise-funds.com/012703forum.html#2.

Poderis, T. (2009d). Capital campaigns: Building for now. *Fund-raising Forum.* Retrieved from http://www.raise-funds.com/1099aforum.html.

Poderis, T. (2009e). *Don't make your organization's statement of purpose a "mission impossible."* Retrieved from http://www.raise-funds.com/1101forum.html.

Poderis, T. (2009f). *Fund-raising forum: How to recruit your volunteer fund-raising team.* Retrieved from http://www.raise-funds.com/999forum.html.

Poderis, T. (2009h). *Gift acknowledgements to annual fund "membership" donors.* Retrieved from http://www.raise-funds.com/exhibits/exhibit39.pdf.

Queenin, J. (2011). The complete idiots guide to grant writing. *BellaOnline: The voice of women.* Retrieved from http://www.bellaonline.com/articles/art53226.asp.

Robert, R. M., III, & Honemann, D. (2011). *Robert's rules of order.* Philadelphia, PA: Perseus Books Group.

Ross, B., & Segal, C. (2009). *The influential fundraiser.* San Francisco, CA: Jossey-Bass.

Sargeant, A., & Jay, E. (2004). *Fundraising management: Analysis, planning, and practice.* New York: Routledge.

Satterfield, B. (2007). An introduction to grant reports: Tips and tools for preparing reports for your funders. *TechSoup.* Retrieved from http://www.techsoup.org/learningcenter/funding/page7036.cfm.

Schar, M. (2009). Making a case for support: Fundraising case statements that win donors' hearts. *suite 101.com: Insightful Writers. Informed Readers.* Retrieved from http://nonprofitfundraising.suite101.com/article.cfm/making_a_case_for_support.

Schmidt, E. (2004). How ethical is your nonprofit organization? *GuideStar.* Retrieved from http://www2.guidestar.org/rxa/news/articles/2004/how-ethical-is-your-nonprofit-organization.aspx?articleId=827.

Schwartz, N. (2010). Nonprofits' most missed marketing tool—Email signatures. *Fundraising for Small Groups Newsletter.* Retrieved from http://www.fundraising-newsletters.com/nonprofits-most-missed-marketing-tool-email-signatures.html.

Seale, A. (2010). How to build a gift chart. *About.com: Nonprofit Charitable Orgs*. Retrieved from http://nonprofit.about.com/od/fundraising/a/giftchart.htm?once=true&.

Selby-Harrington, M. L., Donat, P. L., & Hubbard, H. D. (1993). Guidance for managing a research grant. Nursing Research, *42*(1), 54–61.

Siege, A. (n.d.). Find and reach your target market. *Creative Fundraising: Custom Development Solutions, Inc. (CDS)*. Retrieved from http://cdsfunds.com/find_and _reach_your_target_market.html.

Small Fuel Marketing. (2009). *5 must-know facts about printing marketing materials*. Retrieved from http://www.smallfuel.com/blog/entry/5-must-know-facts-about-printing-marketing-materials.

Sprinkel Grace, K. (2006). *Overall goal: What you must know to excel at fundraising today* (2nd ed.). Medfield, MA: Emerson & Church.

Square (2010). *Accept payments. Everywhere*. Retrieved from https://squareup.com/.

TransFS. (2009). *Financially speaking: 3 tips for non-profits accepting credit card donations*. Retrieved from http://transfs.com/blog/3-tips-for-non-profits-accepting-credit-card-donations/.

Unified Registration Statement, The. (2010). What is the Unified Registration Statement? *The Unified Registration Statement: The Multi-State Filer Project*. Retrieved from http://www.multistatefiling.org/b_introduction1.htm#why.

United Way. (2010). *United Way*. Retrieved from http://national.unitedway.org/.

U.S. Department of Education. (2011). Grants/apply for a grant. *U.S. Department of Education*. Retrieved from http://www2.ed.gov/fund/grants-apply.html.

U.S. Department of Health and Human Services. (2011). Grants/funding. *HHS.gov*. Retrieved from http://www.hhs.gov/grants/.

U.S. Equal Employment Opportunity Commission. (2010). *U.S. Equal Employment Opportunity Commission*. Retrieved from http://www.eeoc.gov/.

Usenet.com (2009). What is Usenet? *Usenet Information Center*. Retrieved from http://www.usenet.com/usenet.html.

Usry, J. (2008a). Charitable solicitation regulation for the nonprofit sector: Paving the regulatory landscape for future success. *Policy Perspectives: Center for Public Policy and Administration: The University of Utah*. Retrieved from http://www.imakenews.com/cppa/e_article001162331.cfm#_ftnref2.

Usry, J. (2008b). Charitable solicitation within the nonprofit sector: Paving the regulatory landscape for future success. *Policy In-depth: Center for Public Policy and Administration: The University of Utah*. Retrieved from http://www.cppa.utah.edu/publications/nonprofit/Charitable_Solicitation.pdf.

Volunteering Ireland. (2010). *Managing volunteers: Volunteers and paid staff … a challenging relationship*. Retrieved from http://www.volunteeringireland.ie/page.php?id=7.

Walker, J. I. (2009). *Jump-starting the stalled fundraising campaign*. Hoboken, NJ: Wiley.

Walsh, I. (n.d.). *How to write a needs statement document*. Retrieved from http://www.klariti.com/templates/How-To-Write-Business-Needs-Statement.shtml.

weazelgrl. (2010). How to identify targets in nonprofit marketing. *eHow: How to do just about everything*. Retrieved from http://www.ehow.com/how_6093500_identify-targets-nonprofit-marketing.html.

Whole Auction Fundraising Solutions. (2010). *Build your own online auction*. Retrieved from http://www.wholeauction.com/online_buildyourown_auction.htm.

Wikipedia. (2010). *Wikipedia: The free encyclopedia*. Retrieved from http://en.wikipedia.org/wiki/Main_Page.

Wilson, R. F. (2009a). *The web marketing checklist: 37 ways to promote your website*. Web Marketing Today. Retrieved from http://www.wilsonweb.com/articles/checklist.htm.

Wilson, R. F. (2009b). *Using banner ads to promote your website*. Web Marketing Today. Retrieved from http://www.wilsonweb.com/articles/bannerad.htm.

WWF. (2006). *Resources for implementing the WWF project and programme standards*. Retrieved from http://assets.panda.org/downloads/3_2_fundraising_02_26_07.pdf.

X Factor Consulting, LLC. (2010). *Questions about major donors and major donor programs*. Retrieved from http://www.xfactorllc.com/resourcesArticlesDetail.asp?id=94.

Yuen, F. K. O., & Terao, K. D. (2003). *Practical grant writing and program evaluation*. Pacific Grove, CA: Brooks/Cole—Thomson Learning.

Zimmerman, R., & Lehman, A. (2004). *Boards that love fundraising: A how-to guide for your board*. San Francisco, CA: Jossey-Bass.

Index